P9-DHN-580

Not the Thing I Was

THIRTEEN YEARS AT BRUNO BETTELHEIM'S ORTHOGENIC SCHOOL

ST. MARTIN'S PRESS NEW YORK

STEPHEN ELIOT

Not the Thing I Was

www.stmartins.com

All photos, except where otherwise noted, are courtesy of the author.

ISBN 0-312-30749-7

First published in France under the title *La Métamorphose* by Bayard Presse

First U.S. Edition: March 2003

10 9 8 7 6 5 4 3 2 1

To the Mohawks and Teddy, Michael and Timothy; to Bruno Bettelheim, who, in spite of it all, lit a candle that still burns; and, finally, to Diana Grossman Kahn and Margaret Carey for more than I can say

Contents

Acknowledgments

The genesis of this book began a dozen years ago, when tired of banking for a while, I moved to Los Angeles to work on a screenplay about my experiences at the Orthogenic School. I had hoped to try to return the School to its former glory by generating the type of publicity that only Hollywood seems to provide.

What I hadn't counted on, however, were the limits to imagination that I found there—one producer wanted more of a love interest for one of the characters. When I protested that the character was merely a twelve-year-old autistic boy, he couldn't see any problem.

That sojourn, which lasted three years, began the process by which I finally learned to write. I got to understand the essential elements in telling a story. Almost ten years later, I wrote another screenplay on my experiences at the School. Again, no one was interested. Thus, I decided to write this book.

From my time in Los Angeles, I have to thank my grandmother, Dorothy, who gave me a sense of family in that city of multiple illusions.

For my continued writing, I need to thank my father, a publisher and legendary editor, who has patiently edited my pieces for as long as I can remember. As usual, I brought him my completed first draft for his comments. Initially, he feared to read it, unsure of its quality, not wanting to disappoint me, until my mother finished reading it and gave him the thumbs-up. In the end, he, too, judged it publishable and worked with me to improve its structure and weed out my excesses. Both he and my mother have supported me and given encouragement throughout my life. While we didn't have a smooth start, we have moved on to a comfortable relationship in such contrast to what we might have expected so long ago. I owe them the enormous debt that any child owes parents who have sacrificed and encouraged their offspring. In addition, they are skilled readers who cast a professional eye.

When I finished the draft that my father had edited for me, I brought it to France to get my good friend Genevieve Jurgensen's opinion. She is an editor at Bayard Presse and passed the manuscript on to her boss, Frederic Boyer. The two of them purchased the rights for France not quite four months after I had begun the work, giving me hope that it would sometime see the light of day, which is why the French translation precedes the English edition.

There have been a number of friends whose advice and judgment, both literary and otherwise, have long counted in my life. Among them are William and Nancy Barbe, Robert W. Baylis, Penny Lee and Jim Brown, François and Ariane Heilbronn, Joan and Theron Raines, and Philippe and Amila Tromp, all of whom contributed to this book and my life in ways for which I am deeply grateful.

I want to thank the staff at St. Martin's Press for their professional and skillful assistance, especially Michael Denneny and Jane Rosenman for their sensitive editing and support and Ethan Friedman, whose patience greatly exceeds my own.

Finally, the first pages of this book were written somewhere on the top floors of the World Trade Center. I think often on the people I saw passing in those halls, most of whose names I never knew.

—Stephen Eliot
New York City
June 1, 2002

Presume not that I am the thing I was,
For God doth know—so shall the world perceive—
That I have turned away my former self.

—William Shakespeare,
Henry IV,
Part II, Act V

Not the Thing I Was

Prologue

It seems as if my life has been surrounded by stories—mine, others, books, fairy tales, movies, even conversations overheard on the bus or subway. As a child, I would read almost a book a day, transported to some other place in time or the galaxy, where I could contemplate what life would be like as a Trojan, Roman, or even a Norman riding over to England, ignorant of a dinner table fork, ready to claim my patch of countryside to ennoble myself and my children. I had all of these worlds in my head, and by the time *Star Trek* came on TV, it seemed quite normal to me to seek out strange new worlds because I had already been doing so all my life anyway.

As is often the case, the stories I read served to help me escape from my life and circumstance—from a school that I lived in from the time I was eight, where I was a prisoner as surely as any prince locked in the Tower or the Bastille. Indeed, from my readings, I knew (or at least believed I did) what it was like to be Louis XIV stalking down the halls of Versailles, or Catherine de' Medici rifling through her chest of poisons, or Alexander the Great contemplating the world from Persepolis after conquering Persia, all of which was his.

The stories that moved me most, however, were the ones of the other children with whom I lived. Those have stayed with me, a bit foggier now than they used to be, but the stories and lives I spent so much time trying to ignore and avoid have turned out to have more meaning for me than any of the other worlds I ever inhabited.

Kirk Douglas has written a number of books and said something that I have always remembered: If you want to tell the truth, write a novel; if you want to lie, write an autobiography. I thought about that remark often. Because while I profess to love the truth, in truth, I love my stories even more. The truth locks you into the worlds you know, and, to me, it was the worlds I didn't know that held the most promise. So I laughed at myself whenever I thought of telling my own story, because I wasn't sure I knew the truth, even though I have spent all of my life trying to make sense of who I am, and the part that I did know, I wasn't sure I wanted to tell.

But there were others I knew whose stories were important to me and I was afraid that when I die, theirs will be forgotten along with mine. In the grand scheme of the universe, with billions of stars in billions of galaxies, none of it really matters, I suppose, except to me. Of all the stories I have read and heard, I decided to tell the one that I know best, my own, because in its telling, I could also tell the story of quite a few others whom I came to know in my travels. I don't promise to tell the whole truth and nothing but the truth, but I will begrudgingly agree not to lie. Some things will be hidden, because I do not remember them accurately, or I have forgotten crucial details (how Freud would approve of this acknowledgment), or I wish to protect myself and others from being judged by those not in a position to do so.

Others may remember events far differently than I, which is probably a good thing. Not all my memories are clear, and many are colored by my childhood perception of the world, which was admittedly not seen through the clearest of lenses, for I grew up in the most famous children's mental institution in the world. In an interview for a book on the School, I was once asked how it felt to be crazy. My response: I never considered myself crazy, merely unhappy. As for the other children around me, many of whom were in far worse shape than I was, I only considered a few of them to be nuts. The rest, the vast majority, even the autistic ones, seemed to me to be unhappy, too. I preferred to see my world that way, because living with a group of crazy children would have been terrifying; living with a group of kids who were unhappy, however, didn't seem so strange. They were just like me. (All of their names have been changed to keep their identities confidential.)

I have been asked what made it necessary for me to go to the School in the first place, how was I crazy, what could have been done to prevent my problems, and what would have happened if I hadn't gone. To describe exactly what happened to me and why is beyond my ability. Much happened when I was too young to remember it. I wanted to write what life was like for me in the Orthogenic School. That was my reality. Describing the events leading up to any child's going to the School, perhaps as a means of preventing others from undergoing the same fate, would be the work of a superb clinician. Some clues may be found in a careful reading of Dr. B.'s case histories. Whatever occurred in my family happened prior to the period this book covers. Although clearly much fallout came from those events, my troubles came from what I carried with me. I had internalized a certain view of the world, and understanding that view was both the School's and my mission.

In retelling the story of my early life, I was assisted by my records from the Orthogenic School, primarily the staffs' transcribed dictations about daily events affecting me. A selection of those dictated observations is included in the notes at the back of this book. They are contemporaneous with what is being discussed in the text and, I hope, elucidate and corroborate the narrative. While the story stands without them, they may perhaps be of interest to the reader.

The historical files were provided to me by Dr. Jacqueline Sanders in 1992, when she was director of the Orthogenic School, some sixteen years after I had left. I did not open the files until September 2000 because it took me until I was forty-five before I could bear to be reminded so intimately of my childhood history. The files remained sealed in my possession for over eight years.[1]

Staff were supposed to dictate notes about each child after each shift or after major happenings; thus over the years a large dossier was created. Dr. B. would read all such transcribed notes (for fifty kids, that alone took an enormous amount of time), making little hatch marks along the outside margin. One mark was a mention, two was important, three was very important, and four lines meant hitting the psychological jackpot. I have extensive records from Diana Grossman Kahn and Margaret Carey and partial notes from Julie Neumann Dunn from 1963 until 1972. From that point in time, after

Dr. B. had left the School, the only notes I have are general ones written in preparation for meetings about me with the School's outside consulting psychiatrists. Such notes cover 1973 through 1976, my last four years there.

To get as fresh a perspective as possible, in September 2000 I first wrote 270 pages, setting down my memories and immediate thoughts covering the period of 1963 to 1976. Only then, and for the first time, did I look at the historical record. In a sense, it was like looking at someone else, for the child that I was had long since vanished. In his place has arisen, through a lot of very dedicated people's hard work, including my own, a saner, more refined version of that child. It was interesting to see how early certain themes arose in my life and how persistent they have been in forming my personality and interests. One thing did surprise me, however: How much I could appreciate and the affection I bore that little boy who lived so long ago. For a long time he embarrassed me and made me cringe. Now, after so much time, I could see that despite how obnoxious and scared he was, he also possessed a certain imagination and resilience that permitted him to survive. Those gifts, despite all the difficulties and frequent barrages of rage, are what Diana Grossman Kahn, Margaret Carey, and Bruno Bettelheim could see and enabled them to hang in there for a struggle that no one has a right to ask another human being to undertake. If ever there was a debt of gratitude and of obligation from one human being to another, for love and action beyond what could be humanly expected, it is what I owe those three primarily, but also Ugo Formigoni, Luitgard Wundheiler, Julie Neumann Dunn, Marsha Greenwood, Len Atkins, Mary Margaret Bell, Bert Cohler, Sue Gottschall, John Frattaroli, Mary Halboth Schwartz, David Lerner, Marc Lubin, and Jacqueline Sanders.

Here we are, so many years later. Once upon a time, there lived a small boy in a strange school in prewar Vienna long after the empire had ceased to exist, as if it had been imagined by a brilliant yet imperfect man who carried in his heart a memory of his homeland that he imparted to many others in a way that would change them forever. That is my story.

I

Setting the Stage

The time was July of 1963, I was eight, and my parents had just dropped me off at the University of Chicago Sonia Shankman Orthogenic School run by Bruno Bettelheim. It was located on Chicago's South Side, situated on a vast ribbon of park three blocks wide, called the Midway, which connected the lakefront parks to the east with Chicago's parks in the west. The University of Chicago's main campus was just across the Midway to the north.

I wouldn't see or speak with my parents for a year. Bettelheim, however, who was called Dr. B. by all, I would see several times a day for the next ten years whether I wanted to or not—and I mostly didn't want to. He has been dead for ten years now, and it has only been in the past year or two that I have finally begun to miss him. As I write this, I have a lump in my throat that I never imagined I would have when I was a child thinking about him, unless it was because he had just slapped me in the face. He was not only my greatest teacher, which I readily could acknowledge, but also a friend, although it has taken almost forty years to see it.

Like other geniuses, he was complex, mercurial, and not always appreciated. He grew up in prewar Vienna, had had a wet nurse, a story that fascinated me, since it was so ancien régime, and had suffered from being a Jew in Europe at a time before the Nazis—when even Freud's professorship was delayed for years since he was a Jew. Things worsened. Dr.

B. was in Buchenwald and Dachau before he got out and came to the United States in 1939. Armed with a Ph.D. in art esthetics,[1] fierce determination to make a life for himself in the new world, and a reputation from having written a treatise on how the Nazis used the camps systematically to destroy personality[2] that Dwight Eisenhower made required reading for senior officers, he arrived in Chicago. In 1944 he was appointed director of the Orthogenic School.

Dr. B. believed that if the Nazis could create an environment to destroy personality as they originally intended with the camps, he could build an environment that could foster and re-create personality. Some may say What arrogance! and yet he did it. He took one of the worst blots in twentieth-century history and used it to build something lasting, truly lighting a candle rather than cursing the darkness.

For me, more than what he said or did, this fact remained strong and powerful: that he could rebuild his life and take from his admittedly painful past things that I could only imagine and use them to further his life. Yet like so many of the other stories that I read and imagined, I was convinced that I knew what it was like to be in a concentration camp. I was sure that I knew the terror of the knock on the door in the middle of the night and its consequences. Living in a mirror image of something so terrible has been a burden. Survivor guilt has hit me two ways: I always have been troubled that I could profit from what Dr. B. learned in the camps—that so many millions had to die horrible deaths—and I got to go to a school based on their bones, as it were, where we could be helped from the knowledge gained from their deaths. Then, too, I have survived when so many of the children I grew up with have not. Some who I grew to love dearly are still in institutions where they shall live out their natural lives. For them, the times that I look back on with so many mixed emotions were the best years of their lives. I, on the other hand, have the luxury of dismissing those years and being angry for what they cost me. And I got to leave and go to Yale, not a locked ward somewhere, so what do I have to complain about? Nonetheless, full knowledge of the facts hasn't stopped me from being consumed with rage and frustration about the details of my life, which I have often wished were different. How spoiled I was.

At any rate, I got dropped off that day in July 1963 with all of my worldly belongings, those I was permitted to take, contained in a medium-size gray suitcase that had once been my mother's, which still had a pink stain inside in the blue silk lining from where a bottle of nail polish had broken. I also brought a small carton of what few toys I had and some books. They wouldn't let me take my bike, which seemed most unfair, although the staff of the School had told me there were bikes there I could use whenever I liked. I later learned that whenever I got to use them, it was whenever *they* liked.

At the School, we would refer to the "outside world" because all of us, kids and staff, lived in a place that was a world unto itself, with its own laws, customs, mores, and culture. It was both a magnificent edifice to the powers of light over darkness and, at other times, a nightmare from which there seemed to be no exit. All of my books and worlds worked to keep those nightmares in abeyance, chased into shadows that would return with a vengeance, all the worse for being called back thousands of years or millions of miles to meet my daily suffering.

I hadn't been happy at home, didn't have any friends, was a revolutionary who hated being a child, because all it meant was that these grown-ups who were bigger and stronger could tell you what to do and could make you do it even if you put up a fight.

Adults, it seemed, existed to say no. One example occurred when I was in first grade. My teacher would at times talk about the colored people on the South Side of Chicago. My brother and I had a set of red, green, blue, and yellow toy soldiers. I assumed that somewhere on the South Side lived green and blue people. (I mean, I was six, after all, and since teachers were like gods and she had said so, who was I to doubt her?) When I would ask my grandmother and mother to take me to see the colored people, they would look at me as if I were crazy and say absolutely not. It never occurred to me to ask them about the red and green people because being told I couldn't do something I wanted seemed so normal. When I finally learned that colored people meant black, it was as bad as finding out that the tooth fairy or Santa Claus didn't exist—I had liked the idea of green or blue people. Black people I knew; they were not exotic: They were just like us.

It didn't seem strange to me that I was sent away. I think most children, no matter what happens to them, assume that it is normal and whatever it is happens to everyone else, too, since as children we have no vantage point other than our own. My books provided other vantages, but I seldom read any stories or reports about children with normal childhoods that seemed believable. Even *Heidi* seemed exotic, located in an Alps I had never seen, although I understood the part about her hoarding dinner rolls, since I liked the idea of having enough food around me once I got to the School and couldn't go to the kitchen whenever I liked as I could at home.

My father had explained to me before I went to the School, when I asked why I was going, that it was because the wiring in my brain was crossed—as if when someone went into the bathroom and turned on the light switch, the water went on instead of the lights. I spent a long time imagining what the wiring in my brain must have looked like. My father and I didn't communicate well. I was scared of him and he was self-absorbed. I realize now that my father loves me and is proud of me, but for many years there were so many battles that being able to relate to him relatively normally was for me a major achievement. I do not believe he meant to be so difficult but he always had to be right, no matter what the cost. And the cost for me was very high—I spent thirteen years at the Orthogenic School trying to figure things out. A Harvard graduate of the same 1950 class as Henry Kissinger, Dad has always been able to argue rings around anyone he chose. I inherited his ability with language, which he in turn inherited from his mother, and began talking in full sentences at ten months. As has been pointed out to me a number of times, I haven't shut up since. I also inherited his ability to read, learning prior to age two—the first book that I could follow by myself was Dr. Seuss' *One Fish Two Fish Red Fish Blue Fish.* My mother had read it to me until I knew each word by heart and then I made the leap of understanding to recognizing each word and being able to read it myself. I followed this intellectual achievement with *Green Eggs and Ham.*

My mother had taken me to visit the School a couple of times to be interviewed. The last time was just a few days before I went for good. I remember getting ready to go—my mother wore this slip with a hole cut out for her belly since she was eight months pregnant with my youngest brother. The slip with a hole cut out struck me as funny, since I knew a lot of men who had bellies at least as big as my mother's and they didn't wear stuff with holes cut out for their stomachs. I must have asked my mother, who, I am sure, took this as another sign that I really was strange, because she must have thought I was asking why fat men didn't wear maternity slips, but that wasn't what I meant at all!

On these visits I must have met Dr. B., but I have almost no recollection of meeting him or what we talked about, except that in his office he had a big bowl of candy, of which he told me I could take as much as I wanted. I also remember telling him that I wanted to go to the School, after he asked, because I thought that was what I was supposed to say. I added that I didn't really think I needed to, since I was not a child at all, but a grown-up in a small body. Maybe, however, I could work there. This conversation was probably as good a description of how I viewed the world as any. Looking back on how I must have appeared, the wonder of it all was that he let me out to go back home for a few more days and didn't lock me up immediately.

I do remember meeting my counselors, Diana and Ugo, who visited with me. I remember a few other things vividly: that Diana, who later was to be the most important person in my life, stayed with me less than Ugo did, a fact that I would remind her of over and over again as a joke as we got to be close. The sheer number of toys in the dormitories—when I got Dr. Perkins, the School's consulting psychiatrist, to take me back so I could see the dorms—amazed me. I wanted to play with some of those toys, since each child had a dresser and closet overflowing with toys, stuffed animals, and books, but Dr. Perkins wouldn't let me, since they belonged to the other kids. There was one other fact of absolutely no importance whatsoever, which of course was the one I remembered most strongly and had the most obvious impact on me: I had looked out a window and seen a building and derived a mental map of how the School was laid out. My spatial sense is somewhat handicapped: Whenever I park in one of those garages that go both up and down, it always confuses me and it seems like I have to walk from the top down before I can find my car. I spent a long time looking for that view from the window, trying to understand the layout as I had first seen it. It took me months before I finally had to assume I had remembered it wrong.

My parents dropped me off that first day and Diana and Ugo took me upstairs to the dorm. I had no way of knowing, nor did it occur to me, that the other children would wonder who I was and how big a disruption to their lives I might be. I thought about whether I could run back to my parents without being stopped. Chicago had the strictest fire laws in the country, and there were two heavy metal fire doors separating the dorms from the older, less fire resistant, front offices, which were at the front of a twisting corridor and then down a flight of stairs. I knew I could never make it up front in time without being caught by Diana or Ugo, but I tried a couple of times, anyway. Eventually I figured my parents had left since my father had to go to work. I just sat in the dorm playing with a battery-powered helicopter and talking to Diana and Ugo from about ten in the morning until one or so, when I got hungry and they took me down to get some lunch in the enormous dining room. Already a foodie, I remember there was a chef's salad with olives, bologna, and mayonnaise that I always loved and I haven't had since my childhood. It was after lunch that I made my first introduction to the kids with whom I would spend the next thirteen years of my life.

I learned much later that my parents were overwhelmed at having left their eldest son at this school, concerned whether they had done the right thing, yet knowing that something had to be done. They went to my mom's oldest friend from high school, Ruth, who lived nearby in Hyde Park. Ruth and her family are among my closest friends and as a child when my dorm mates and I would go out in the neighborhood, I would often run into her. Since I was the only one in my dorm who knew anyone in the neighborhood unconnected with the School, she became a cult figure for us. Often other kids would come up to me and tell me that they had seen Ruth in the neighborhood. In time, Ruth got used to having strange kids wave and smile at her. She was a psychiatric social worker married to a psychiatrist, so it was all in the family, so to speak. Ruth's husband, Gerson, also earned some measure of fame, since he specialized in the criminally insane and was a frequent expert witness when certain prisoners were coming up for parole. Once, after a notorious mass murder at a hamburger place in California, he was asked about his medical view of the murderer's state of mind. His reply: "I guess he had a bad burger."

At any rate, my parents went over to Ruth's to attempt to deal with their worries about me as well as their guilt as parents for institutionalizing me. Now, the fact that the School was unlike any other institution in the world, had a long waiting list of children needing to go, and had a history of good results didn't change the cold hard fact that I had been sent there for a period likely to be years. None of us dreamed it would stretch to thirteen and I would be twenty-one until I returned home for ten weeks before leaving for college. My father told me much later that he and my mother didn't think I would be able to complete high school, let alone college. Not that I wasn't smart or couldn't study, but I was unable to get along or manage with others.

In fact, at the time, my parents were relieved that I was permitted to enter the School. My father had gotten his uncle, a dean at the University of Chicago, to vouch for the family. One of the world's greatest algebraists, Uncle Adrian had worked with Einstein at Princeton, so that fact attached to my dossier, my father always believed, helped to get me into the School. Although Uncle Adrian might have helped, I got in on my own merit, a dubious honor to be sure. When it came to being crazy, I could hold my own.

I never lived with my parents again.

2

Some Additional Backstory

Now, what had transpired to bring me on that July morning to step across the threshold of the Orthogenic School and out of the real world for the next thirteen years? The short answer: Essentially I believed at that period of my life that all the options presented to me were deadly. I was damned no matter which way I turned, and my rage from being cornered by life, so to speak, knew no bounds. All my emotions were blocked out, so I turned inward, ambled through life, and ran from or fought whatever dangers I perceived. I could trust no one and was wise enough to distrust myself. I felt that I lived in mortal danger and only I could protect myself, but as a child I had not the knowledge to comprehend the world. I did, however, know how to fight, which is what I did. I fought everyone off, and my parents, finally, had enough.

At that time, I thought being a man meant that you worked ceaselessly but got nothing for yourself, and, worse, in the end you would be devoured by a woman in the manner that a black widow devours her mate when she has taken what she needs; being a woman meant that you were surrounded by babies with nothing for yourself other than misery and frustration with no support; and, finally, worst of all, being a child meant you lived under adults who were not to be trusted and who existed only for themselves. What little attention or care you got had to be shared with a never-ending series of brothers, and whatever security that could be attained was subject to sudden removal at any time without warning for reasons beyond your control. If it was not safe to be a man, woman, or child, there were not a lot of other options. I had the depression and desperation of a trapped animal. Except I created a world such that I felt nothing, except rage against my situation, thus escaping the worst of my existence.

Margaret, who was my therapist for over ten years at the School, reported that once I told her that when I was small, I had believed that to make a baby, a man needed to lose his penis to fertilize the egg, although eventually he would grow another one like a lizard growing a new tail or like a child's tooth falling out. The fear of castration, which has become a punch line for so many jokes about shrinks, was no laughing matter to me.[1]

I always had a love/hate relationship with things that scared me. I didn't like to be scared of things, particularly when I knew it just to be weakness on my part. I was scared of the dark. At the School, off the dining room, the bathroom had no window, so if you went in there and switched off the light, it was pitch black. I started going in there to turn off the lights, because I wanted to get over my fear. Eventually Diana figured out what I was doing. She tried to get me to stop but in the end just joined me in the bathroom with the lights switched off, so that I could get over this fear without being scared all by myself. Eventually it worked. I realized that in a safe place, the dark didn't mean that robbers or Nazis would come and get me. I think I played this out longer than necessary because I liked having Diana all to myself in the dark.

My gender identity was shaky and played into my castration fears. Perhaps my identification with a woman paralleled locking myself into a pitch-dark room: I thus would find out what life would be like if the worst happened and I ended up penisless. I didn't know with whom to identify, either, since everyone was equally scary, so part of me identified with my mother and developed feminine mannerisms, which became more pronounced when I was anxious. From my father, I inherited the facility that permitted me to go on the verbal attack. I learned how to go for the jugular with a backhand remark. It was effortless for me, and I could, and did, drive away those who might otherwise have been my friends. Added to this mix was a desperate attempt to overcompensate for the total emptiness that I felt inside, which pushed me to be grandiose and arrogant. I had to pretend to myself, let alone others, to be bigger, smarter, quicker, more knowing, and if others couldn't recognize it, then I would fight all the harder. Part of all of this was my need to prove that I could be a better mother than my mother, something that would drive her to her wits' end. She didn't know what to do, and I would shake her confidence as a mother daily because she knew she could not deal with or help me. My father, too, with his eldest son becoming more feminine day by day, could see me fight off everyone, including him and my mother, and became increasingly worried because I had headed past disaster already, clearly arriving there prior to age eight. One did not need to be a professional to see a grim prognosis unless there was a miracle.

I had a lot of trouble in school. In second grade, I was suspended for several days, because I had been accused of scratching one of the girls in the coatroom. I hadn't done it, but my general behavior made it plausible. What I had done was act in such a way that a classmate wanted to get rid of me and succeeded. I had been thrown out of Sunday school. Initially I had complained about it to my parents, and my father said I didn't have to go. Then he thought about it and changed his mind. I waited in the next class until the teacher was looking and then pulled the chair out from under the girl in front of me as she was sitting down. I was promptly expelled. The girl's name was Nina and I had liked her. I was damned if I was going to go to Sunday school, and she became the instrument of my liberation. I have felt guilty about it all these years and have long wanted to apologize to her.

The initial prognosis was worse than grim. The Becks, a husband and wife team who were renowned for their testing skills, performed a variety of tests, including Rorschach and intelligence tests, on me a month before my eighth birthday. The findings confirmed my parents' worst fears. My IQ placed me in the superior category, my vocabulary was off the charts, my mental age was two and half years older than my chronological age, and my future, even with therapy, was uncertain since my "pathogenic processes have already progressed ominously but the residual assets warrant the effort at reversing the present malignant course." Reading this sounds more like a description of a budding Darth Vader than a small child.

My fantasy world was highly developed, and the Becks found that my hold on reality was tenuous at best. They concluded I was borderline schizophrenic, but, fortunately, I was not that far gone and could tell the difference, when it mattered, between my views and reality. As far as intimate human contact went, however, I could not tell the difference between my fears and how people treated me. As a result, I could not be close to anyone. It was a lonely life and, despite my obvious intelligence, I was incapable of managing most normal social interactions.[2]

It is chilling reading the Becks' report now, almost forty years later, to see how close to the edge I had come. The associations to the inkblot images might have been fascinating, given their breadth and originality, but they, too, are chilling in a depiction of a world both deranged and terrifying, with genders uncertain, such as mother-roosters.

It was understandable from this report that I had no friends, which is reassuring in a strange way. If I had friends while behaving as I did, it would show that everything I have learned about human interaction was wrong. It is reassuring to know that gravity works. How could anyone be friends with this little kid, alternately feminine and then as aggressive as hell, who interpreted the world in his own way? Deep inside, I knew that my parents had had enough of me and that I could not have any friends given the state I was in. My grandmother, because she was not a parent, didn't have responsibility or guilt to worry about me in the same way and, despite everything, could love me unconditionally. By this time she had moved to California. Even had she been there, I was too damaged to remain at home. However, to give credit where it was due, unconditional love is a precious gift from wherever it comes, and knowing it once gave me the ability to recognize it when it came along later. Her faith in my worth somehow had gotten through somewhere and would be unearthed as a past treasure in the emotional archaeology to be performed in the long years ahead.

A short word about my parents. This story is not about them, except peripherally, since it is about my life at the School. It is true, if we had had a more satisfactory home life, all of this might have been averted. Maybe not. My parents were not monsters. But my view of them, like my view of the world, was so distorted that it would take me a long time to see them as they were and not as stand-ins for how I perceived the world. As I have changed, so have they. Our tragedy was that I could not live in their home without being thrown back into the old terror of how I saw the world. In the end, I think we could forgive and forget, but for the duration of this story, that was not yet to occur.

One more thing. My maternal grandfather died of lung cancer shortly before I was born. He knew of my mother's pregnancy with his first grandchild, and it was hoped that he would live long enough to hold me in his arms. Alas, that was not to be, for he died a few months before my birth, leaving my grandmother a widow at forty-four and my mother bereft. That loss deeply affected her, as was to be expected, and, through no fault of either of us, her depression carried over to me after my birth. My gift, as well as my curse, was to be so extraordinarily sensitive that I could read people no matter how much they tried to hide. And, as my history documents, I had the capability to observe and to reason far earlier than most. Disequilibrium is, at best, difficult to correct once one loses one's footing. That is where Dr. B. came in, to restore my balance and the balance of my relationship with my family. He was a tough taskmaster to all of us as you will see. The proof that he succeeded is in this book, for I finally achieved the distance and objectivity to write it. He set in motion a process that did not fully bear fruit until years after his death.

3

The Initial Cast

After spending that first morning with Diana and Ugo, it was time for me to join the rest of the kids and meet my fellow inmates. From nine to three the kids spent their weekdays in the classrooms, located in a former church across a side yard where there was a jungle gym, sandbox, monkey bars, and a stone lady whose arms formed pools. I would later like to fill those pools with the hose and sit in them. Diana and Ugo took me across the side yard to the largest classroom of them all where the entire school would meet Monday afternoon to watch educational movies, so that a couple of teachers could attend a daily staff meeting.

The other kids were curious about who I was, but I hadn't even thought about who they were and what they might be like. My world ended at my shoes. Even now, while I understand that the rest of the world goes on in my absence, it is hard for me to imagine that Paris, for example, still stands with its cobblestone pavements and mansard roofs without me. For all it says about my personality at the time, I hadn't had a single thought about the other kids, other than noticing how many toys they had.

I met my teacher, Luitgard, for the first time and sat behind her as the lights were dimmed and the educational movies began to run. Lilly, who was in Luitgard's class, was scared of many things and always worried about getting punished, a reasonable worry since she acted out constantly.

She was eleven or twelve and to me, at age eight, she seemed almost a grown-up, so it was hard for me to fathom that her mental age was even younger than my own. She would call out "la-la" over and over in an anxious mantra. I didn't understand this at all and asked Luitgard if she was speaking a foreign language. Luitgard, who possessed a sense of subtlety that would have done well in any diplomatic posting, replied, "In a way, she is." At the time, that made no sense to me at all, but I couldn't figure it out and the movie had begun, so the answer remained unsolved in my memory to be played back years later, when I could admire Luitgard's cleverness. Lilly did indeed speak a foreign language: her own.

Luitgard was German, born in Hesse, a point that I used to throw in her face when we studied the American Revolution, since Hessian mercenaries fought for the English. She had Ph.D.'s in both German literature and educational psychology, and, with all of her talents, she chose to teach us.

I have no memories of what happened next or, in fact, pretty much the rest of the day. In those days I didn't feel much. Afterward, I would think of myself as a large science fiction–like pulsating brain, able to read, think, and, most of all, argue, but unable to feel or to understand what I was feeling. Anger was the one emotion that I did know, but not always why I was angry. There were times that I would rip my shirt in half, blinded by rage, but I was unable to discern the reasons behind such overwhelming rage. I was just this skinny kid with bright blue eyes and a big mouth.

However, Diana dictated extensive notes that first day, which came to four and half single-spaced typed pages. Her reportage seems familiar, almost as if recalling a dream, since at that time I lived in a dream world. Her notes began, "This is the day that Steve came to live with us."[1]

Upon coming to the School, every child received a stuffed animal—and on each anniversary of their coming, they would receive another animal, as well as one at Christmas and sometimes more for birthdays. In time, every child's bed resembled a menagerie, requiring a chair to pile up these animals in order to get into bed at night. I arrived with an ancient threadbare Steiff cat that my mother had bought me when I was a baby, one of two mementos of my childhood. The other was my baby blanket of green wool that had shrunk to a stiff square a yard across. I kept it folded at the foot of my bed all of my years at the School and later, even, when I went to Yale. Without it, I couldn't go to bed until I was three or four and decided I was a big boy. It was a memory of my babyhood and of the good things that I had had from my parents.

From the School, I received a stuffed lion as my welcoming present. Dr. B. told me that it was something I could hit when I got angry and it would never hit me back. Diana and Ugo were surprised that I had so few toys, which, compared to the riches of the other kids, made me look like a pauper. For a long time, I would receive presents of trucks, games, and other trinkets for no reason other than to make me feel special. I quickly learned to become greedy and demand these extra treats, so that the purity of receiving a gift became tainted with my unceasing demands, which, when sometimes met, could be looked at as giving in to my pestering (or as a bribe to shut me up).

At three o'clock there was the handoff, when the teachers brought their classes back to the other building and we went back to our dorms. Often there would be a meeting and one of the staff would talk to us about something of interest (or so they hoped). After the meeting, at three-fifteen or so, the six dorms—three boys, three girls—each with six to eight kids would go upstairs and begin our afternoons. For a new child, there was a welcoming party with ice cream, cake, and presents for all, probably to distract us for a few moments so that the new child could be made to feel welcome. The rivalries and petty jealousies would have done honor to a sultan's court. Each group had two counselors, and they would have to spend a lot of energy and time welcoming and indoctrinating the new addition into the fold.[2]

I was the youngest and smallest in the group, a position I detested. I never worried about physical safety, unless I figured that Dr. B. was going to slap me, which didn't happen more than a couple of times a month. I did hate the position since I hated being a child at all and to be the smallest was an insult hard to bear. Of course, later, when kids younger and smaller arrived, I hated them, too, for fear they would usurp my position with Diana and get more attention. Over time, and by that I mean years, I learned that no one got more attention from Diana than I did—not that she didn't take good care of the others, but only that she always had enough time for me. Though I would fight with her incessantly, she was the first person in the world who was able to reach me so that I was no longer completely alone. I always knew she loved me.

That first day, when Diana was playing checkers with me, one of the other kids in the dorm, Francis, came over to say a word to her. My jealousy was already in full gear, and I pinched Diana for having the nerve to talk to anyone else.[3]

I had come to the School when my mother was eight months pregnant with her fourth and last child. Although I do not remember permitting myself to acknowledge that I was jealous, my preoccupation with pregnancy and sibling jealousy would last for years. Diana was overweight then, which was always of concern to me, because I feared that she might be pregnant. I hadn't realized that those concerns began the very first day with her, when I asked if she was pregnant.[4]

I told her my mother looked like she was going to have twenty babies. There were later notes that said part of the timing of my coming to the School was out of concern that I might harm the baby or my mother. Diana herself told me that once when I was thirteen or so. Even now I can remember the burn of shame when Diana told me of that presumption so long ago. As far gone as I was, I wouldn't have harmed a child (I hadn't before I went to the School and I never did afterward, either) although I had gotten into fights with my brothers and punched them as they did me.

The other kids in my dorm, which was called the Mohawks, were Daniel, my chief rival for as long as we were in the same dorm together—which was five or six years—and who was also three and a half years older than I was (he would say four years, just to piss me off, since I was damned if I would give him another six months over me). He was like me in the sense that he was articulate, able to study, and could interact real time with others. In fact, in many ways he was far more advanced than I was: He could feel his feelings and relate to his peers. (However, being more advanced than I was is hardly an unmitigated compliment.) He also, from time to time, would wet his bed, which I found repugnant at his age, and yet I enjoyed the fact, since it gave me a sense of superiority.

Andrew, who must have been fifteen or so, was the eldest. At the time, I considered him a big kid so I didn't think about him in more terms than that. If he struck me as strange, I must have thought it was because I didn't understand—not that there was something seriously wrong with him. In actuality, as a child he had been autistic or pretty close to it, and the fact that he was communicating and being part of the group was an amazing achievement. Score one for Bettelheim. Later, despite all of that, I thought he was pretty weird.

Hank was next oldest at thirteen or so. He had been adopted because his father had fooled around with firecrackers as a kid and a spark went up his pants. I never found out if in fact the father had blown off his balls or not, but I have never felt comfortable about firecrackers since. Hank was quiet, but, as someone so much older than I was, he didn't really figure in my world.

Paul was eleven or so, which again seemed almost like a grown-up to me. He was autistic and clearly struck me as a weirdo. He didn't really talk but echoed back to you what you said to him. I remember him as having a sweet face with dark hair and eyebrows. He was just about to enter puberty, which must have been terrifying for him, since he couldn't understand what was happening to his body and all of his new feelings when he had so much trouble with the old ones. One of the regrets of my life is that I didn't get to know him better. I had no means of doing so then; yet I lived with him for several years, until he was sent to an institution somewhere, where he probably remains, if he is still alive.

Francis, who was ten or eleven, was our fruitcake. He wet his pants all the time, sucked his thumbs raw, and did this thing called flupping, whereby he could generate a stream of air from flipping his wrist and snapping his fingers against his palm that could keep a small piece of fluff in the air for several minutes. The rest of us spent a lot of time trying to imitate this, but none of us ever developed his proficiency. Of course, there was the time we were all having a flupping contest in the dorm and a visitor was being shown around the School. He walked in, saw a roomful of us flupping, shook his head sadly at this village of the damned, and walked out. All of us, including Diana or Ugo, I forget who was on, laughed until we had tears running down our faces at the expression of horror on that visitor's face. Any explanation would have just made things worse. As my father is wont to quote to his children, "To those who understand, no explanation is necessary. To those who don't, no explanation is possible."

One of the wonderful things about the School was that Francis never was made to feel like a freak because of his flupping. It was a sense of pride for him that he could always win a flupping contest—and we respected his skill. You try it. Although there were times I hated him, like when he peed in his pants while sitting on the rug, in time I learned to see he was just the way he was. All of us knew somewhere that he was definitely outside the normal, but then so were the rest of us. Once I told someone, probably Diana, in a screaming match that he wasn't human. Her response has haunted me forever: "To the extent you deny his own humanity, you deny your own." I couldn't have been more than age ten.

Dr. B. used to say that to understand a child, one had to see the world the way he did; and a symptom was a child's highest form of coping, given how he saw the world. Once the staff saw the child's vantage point, they could begin helping him to see that, perhaps, there might be another point of view that might be more helpful and fulfilling in the long run. He would long elaborate on this theme.

> *Psychic economy says that we can't in every new situation analyze it from scratch. So we carry things over from previous experiences. Like a child who can get attention when sick—later when things get too much, then such a person collapses to get rest and attention he wants and needs. In the concentration camps, large numbers fell into this passive defense role. A large percentage died in the first week. They went back to old defenses, which were dangerously inadequate for meeting the new demands. However, in the American army, they would have gotten discharges. So there, such a defense would have worked.*[5]

Francis was an original and to stand out in that School took some talent. Unfortunately, it was the wrong kind of talent to manage any sort of normal life. I'm afraid he wasn't one of the School's outstanding successes.

The other original in our dorm, I am not proud to report, was me. The School, by which I mean staff and kids, had seen all kinds. The fact that I could get into so much trouble, argued with everyone, and could barely play with another soul was my measure of fame. I annoyed the other kids with my bragging, and I could play with them only when I could commandeer whatever they were playing to fit into my fantasy world. That first day I played a lot of checkers and dominoes with Diana, and she reports that I cheated like crazy. I would make up my own rules. Diana won one of the games I had made up three times in a row.[6]

Diana wouldn't let me cheat and would point out to me some of my more outrageous claims were clearly untrue, like my announcement that I worked for the secret service at $5,000 per year (which would be $30,000 today). I hated being brought up short, even though I knew I deserved it, so I would fight with her just to protest. One thing that I did not do was steal, although some of the early records suggested that the staff thought I did. I had stolen some things when younger, but my father took care of that. I had stolen a transistor radio and my father found it. He asked me how I had gotten it, and I confessed that I had taken it from the local gas station, which had all the doors open during the summer heat. My father drove me to the gas station and made me return it and apologize. I never forgot how humiliated I felt confessing to the very people I had injured by stealing from them. I was truly sorry and never did it again. My father was very wise—he knew his yelling at me wouldn't do any good. That did.

My stories continued unabated and would grow worse when I was scared or felt that I needed to impress people. Sometimes they were merely amusing.[7]

The rest of the community got used to hearing me fight with Diana, who was known to fight back, from dawn until dusk. The girls' dorm on the floor below our own used to complain about the noise. They also used to complain about our running and jumping around so that the light fixtures would swing. Once Diana and Kathy, the girls' counselor, arranged a trade. The girls came upstairs and jumped around while we were downstairs so we could see what it was like. The arrangement backfired. We were so proud that we could make the light fixtures swing. It is ironic, but even there, in such a situation, the girls got the lower hand and suffered from the selfishness of the boys. And that's just the way it was, because we were on top.

Remembering back, Dr. B., who scared me and yelled at me several times a week, never said a word to me about my fighting with Diana. That was no accident, since he could read a child and interpret what actions meant to that child the way other people could a book. He knew, I am sure, that the only way to save my life was to have Diana establish a relationship with me. Thus, since the only way I could relate was to fight, he left well enough alone.

I am struck now, so many years later, that I have so few memories of this time of my life. I ask myself how could I not be terrified, that I must have missed my parents, and why do my reactions to my dorm mates feel so muted? I don't have an answer. I am forced to guess because I was so cut off from my emotions that much of my life remained a blur. I looked at life and those around me as if I were looking through a glass-brick wall. What came back reflected through the thick glass was an image based on what was there, but wavy and distorted. I can't remember who I was. The problem was that I didn't know.

Most people can't remember anything prior to being three or so. I can. Not everything, and not much, but distinctive memories of my grandmother's apartment at Sunday brunch with the crystal and silver gleaming on the tablecloth (she moved before I was one); I remember learning how to escape from my crib by putting my hand through the slats and pushing down on the metal foot bar to lower the side wall of the crib—and I remember the terror of having to pull my hand and arm through the slats as fast as possible so they wouldn't get smashed when the side fell down; I remember climbing out, leaving the apartment, and sliding down the red carpeted stairs on my bottom, because I was still too young to know how to walk down stairs; and I remember walking around the neighborhood, waiting at each corner for a grown-up to arrive, so I could cross the street, since I didn't yet know how to cross by myself. This was not unusual, for I did this several times, waiting for my mother to take her nap, since she was pregnant with my next brother, who was born when I was two months shy of my second birthday. When she woke, she'd find me missing with the front door open and would have to go search frantically for me. Being my mother was not easy.

The reason most people can't remember the early parts of their lives, I think, is that we store memories in words—which is how we file and retrieve the facts of our lives. Prior to words, the filing system doesn't work, so it is hard to retrieve anything concrete. Most people become articulate at three or four, when memory seems to begin. Because I began talking so early, I had a primitive filing system that I could later access. Feelings, however, color memories, and the important events of our lives are stored with the feelings attached to the memory, which is why certain songs, smells, and faces bring back a wealth of emotion as well as data that is more than just hard facts.

Thus, I lacked a crucial factor of memories, the feelings associated with them. I did not know what I felt, and, besides, I lived too much in my own world to truly acknowledge anyone else. I have more memories of Diana than anyone else back then, but even for her, many of them were later when I was eleven or twelve, when I had already made "first contact" with her.

Now, thinking about those first meetings with the Mohawks and trying to tell you what it was like, I am sad that there is so little there to retrieve. Of those first few months, my memories are sporadic. Once, after the lights were out and I was trying to get to sleep, I was thinking about my mother. There was a flash and I could see her face in front of me, almost lifelike. It vanished and try as I might later to make it happen again, it never did. By the time I did see my mother a year later, so much had passed, and I had already begun to step outside the family orbit. I remember my first visit home, a year and a half later, when I saw my brothers again and met my youngest brother for the first time. After supper, before taking me back to the School, my mother came into the bathroom with a washcloth and asked if she could wash my face, since the next time she saw me, I would be too big. She washed her eldest son's face for the last time, and, indeed, it was the last time she cared for me when I was a small child.

My first morning, Diana came in to get us up at seven-thirty. The life of a counselor was hard—for she had put us to bed the night before at nine, read a story, and didn't leave until we were asleep at ten or so. Counselors worked ten shifts a week: weekday mornings seven-thirty to nine, then five shifts after school from 3 P.M. to 10 P.M. or so, and four shifts on weekends, mornings from 8 A.M. to 3 P.M. and evenings from 3 P.M. till bed. Two counselors alternated for each group—and when they weren't "on" with us, they had to take us for clothes, the dentist, doctor, any other special trips, not to mention the times they were both together for special trips, birthdays, and parties. One would be hard pressed to find people who would do that today on a stipend of some $2,500 per year—equivalent now to maybe $15,000.

At night, after putting us to bed and reading a story, Diana would sing each of us a song that we chose. For a long time, she sang me "Wouldn't It Be Loverly" from *My Fair Lady*. It was a song of hope for us both—for me that I could have a real home, safe, warm, and secure ("All I want is a room somewhere, far away from the cold night air") and for her that she could weather my stormy rages and constant arguing to help me achieve this. Some twenty-five years later in London where I was working as an investment banker, in the first apartment I ever bought, I sang that song to myself while arranging my first antiques. When alone and no one was looking, I would pinch myself to make sure that this room somewhere in London, like Eliza Doolittle's hope, was not a dream.

Being who I was and the others being who they were, we considered all this attention our due. Both Diana and Ugo had their own rooms past the fire doors that separated the older building up front, so they, with other staff, lived with us although they had their own building, which we were not supposed to go into by ourselves. Nonetheless, despite this workload, even when Diana wasn't on, she would stop by the dorm to say hello, not out of a sense of duty but because she wanted to. To this day, I sit in disbelief: She wanted to see me, with a schedule like that, and still she would show up. Of course at the time I repaid such devotion by arguing, refusing to go to bed, refusing to get up, and demanding to go on all sorts of trips around the neighborhood.

That first morning Diana arrived, opened the curtains, and started some quick baths for the bedwetters. I remember just pulling the covers over my head, since I never was much of a morning person. Once Diana told me that she would rather stick her head in an oven than get me up in the morning; I was proud of that remark and would remind her of it constantly in the years to follow.

Since I was late, I had to race down to breakfast after Diana took the others to make it on time by eight-fifteen. Groups were known to be late sometimes, but if an individual was more than five minutes late, he or she had to eat on the bench outside of the dining room. Food was never withheld, but it was humiliating to have to eat outside where everyone could see that you had been late. I arrived post five-minutes and sat down, since the rule was unknown to me: It was my first morning. From across the dining room, some lady came over and grabbed my arm and ordered me out to the bench. I protested that this was unfair, since I hadn't known the rule. The woman, Jacqui, who would later be the School's director, was then the most senior counselor at the School. For me, she was often the Wicked Witch of the West. I was forced to eat breakfast on the bench my first morning.

Diana, however, had made notes of that morning. She does not report that Jacqui kicked me out of the dining room, but I am pretty sure that it happened.[8]

According to Diana's notes, it took me four days to settle in to the School, although I wouldn't admit it to anyone (or myself) for a lot longer. It is clear, at least to me, from reading these notes that she had my number almost immediately. It was an understanding with affection and amusement, not judgment. I don't remember much of the goings-on, but I was never simple or a fool, and if I could see that I needed to be at the School after four days, then somewhere I didn't doubt that my life was seriously out of kilter. Maybe, however, it was Diana who made me want to stay. For I could see acceptance in how she treated me and the other Mohawks. Looking back, it is remarkable, really, how quickly she won me over. Not that it meant a whole lot of improved behavior or made my life any easier, but she held out hope for something better. Hope at that time was in short supply.[9]

I would turn to Diana but often didn't want to be direct about being babied by her, such as being held by her or sitting in her lap.[10]

Evidently, those first few months I managed to hurt myself constantly—nothing serious, but enough to make Diana concerned. Since I had to tell the counselor every time I did something, and I would feel very guilty if I didn't, there were update injury reports ten times a day and it was impossible to get through a meal without my being kicked or kicking someone. My being kicked was not surprising, since I was so trying and took so much attention that my dorm mates and classmates wanted to get back at me. Even with all the attention, I do not remember being such a baby. In one report, Diana comments that she thinks I have gotten to the mental age of three. It doesn't surprise me, but it was hard for me myself to judge how needy and how backward emotionally I actually was, because I could disguise it with my intellect. My intellectual knowledge was spotty—the Becks had reported that I couldn't tell them all the days of the week (I kept missing Wednesday), and Diana reports that I didn't know the months; I kept forgetting April and November. After thinking it over years later, all I could conclude was those were the months that my brothers were conceived.

There was one morning that Diana overslept and we knew we were going to be really late for breakfast, since we had overslept, too. We jumped up to get ready, someone went to get Diana, and I volunteered to dress Paul. That memory brings a small smile to my face as I remember both my presumption as well as Paul's sweetness. He evidently walked around later protesting in his own way the fact that I had dressed him. Other than that rare occasion, Paul was too autistic to often object to my bossiness. I never considered him a rival.

As far as my destructiveness went, I don't know where it would have ended. I was too out of control at home with my parents, so without Diana stopping me, I might very well have "accidentally" done something to do myself in.

4

Luitgard's Class

In the mornings, when the weather was good, after breakfast we would all go to the side yard, where we could hang out with our friends from other groups. At nine, the teachers would come and call their classes and we would go off, leaving our counselors to catch their breath. I don't remember how many of us were in Luitgard's class: Paul from my dorm was there. Lilly was there, too, of course, la-la-ing her way through the day. There was Jim, my rival in class, as Daniel was my rival in the dorm. Jim was a year older than I, bigger and somewhat of a bully. Daniel I learned to love, but Jim remained someone I never quite respected.

There was Humphrey, a big lug, eleven or twelve, fascinated by knights, always carrying around a big book that he couldn't read in the same way that he would later pretend to exercise all the time to be big and strong, while he remained fat and out of shape despite all the hours he devoted to pretending to work out. He would also talk about going to a great university. As chance would have it, I ran into Humphrey years later when I returned to visit Margaret and the School after I had finished my first semester at Yale. Humphrey was back visiting, too, and when I was on my way back to the front offices to say a few words to Jacqui, by then the director, I ran into him. Jacqui said, "Here is your old friend Humphrey," and I remember praying that he would not ask me what I was doing or where I was in school.

I knew he would feel bad and I had no wish to see him hurt. Somehow he knew not to ask, and I was grateful that the gentle giant had escaped, once more, another piece of painful reality.

Another kid, Benji, semiautistic and maybe ten, was fascinated and terrified by the weather, which was not an unusual symptom. Many kids were obsessed by the weather, one of whom read the word as "we eat her." Benji had to know all about the weather or he would panic. He also saw Margaret, one of the School's two psychotherapists, in session, and, after I started seeing her, too, he never forgave me. His hostility was quiet but ever present and all the worse for its never-ending coldness.

Luitgard pulled us all together and made a place where we could play and learn. She made learning so much fun that she encouraged in me a love for it that has lasted all of my life. Given Benji's obsession with the weather, she put that to use teaching the entire class science, math, and English. In this pre-Xerox era, each morning she would bring each of us our own cutting of the weather map and forecast from the *Chicago Sun-Times*.

We made a barometer from an old Mason jar with a balloon stretched tight over the top with a straw glued on that would move up and down due to air pressure that we would calibrate with a "store-bought" barometer so we could read our Mason jar balloon unit. We had thermometers to measure the temperature, a unit with cups that spun around to measure wind speed and direction, and a hygrometer with two thermometers—one with a wick over the bulb of mercury, which we would carefully wet and then swing around our heads on a string. After measuring the elapsed swing time, we would check the temperature difference caused by the evaporation. From the temperature difference, we could calculate relative humidity, which affected the rate of evaporation as we swung the hygrometer over our heads. We would check out the clouds, and, in those days, I knew the difference between a cumulus and nimbostratus cloud. We would each write up a copy of our weather report in the best handwriting we could and deliver them to the other classrooms. It was an issue of pride to get it right. The entire School knew of our prediction and could check it the following day to see if we were right or not. Sometimes we were wrong and then we had to learn how to deal with making a public mistake.

Our big competitor was the *Sun-Times*, and there was a running tally of whose prediction was right more often. I am proud to report that we usually beat the *Sun-Times*!

From all of this, Luitgard got us to learn a multitude of academic and social disciplines, pushed us to work together, and included Benji in the daily life of the class, no mean feat. What genius! Given that the weather was his obsession, he had a special place in the class, as far as it went, since by choosing to use the weather as a teaching basis, Luitgard honored him. How could he feel strange or bizarre given that we were all doing the weather with him and trying to help predict it?

Another project was our color lab. We tried to make all the colors we could out of Play-Doh which we made by mixing it up. We got all kinds of shades that we stored in round little balls of color placed back in the original containers. Our alchemy to transmute base metal into gold was to develop the color black. We got some dark browns and purples, which were the most valuable of all since they were so hard for us to make. If we traded colors, those dark ones were always worth the most. This project went on for months, until one day Lilly opened all of our stored colors and smashed them into a large mass. I wanted to beat her up, but Luitgard wouldn't let me—and complaining to Dr. B. would do no good; since she got into trouble so much, what was one more thing? So, our color lab came to end, but I remember it well.

Basically, Luitgard let me do what I was interested in and then found some way to make me learn more from it than I had intended. Book reports, spelling, history, science, and math all got tied into my projects.

One was our garden, where I cross-pollinated snapdragons with petunias just to see what would happen. I had to read about Gregor Mendel, his work with peas, and began some work with fractions to try to understand genetic outcomes. I had to wait all summer for this one. Once I eagerly harvested the seeds after waiting seemingly forever, then I stupidly planted them all, instead of saving some in reserve. I hadn't counted on Lilly. They sprouted, all right, and as soon as they were a couple of inches tall, she smashed them all, killing them. La-la my ass! I am sure I must have punched her good and hard when no one was looking. At the time, I vowed I would hate her forever, but as I continued to make progress and she remained the same as she always was, I could no longer hate her.

She didn't matter in my life any more. Years later, when she left to go home and finally ended up in an institution, I felt bad, but it was like hearing bad news about someone you didn't really know; you are almost relieved that it didn't happen to someone closer.

Dr. B. had reported my interest in botany to my parents in one of the regular monthly letters he sent, which kept our various parents informed in a limited way of how we were doing. He had a particular spin on my interest. His twin themes were my interest in reproduction (and where babies come from) and my anxiety about my body (and how it worked). Other themes that would reverberate through these letters were the issue of receiving care and security as well as my (sometimes improving) feminine tendencies.

Luitgard knew so much and I was so interested in nature that I spent a lot of time learning about it, but what I learned often played into what was happening in my interior world.

> *An example of his willingness to use something he learns in school to examine his emotions occurred recently, when the children talked about the breeding instinct of birds and how they take care of their young after they are hatched. The children were told a mother-bird's breeding instinct can be satisfied by eggs other than her own, or, for that matter, by any cool object. Steve was puzzled, but after a while he made two very insightful remarks. He said: "An egg is not a bird yet," and "all eggs are alike, so why should a mother-bird like her eggs." In this way he expressed his insight that one has to be a person with individuality in order to be liked. Since he is feeling more certain that we like him, such insight is now accessible to him.*[1]

This theme of nature was repeated over and over in the monthlies. A few months later Dr. B. wrote the following report to my parents.

> *The children studied seeds this month. Steve was delighted to find the embryo plants in the seeds and to distinguish their parts. At first he found only those parts which an embryo plant actually has: the root and the leaves; but soon he was busy looking for and "finding" parts which it does not have, and which he hoped would develop into petals, the pistil, pollen tubes, etc. This reflects his burning desire to see and understand not only the earliest stages of life, but that which*

causes life. He keeps hoping that seeing those parts of the plant which are involved in fertilization will also help him understand the mystery of the process of fertilization itself.[2]

As part of my interest in nature, Lilly had an attraction that made me curious. She peed in her pants all the time, often removing her underwear and running around with her skirt hiked up. Female anatomy to me was a mystery, since I had all brothers and I lived in an all-boys' dorm. Jim and I used to check out Lilly every chance we could in the beginning. After months of this, we were bored, had studied enough female anatomy, and just wished she would stop peeing, which smelled. Worse, we didn't want to sit on anything she had sat on until it had been washed.

This interest in nature, since it included female anatomy, also included sex. Luitgard was a widow. As a child, particularly in a place like the School, one could ask questions that in any other place or situation would be considered bad form. I remember someone asking her about sex, what it was like and whether she had it with her husband and had she liked it. It seemed normal to ask such a question of a widow in that place, and I still remember the quiet, dignified answer: "It was beautiful."

In the same letter that Dr. B. wrote about the mother-birds, he also reported that I had read a children's version of *The Story of Helen Keller*, a celebrated American who had attended Harvard despite being both deaf and blind since infancy. Her autobiography, which detailed how she had been taught sign language by Annie Sullivan and finally emerged into the world, was made into a major Academy Award–winning motion picture, *The Miracle Worker*.

He was very moved and intensely admired the teacher who was able to reach Helen Keller, who until then had been as if "locked in a prison." He said that he would like to be such a teacher when he grows up, and "turn the key to open the prison door for more than one person." For a few days he practiced the hand-sign alphabet.

Clearly, I identified with someone who lived in a mental prison since I felt that I lived in an actual one. Luitgard, whom I admired and found comfort with, was like an Annie Sullivan to me, by slowly getting me to join the class and to do some simple things that

I could manage to build my confidence and organize me. Just juggling all of this and managing to keep us together, safe, fed, taught, and not fighting, must have taken incredible strength of will. Luitgard did it so that I never saw the seams.

One of the nicest parts of our week was a Good Humor truck that used to come around the neighborhood. We would yell at the driver out the window to make him stop. Luitgard used to take us outside for a break and buy us all ice cream bars—mine was always toasted almond. In time, we got to know the Good Humor man, whom we liked. He was always cheerful and patient with us, even the kids who couldn't make up their minds or who could barely talk. He gave us a sign to put in the window, so he would know when to stop when driving along. I think that was also to make his life easier, since we would try to get him to stop all the time, otherwise, and Luitgard would have to tell him that today wasn't the day.

None of the School's doors were locked from the inside. Only the outside door was locked to keep strangers out. We could always go outside whenever we wanted, although it was strictly forbidden without a counselor. They didn't need locks on the door, since the mental locks were so good. It was those that kept me from running away—besides, I didn't relish the idea of facing Dr. B. after having run away, since it would have been equivalent to facing a firing squad. My father told me that he figured that the School was okay for me since I never ran away and I was perfectly capable of making it downtown to his office on my own, even at age eight. I never told him that I thought about it often but knew that I would get into big trouble. Somewhere I must have known this was a good place for me and there was always Diana, whom I didn't want to give up.

One day the ice cream truck arrived—and by this time the whole School was going to the truck, following Luitgard's class's example—and some people ran outside to the truck before the rest of their class, without their teachers. They had the misfortune of running right into Dr. B., who had an uncanny way of appearing at the worst times. He yelled at them, humiliating them, and punished them by not allowing them to have any ice cream. It could have easily been me, but by sheer luck, it wasn't.

The reason, I think, Dr. B. said no ice cream for the kids who ran outside before their teachers wasn't about the food; it was punishment for going off School grounds alone without permission. If they were not allowed off the grounds, they couldn't chose their ice cream; hence no ice cream was a consequence of their punishment but not the actual punishment. Just the result appeared the same although the meaning behind the action wasn't. Dr. B. did this kind of thing over and over, where one had to try to extract the meaning behind his decisions. Some kids (and staff, I might add) never got him, but I generally could figure out what he was getting at.

One advantage in all my reading was that I thought in metaphor and simile as he did. While I had to puzzle things out often, Dr. B. trusted that I was smart enough to eventually figure it out on my own. As I got older it got worse, and his comments got even more cryptic. By the time he left, when I was eighteen or so, he began holding me to some of the same standards to which he held the staff when I worked with some of the younger children, a difficult honor to be sure. But I am getting way ahead of myself.

This business with the ice cream truck was the only time that I can remember that someone was punished by withholding food. Well, there was the time I was threatened when I dropped a piece of fried filet of sole on the floor to show how high it would bounce, but I suppose even then, they would have gotten me something else to eat (although it might have been in the hall, on the bench). What got me into trouble was being rude to the maids. You have to understand how big a deal food was at the School. Many of us had eating problems. There was a candy closet from which any child could take as much as he or she wanted. In fact, most kids, when they got to the School, hoarded piles of licorice, chocolate bars of all kinds, plus a variety of other brightly colored confections and put on weight. The staff never said no, unless someone was in the process of eating enough to make themselves sick. There was a cookie closet, too. Coke was the only thing that was limited, I think to twice a week, both because of the caffeine and because we were supposed to drink milk since we were still growing. We got the twice-a-week Coke rights because someone complained to Dr. B. (in his weekly three o'clock meeting at the handoff) that we hardly ever had it, so, in fact, this was an extra privilege that Dr. B. gave us on the spur of the moment just because someone asked for it.

Also, once every quarter Jacqui, who among her other duties as a counselor and assistant director was in charge of the kitchen, came around and every child got to request one dish, unimaginatively called a special request, from roast beef to chocolate cake to whatever. Some of the more bizarre requests were politely turned down. I never got to have chocolate-covered ants.

Even the staff got to make requests, for many of them lived in the School, as I've said. For the youngest and sickest kids, a special request was a big deal. Making a decision on such an important issue provided a wealth of opportunity to look at oneself, or to have oneself looked at, not necessarily so delicately, either. Also, on the menu it would say so-and-so's special request, thus everyone knew in advance whose special request was being served. It seems silly, but people would get a lot of attention over their choice. Good ones got a lot of compliments, so there started to be some competition. Naturally, fights started over who got to be the first to order steak or lobster, so one steak night and one lobster night were added to the quarterly special request list to lessen the infighting.

This all seems vague now, except for once, when I requested sweet and sour meatballs, meaning the Jewish kind that my grandmother made. We got back meatballs in some Chinese sweet and sour sauce with pineapple. Since a number of us in the dorm were Jewish, as was Diana, we giggled and started making up scenarios for various Jewish-Chinese sweet and sour dishes, until we got to the sweet and sour gefilte fish, which we imagined was still alive and trying to jump away from the sauce, since it didn't like the pineapple. I think we ended up getting into trouble over this, since we were making such a commotion, it was deemed as being rude to the cook. Later I got my grandmother to send the recipe.

I put on nine pounds the first month I was at the School. For the first few days, I hardly ate at all, but then I started making up for lost time. Diana reported that I would even bring Nestlé's Crunch bars to breakfast to have for dessert. She was delighted, because it was something I could enjoy and she felt the extra weight made my face, as it got rounder, look more boyish, or even babyish, and less feminine. All of the weight went directly to my stomach, and since I had terrible posture, my stomach stuck out in front like a pregnant lady's. As vain as I was, and still am, I hated being fat, so I went on a diet and, in two to three weeks, took it all off. It was the only time in my life I was overweight. Preoccupation with food and my body was a constant theme. I was always sore or hurt or feeling sick and worried that something was terribly wrong with me. I hated my body, so clothes shopping was excruciating for me and often for Diana, too, since I liked so few things and felt I looked bad in most of them. I did like black, however, but since I also didn't want to have what anybody else had, my choices were further limited. I was still eight.

Going back to the issue of being rude to the maids and cooks, who were referred to as the technical staff, this was always a major transgression. We weren't always sure what Dr. B. would come down on us for, but one thing resulting in deep trouble for anyone was to be disrespectful to any of the maids and woe to the one who asked them to do anything like a lord or lady of the manor. There were easier ways to commit suicide. In some things, Dr. B. ran the School like an upper-class Viennese home: Dealing with the technical staff was one of them. Since there was a boys' floor maid, a girls' floor maid, a third maid for the rest of the main building, plus laundresses, gardeners, maids, cooks, a seamstress, janitors for the classrooms, and engineers to maintain the boiler, there were a lot of technical staff around. They were mostly pretty special people who at times found themselves in some pretty strange situations, but often their common sense did better than some of the staff's more Freudian-based reactions.

Often special relations developed between some of the technical staff and us, all the more special since there was no pressure. An intimacy developed, of which Dr. B. was well aware, since he had grown up in a society that took servants for granted, something his more modern-era staff missed.

Theresa worked on our floor. She seemed to be already in her fifties when I first met her, when I was eight, and she knew me until I left for college. Quietly she looked after me when she thought I wasn't looking. At age eight once I was running late (again) for breakfast and she asked if she could help tie my shoes. Terribly embarrassed, I turned her down. What was I, a baby? When I was twelve or thirteen, I had one of my first nocturnal emissions. Theresa was making my bed in the morning and felt the damp spot. She turned to me and asked me how old I was. It was horrifyingly obvious what she meant. Talk about embarrassed—she was like my grandmother—but she never said a word to me about it again or, more important, to my counselors, for which I was eternally grateful.

The thing I always remembered about her: Here she was, a black maid in Chicago in the 1960s and '70s, with huge personal dignity. She was never demeaned by being a maid, as I would have been; it was her job and she took great pride in her work with us. Being a maid had nothing to do with her value to others or to God. It was a good lesson for me, focused as I was on power and status. There was a reason why I read so much history about kings and dictators. (One of Dr. B.'s major works was titled *Truants from Life*. We had to ask permission to read his books and he was vastly amused, the reason for which I didn't understand at the time, when, at age eleven, I asked if I could read *Tyrants from Life*. No Freudian slip there! All he said was that I had to wait a few more years. Then he turned, asked, "How ist e'ryboty?" No answer. "Zhat's goot," and left the dorm, shoes squeaking.)

I only saw Theresa get mad once, which was during a postal strike, when she said incredulously, "These men are out there day after day in the rain and snow and they don't want to give them any more money?"

But when the University of Chicago unions went on strike, the one place that they would not picket was us despite the fact the School was part of the university. One of the kitchen staff was on the union board, and she didn't want us to worry about food coming in or staff crossing the picket lines. Whenever a strike began, we never suffered from it and actually enjoyed it, since we got to take the garbage out and help in the kitchen. We only really knew about its seriousness from seeing the pickets in the rest of the neighborhood.

Luitgard had ties back in Germany. Every Christmas for the two I spent with her, she would order from her hometown a special candy made of quince, which resembled the French *pâtes de fruits*, which are squares of pure jellied extracts of fruit and sugar. They were elegant, simple, and pure and such a new taste that I looked forward to each one. It was a lot of trouble to order them, not to mention the problems of making foreign exchange payments to a local village shop.

Once when she came back from vacation in Germany, in addition to sending all of us several wonderful postcards, she brought us presents. Mine was a wonderful straw turtle, but the brat that I was, I felt it was too babyish. Luitgard got me a beautiful pack of playing cards instead. I am sorry now.

Luitgard succeeded in opening a window for me of a life and culture about which I knew nothing; through her, Ugo, who was Italian, and Dr. B., who was Viennese, I had a sense that the huge world about which I read truly existed, unlike some of the other worlds that I saw daily. In time I became adept at seeing most of the other kids' worlds, too, but most of them were not of this earth. Years later, when I went to Europe for the first time, as I left from O'Hare in Chicago, I had tears in my eyes as we took off, because I was getting a chance at last to see what I had only been able to read about for so long. It was like a blind man finally being able to see. This was the summer of *Saturday Night Fever*, when the Bee Gees' "More Than a Woman" played every ten minutes on the radio. I was somewhat disillusioned when I disembarked at Heathrow eager to see all the culture I had been missing and, surprise!, the first thing I heard was the Bee Gees blaring from every jukebox from customs to the Underground.

But in Paris, at the Place de Madeleine, I found Luitgard's *pâtes de fruits* at Hediard, in all flavors, including quince. I must say, no offense to Chéz Hediard, that they didn't taste as good as the ones from Luitgard's hometown. To this day, I think of Luitgard every time I see one of those candies.

Luitgard left after I had been at the School for two years. She taught me that learning was fun, something I have tried to show a few other children when the situation arose. She seemed to disappear off the face of the earth for a while, but many years later, when I was in my mid-thirties, I found out where she was and went to visit her. I recognized her instantly but was saddened: She was alone, ill, with a sadness that I didn't like to see. She was pleased to see me, but I was disquieted on opening this Pandora's box from the past. I wasn't yet ready to go back that far in my life. I felt too much pressure for me to be a bridge into a past for Luitgard and me. If she reads this, I hope she can forgive me.

The School has weighed on me for a long time. The impetus for writing this book arrived with a series of dreams of my being about to leave the School. Instead of being terrified as I usually was when I had those dreams in the past, I realized it was now time. Almost since I left, I have dreamed that I am still at the School and it is bedtime. In the dream, I do not want to go to bed with all of New York around me, since it is way too early; however, I am too scared to leave yet, so I suffer knowing all that I am missing by remaining at the School.

Finally I had achieved enough distance from my past to be able to see it and to suffer through once more some of the feelings that I had so much trouble with the first time around. Life was finally good enough so that I wanted to remember what it was like when it wasn't so good.

5

Settling In to the Mohawks

There were a couple of cardinal rules for all of us. Number one was that you weren't allowed to hurt yourself or anyone else. This was the key that let all of us know when the line was stepped over into destructive behavior. Like most laws, however, this one was open to interpretation, and occasionally there were staff members who were less than intelligent in its application. Physical injury was easy to determine (like hitting someone); besides, it happened so rarely that it was not a major part of our lives. However, more subtle variations, such as people injuring themselves by not eating, were more difficult to judge. There were kids with eating problems and some kids who arrived with severe anorexia. Sometimes, though, someone was merely not feeling well, was too angry to eat, or tripped running up the stairs (usually me). The good staff would make the good calls; as for the others, they could end up in left field. The rest of us, as long as the less intelligent staff's victim hadn't slugged someone, just rolled our eyes. We knew when other kids crossed the line—and when they did, we let them know we knew.

Encouraging someone to do something destructive to himself was another cardinal sin. Group pressure, as we all know, is a powerful force. Corraling all of us together so that we encouraged healthy behavior, or at least didn't assist our fellow inmates in destroying themselves, was a great accomplishment. Its origin, long before I arrived, had to have been from Dr. B. He never worried about accomplishing the almost impossible.

The other rule, which was almost as big a deal and much harder to police, was not to tell secrets. Dr. B. would really get bent out of shape over this one: He didn't want us worrying about betraying one of our classmates if we were told something in confidence or we learned something that the staff didn't know. The only betrayal he cared about was any betrayal of the principle of helping one another to get well. We all knew that if we told anyone anything at any time, we should expect to have it come back and bite us in the ass as surely as if we were any Hollywood star confiding something really juicy too loudly over martinis in a crowded restaurant. Every now and then someone would forget themselves, it would always come out, and then both parties would get screamed at plus held up as poster children for bad behavior in Dr. B.'s next three o'clock meeting.

Even though we were under supervision twenty-four hours a day, there were those moments in the bathroom, or in the hall, or in the swimming pool or wherever, that we could always find to make a crack or a confidence. But the system worked because our guilt would often, in the end, make us cough up the goods.

"Whatever were you thinking?" Dr. B. would shout. These "honorable mentions," as we called them, during the three o'clock meeting were our version of the most wanted list at the post office. The old WASP adage that you only wanted your name in the papers three times—birth, marriage, and death—certainly applied here. Nonetheless, this subject came up with great regularity. You'd think people might learn, but I guess that was expecting too much or, perhaps, they wanted to get caught. And caught they were.

Juicy gossip nonetheless livened up our lives, and what we couldn't interpret we would make up about the clues we'd received by and about the staff. We would later, of course, try to look stupid, not understanding what the big deal was when we had offended someone, especially when they tried to turn around whatever we thought and used it to "psychoanalyze" us. When older, of course, I had trusted friends, but even with them, I was careful not to tell them anything that burdened them if I didn't want them to repeat it. As I got older, I worried about this less, because my attitude became that even prisoners have rights, which didn't do much either to ensure my popularity with some of the staff or to keep me out of trouble with Dr. B. But concerning the principal rule, not aiding or abetting people's problems or interfering fundamentally with their getting well, I tried not to break that commandment.

We understood the implications about aiding and abetting craziness. It wasn't always possible to describe all the myriad possibilities; like pornography, however, we all recognized it when we saw it. The only sanctuary I had was in session with Margaret. Our deal was whatever I said to her was not going to come back to me. Margaret ensured that it never did. Some of the other staff was not as good in protecting their kids. It was one thing to tell another kid something provocative or loaded, because if he or she had their own reaction, he or she was perfectly entitled to talk about it. On the other hand, if you were already discussing something privately with a staff member, such as being angry with someone for whatever reason, the last thing you needed was having Dr. B. standing over you, yelling.

For a long time after I came, my behavior was sufficiently bad that Diana worried about how to restrain me. I had such little self-confidence she didn't want to damage it further. On the other hand, she couldn't let me careen around the dorm unchecked.[1]

I could tolerate the structure of solitary activities, such as building models or reading, but not playing with other kids. I tried to join in the games sometimes but was always hurt because the others didn't want to play with me. Of course, at that point I couldn't see that my rejection may have had something to do with how bossy I was. The game had to fit in or otherwise reinforce my ideas or fantasies. My imagination would run away and could not be corraled. In one report, Diana describes how I tried to join a game of rocket ship with the other kids, but scared them with my discussions about aliens, monsters, and space mishaps. It was not appreciated that I had the spaceship take off without their consent to escape the alien invaders. My bossiness and my need to indulge my fantasy life meant that the next time, they would play without me. While the others didn't want to play with me, my imagination, however, did earn me some grudging respect.[2]

The School had outside consulting psychiatrists who would see the kids a few times a year. Dr. George Perkins, who was there for the first ten years I was at the School, would later figure more in my life since I would see him when I was home on summer visits. I always liked him. He had seen me once for diagnostic purposes before I came to the School (he wouldn't let me play with the other kids' toys when I visited the dorms with him). After my arrival, in my first formal meeting with him, the staff met to discuss me. He felt that I was not schizophrenic at all but suffered from underlying depression. He also pointed out that I had a good imagination, which could get very wild, and that I was scared about my body. Like some of the other kids, I was quite primitive in my emotions, which were very undeveloped despite my pretense of being intellectual. Diana was also concerned about my feminine identification with my mother, but Dr. Perkins felt that it was merely my way of trying to get what I needed as opposed to trying to become a woman.[3]

Evidently, too, I was concerned because Dr. B. was on vacation at the time. I had remembered being scared of him, but the notes indicate that as a small child I was more comfortable talking to him than I was later. I had also forgotten, until reminded, how he would sometimes come in and pat us on the arm or put an arm around us, which I always liked. He didn't do that to the older boys, and I remember more of him from the vantage point of an older child than I do as a younger one. Still, it was curious to me that, at least in the beginning, he was less of a distant figure. He was important as the arbiter of my new world and, given all my guilt over my actual transgressions as well as imagined ones, he could also provide absolution, thus cleansing my crimes away.[4]

The next year or so whirred by, probably a lot slower for me then than I remember it now. I do remember getting into trouble a lot. Dr. B. took his vacation in August, as he usually did, which was more unsettling to me than I remembered. He wrote me, as he did all of the kids, several postcards, always signed "Your Dr. B." I have saved them, written in elegant Old World script, and the one that I remember most is of an ornate solid gold cradle for some sultan's child with a coverlet embroidered with heavy gold thread and pearls. He wrote of the encrusted swaddling, "It must have been most uncomfortable for the poor infant." Even the postcards were therapeutic. I was always flattered that he took time from his vacation to write to all of us, for we all knew how busy he was. This was the period of his greatest fame. His books were widely read; he wrote a column for *Ladies Home Journal*, called "Dialogue with Mothers," where he answered parenting queries; he was interviewed left and right by the media; and he wrote a series of pieces for such publications as *The New Yorker* in addition to his scholarly work. He would be seen on the talk shows, which we sometimes got to stay up and watch. Even Ann Landers came to visit us, taken on a tour by Dr. B. One of the smaller kids was in the bath (thank God it wasn't me. I wanted to check out Ann Landers, who was already even more famous than Dr. B., without being embarrassed by being in the tub). She came in, saw the kid in the tub, made a comment about "going back to the womb, eh?" and walked out.

We laughed about that for months. Later, when we asked Dr. B. during a three o'clock meeting whether she had visited because she was going to contribute money to the School, he snapped, "I don't want that woman's money," so I figured that he didn't like her, either.

Later, in another three o'clock meeting, someone else asked Dr. B. if life had changed for him now that he was famous. For some reason, I have always thought about his response, since it struck a chord in me. He answered, "Yes, now when I think someone is a horse's ass, I have to keep my mouth shut." It was an amazingly revealing comment for a first response out of all the choices he could have made.

He also usually taught a graduate course or two plus an undergraduate course while running the School, where he could be found most of the day until eleven at night. We would see him every day at lunch; he would come around the dorms after school to see us—in what were called afternoon rounds; he made an appearance at dinner, staying to chat with the staff at the staff table for fifteen to twenty minutes, before going home to have dinner with his family—and he came around every night, sometimes before we were in bed, sometimes after. He would make this sweep in the dining room, going by each table, circling the room. In the dorms, it was a modified sweep, which was basically just going in, turning around in a small circle, and then leaving, unless something caught his eye or he needed to speak to someone, which usually meant getting into trouble. In the dorms, he would always ask in his German-accented English, "Vell, how ist everybody? Is everybody okay? Vell, zhat's goot."

He usually wore dark-gray wool slacks, an open, white short-sleeved dress shirt, and black leather, rubber-soled shoes. The shoes were important, since they squeaked, and in order to give a good Dr.

B. imitation, that squeak was vital. We spent hours perfecting it and found that gym shoes were an acceptable substitute. We also worked on the accent. After several hours of listening to a dormful of kids speaking with fake German accents, I am sure that our counselors were driven nuts. I don't think we ever tired of it. There wasn't one former Mohawk who can't still do a decent fake German accent, which I have been known to use when making restaurant reservations.

Even when we would go down the hall to another group to visit (or start trouble), it was not unknown to do the Dr. B. sweep, which included squeaks and "Vell, how ist everybody?" The other stock phrase, used almost as much by us and, fortunately, not as much by him, was "Vell, do you need a beating?" Usually, if you got asked, you knew you were going to get off, because otherwise you just got smacked. In my case, it was not often a rhetorical question.

Dr. B. had to know that we imitated him all the time. Some of the older kids nicknamed his wife "Edelweiss," after the song in *The Sound of Music*. I didn't know this until my second Halloween. During dinner, we were each called by Dr. B. to parade our costumes up and down the dining hall, after which he would give us our present. After dinner, we would trick-or-treat and he always had a Drostë chocolate orange and a quarter for each child. Since back then my allowance was fifty cents a week, that was a lot of money.

At any rate, someone asked him if he had a costume to wear after dinner, when he went home. He replied that he and Edelweiss were going to stay home and answer the door, since they didn't want to have their windows soaped. When someone had explained to me who Edelweiss was, I figured that he might have a sense of humor, after all. I just didn't experience it much.

Every now and again, he would catch someone doing an imitation. Often Dr. B. would pretend not to notice, but sometimes he would call the victim on the carpet for being disrespectful. Looking back, I think his response was tailored to what else was going on in that child's life. Why else would he care that we all imitated him?

During August, when Dr. B. was away, the older kids would go home to their parents for summer visits. I would be twelve before I would go home for my first overnight visit, which was in some ways like being on parole but in other ways like being thrown back into the lion's den. Dr. B.'s postcard writing chores were cut down considerably, since he didn't write to those who had visits: The School shrank to half size. Sometimes dorms would combine, since it didn't make sense to have a dorm with two kids in it. Those of us left behind were the newest, the youngest, and those who did not have any families to go to.

The staff tried hard to make the summer fun for us, with several weekly trips to the zoo and the North Pole, a children's amusement park in one of the suburbs; trips to the Dunes in Indiana; picnics; trips to the beach and the movies. We'd go in big yellow school buses, and it made being watched over the entire time a bit more bearable. That first summer we went to the Lincoln Park Zoo, which had an excellent children's zoo, where they generally had a baby chimp and rabbits one could pet. Once the baby lioness had gotten too big to remain there and was being moved into the big cat house, so she was in a small cage waiting to be moved. All my life I have loved animals and they have loved me back, so I have absolutely no fear of them. I stuck my hand through the railing (I may have climbed over a barrier to get to the cage first) and began petting the lioness. She didn't mind, but the zoo people sure did, and I got hauled out of there pretty quickly. From the School, everyone yelled at me—Diana and/or Ugo plus the senior staff member there. Still, it was cool. However, there is no mention of this in the notes—so maybe this happened before I went to the School on a prior school trip.

Living in a dorm with six other people was hard work. There was no privacy, and this became more and more unbearable as I got older. On occasion I just needed to be alone, and I never got that opportunity. I did learn how to build a wall around myself and lose myself in my books, but that was the last thing Diana and Ugo wanted. Sometimes, though, it was preferable to fighting with me all day.

One other thing about life in the dorms that I hated was the night-lights. There were two in each dorm and on a separate emergency system. They were little blue bulbs that bathed us in a shadowy twilight while we slept. Although they may have been there due to fire regulations, we were told they were there so we wouldn't be scared by the dark. After I got over my fear of the dark when I was eight or so, I and my dorm mates would cheer when one burned out in the middle of the night, giving us one evening of darkness in which to sleep. As an older kid in the Adolescent Unit, I disconnected the one in my room and counted it a great luxury to sleep in the complete dark. Of course, every time some officious counselor noticed it (one counselor was on at night—the night counselor—and would make rounds after we were asleep, which I really hated when I was older), they would change it. I just played dumb, waited for them to get the hell out, and then unscrewed it.

One of the activities that we all did was swimming twice a week across the Midway in the big Olympic pool of the University of Chicago Laboratory Schools. These were the lower, middle, and high schools of the University of Chicago—originally an educational laboratory, hence the name. I think it was Tuesdays and Thursdays we would go swimming, taking turns whether the boys or girls would go first. Some years later, in a revolutionary decision due to the effects of women's liberation, we would all go at the same time. In the beginning swimming was fun, but as the years went on, I hated it. One of the privileges of being a big kid in high school was that I could refuse to go, unless I was needed to look after some of the little ones, in which case I might be persuaded. Otherwise, I'd study or go to the library. We'd roll up our bathing suits and flip-flops in a towel and cross the Midway. In the winter, you'd freeze your ass off on the way home, and I remember how my hair used to turn to ice. We were supposed to wear hats, but I always hated them.

Mr. Zarvis was the School's lifeguard for twenty years; his real job was directing the athletic program at the University of Chicago Laboratory Schools. When I finally went to Lab School (as we called it) for my last two years of high school, it was nice to see him, since he was the only faculty member I knew. In fact, he had known me all of my life at the School and taught me how to swim, play water polo, and dive.

We used the locker rooms next to the pool. Since the staff would change separately from us, because it was felt it was not a good idea for us to see them naked, some older kids were necessary to watch over the younger ones. Once when some new potential staff member hadn't been warned and changed with us, one of the kids complained. Dr. B.'s response was a sarcastic classic: "I am sure it came as a big shock to you to find out that he had a penis."

The little kids swam in the shallow end—each season in September, there was a swimming test where everyone who was allowed in the deep end had to swim two laps in a minute. Sometimes at other times of the year, there would be a special test for one kid who was deemed ready, but that meant swimming two laps in front of half the School, and you didn't want to mess up in front of everybody. Of course, what that really meant was that your counselors wouldn't let you take the test if there was any possibility of failure, since, for our frail egos, it would be devastating. It also meant that you might get held back longer than you needed to. I so wanted to get out of that shallow end with the babies as soon as I got in it. I think I finally got to take my test when I was ten or eleven.

Of course, later, as an older kid, I chose to spend a lot of time with some of my favorite younger kids in the shallow end that I had tried to flee for so long. Mr. Zarvis tried to run a tight ship but he was a man of great patience, who often used his authority in an unobtrusive way to help out some of the newer staff. Many years later, I spent a lot of time with Teddy, a four-year-old who had come to the School as the youngest child ever and who liked me a lot. Teddy once yanked off his bathing suit and began running to the edge of the deep end. I was already in the water but was concerned he might fall in—silly me, since that was not his intention. He raced to the corner of the pool by the ladder in the deep end and, as I was pulling myself out to grab him before he could fall in, he began peeing. With no suit, the stream was about to hit me in the face, so I grabbed him with one hand over his penis and spun him around as I vaulted out of the pool. I will always remember the look on Mr. Zarvis' face as he walked over and wagged a finger at Teddy. "You are not to pee in my pool!" This had some major effect on Teddy, who for months following would walk around repeating "You are not to pee in my pool." As for me, I survived being peed on and lived through the germs.

Another memory of my first summer at the school: We had gone swimming and I dropped my flip-flops on the way to or from the pool. They had my name on them and one of the kids from Lab School must have found them and stuck them in one of the door handles outside the pool so I could find them later when I left. It was then that I made my acquaintance with Sandy Lewis. Sandy had been a kid at the School himself and came back to work as a counselor after college. I would run into him years later when I was looking for a job on Wall Street, where he was a big success. He was less successful as a counselor than as a banker and left shortly after I arrived. It was he who found my flip-flops in the door. He came over to give them back to me and asked me why I had put them in the door handle, thinking it might have some special meaning to me. I explained or tried to explain that I had no idea; that they must have fallen out of my towel and someone else put them there. Sandy refused to believe me. The more I protested, the more he felt certain that there was some hidden meaning there. He was not pleased when I finally retorted that the only hidden meaning here was that he was a moron.

I was so frustrated at not being believed. It was like those old movies where someone, usually Bette Davis, wasn't crazy at all, but no one would believe it. How I hated being a kid and not being taken at my word. Years later, when we met up, I asked Sandy if he remembered any of this, but he didn't. It was one of those little memories that had meaning only for me.

Back in the dorm, while Ugo and I had our battles, it was easier to get along with him than with Diana. I remember him smacking me a couple of times, but he was a wonderful Italian who had a contagious sense of *la dolce vita*. He was always amenable to letting us play ball or ride bicycles or even, most holy of holies, watch TV, which was more tightly regulated than in the Soviet Union. He was a physician who was studying for his U.S. medical boards, so he was often consulted whenever someone had a medical problem. We got used to him bandaging people up in our hallway, next to the locked closet, where he kept some medical supplies, along with all the dangerous stuff that was locked up, like poisonous glues, scissors, miscellaneous household items, and our allowances. (In case kids wanted to run away, they wouldn't have any money.)

Ugo did things that none of the other counselors would dare, which is why we liked him. Normally, we would be taken one by one to go shoe shopping: Once we all went with him and we each got a new pair of shoes and sneakers. I think that for all seven of us, the bill was an astronomical $200. We had a gas. Another time, Sophia Loren was on TV giving a tour of Rome. I didn't know who she was, but Ugo sure did and he wanted us to get an idea of what his home country was like. Since it was on late, we watched it instead of having a bedtime story. I remember four things from that show, depending on if you count Sophia Loren's breasts as one item or two.

The other three things: First was a huge fortress in Rome, surrounded by cannon. Ms. Loren commented that if you got hit on the head by a cannon ball, it would really hurt. I found that funny. Second was that she changed her clothes every two minutes. Three, she carefully explained how to pronounce prosciutto. Now, whenever I see it on the menu, I always remember that Sophia Loren taught me how to pronounce it.

While I was very attached to Ugo, Diana had quickly become the center of my world.[5] The reason I never had the same fights with Ugo as with her was because not only was he less important to me, but also I was less important to him, which was why he didn't challenge me as much. He was closer to Daniel and I would infuriate Daniel when Ugo would sit on his bed talking to him by climbing into Ugo's lap. I would also do this with Diana, and this did not do much to further my already low popularity. Daniel battled Ugo, not as badly as I battled Diana, but they had their war and we had ours. I was jealous that Daniel seemed to be Ugo's favorite. Daniel, on the other hand, thought that I was the favorite, since Ugo let me get away with far more than he could.

Daniel was one of the big kids and got to do stuff that I couldn't. I had never had a bigger brother—he was it. As with all big brothers, no matter how old I got, he was still bigger. Even after two dorm changes, the first separating us as he moved into the older kids' dorm, and years later, when I joined him in the new building, the Adolescent Unit, so we were back together again, he was still ahead of me, going out to high school, going on dates, and generally having a lot more freedom than I did. It seemed as if I was always following in his footsteps, but in the end, in our second reincarnation together, I was able to get along with him much better. If truth were told, part of me always looked up to him, not just because he was older; he had a good soul. I would never, ever have admitted it at the time, but he looked after me in a way and did a good job.

Part of the School's ability to operate was that in time, the older kids looked after the younger ones. This served dual purposes. There was usually one autistic child per dorm and another extremely difficult child plus five or six other kids. In a crisis, or if one kid ran out of the dorm, there was only one counselor, although there were other counselors down the hall. Without the older kids to keep the lid on, the system never would have worked. A counselor could count on having support. Even new counselors, or substitutes, who worked when someone was on vacation (or were with us once a week, to give Diana and Ugo a break and to give us someone new for a change), got the benefits of this, even if they did not know they could count on it. In all my time in the School, it never happened that a group got out of control, because in an emergency, there were always enough kids around with enough sense to take control and protect the others from themselves, if necessary.

The other reason was that it was good for the older kids to learn how to be responsible. Once, when some of the older girls were complaining about the newest addition to their dorm, who was five, Dr. B. said, "How do you expect to learn how to be mothers if you can't take care of a five-year-old?" That shut them up.

He was good at shutting people up sometimes. That first year, one of the many times that we couldn't go outside because one kid or another was upset, I complained I would rather be at home than in this prison. True to form, Dr. B. walked in just as I said it. He hauled me in the hall for a private conversation, which consisted of him telling me "Do you know why you are here?" I just looked down. "I'll tell you why you are here. You are here because your parents can't stand you, so don't talk about how much you like being at home."

I felt about an inch tall after being hit in the head with a baseball bat. In the entire time I was at the School, I never again said that I wished I was at home or that I missed my parents. I wasn't going to lay myself open to that kind of humiliation.[6]

I could forgive Dr. B. much, but not that. Even now, as I write this, I remember all those years of terror—please don't humiliate me, please don't. He just never got it. For an autistic child, Dr. B. could see things nobody else could. He was not as good with the older children—and among the older kids, he did better with the girls. He was tougher on the boys and tended to see them, or wanted to ensure that they didn't see themselves, as a threat to his authority. He was also harder on male staff, which was why in part there were always far more female counselors. At times, he delighted in controversy. Part of me always appreciated that, because so did I.

God is so jealous of Adam and Eve because he could not enjoy intercourse because he had no partner. That's why he kicked them out of Eden.[7]

Dr. B. would also joke about being the Big Bad Wolf. He knew that was his image and justified it to himself. He explained that we needed a strict framework to feel secure and to permit us to do the internal work necessary to get well while he would see to external regulations. I paid for that in ways I hope he didn't realize, because if he did, it made him a real monster. Twenty-five years later, I went to visit him in Santa Monica a few years before he died. Curiously, it was his son, with whom I had become friends after I moved to London, who had urged me to go see him, since I was still so ambivalent about my experiences at the School. As his son pointed out, no one lives forever. So I went see Dr. B. and it was good to see him again. He was a lot older and frailer than when I had known him, which saddened me. It was also not easy to hold on to anger when its object was a man struggling to survive the scourge of old age as I had once suffered the scourge of my emotions. At the end of our visit, I told him I had been mad at him all this time for his being the Big Bad Wolf. He responded, "Vell, it doesn't appear to have left any lasting damage." I went back to California to see him one more time before he died.

Yet writing this down can't convey the ambivalence with which I lived and the ambivalence of my memories. The written word, necessarily, follows one thought at a time, topic sentence, following paragraph, and concluding thought. The next paragraph can state the exact opposite, which makes the author look confused, hypocritical, or merely all over the place. It is hard for me to convey all of this clearly. Dr. B. did some bad things. He also had surprising compassion (probably all the more surprising when contrasted with his put-downs), true decency, and did a lot of good things. He was human and thus flawed, except his good and bad traits seem magnified since he did little that was ever halfway. I remain conflicted, aware of the bad but appreciative of the good. It is difficult for me, even now, to make up my mind. I think I come down in the end to this: Here was a man, despite some of the wrongs he did, who re-created his life and helped make a life for numerous kids who had no hope in hell of surviving on their own. Desperate times call for desperate measures, as they say. And there were times that I found him very comforting and appreciated his mind and wit.[8]

Diana had a different take on my feelings about Dr. B. I was often curious about her relationship with Ugo, since I had initially assumed they were married. When Diana finally persuaded me that she was not Ugo's mate and was not going to have a baby with him to usurp my special position with her, I finally assumed that my oedipal rival had to be Dr. B. I remember wanting to have Diana all to myself—I do not remember that I wanted her sexually (I was eight, after all), but I think I was scared often of what she might do to me, since I was innately distrustful of all adults, even her, but the ambivalence, particularly with Diana, was very hard for me to cope with, so I acted it out all over the place.[9]

It is also interesting to note, despite my feeling of being totally unimportant on one hand, here I was assuming that my rival had to be the head of the School, not just anyone, which was pretty grandiose, on the other.

One event that marked that first fall at the School was the assassination of President Kennedy. Like everyone else who heard about it, I remember. It must have been just past two o'clock that November 22, 1963, that we were all called together in the largest classroom. Dr. B. came in and told us the president had been shot and killed. I had worn a Kennedy-Johnson button in 1960 since my parents were Democrats; at five I couldn't possibly have known anything about the election. Later JFK became a hero to me and I read everything about him I could lay my hands on. Diana's notes are replete with my mentions of the Kennedys and how they fitted in with my personal ideology. Given my oedipal ideas about Dr. B., it was in the same vein that I would have so many ideas about JFK's family, which had four children like mine (two of the Kennedy children died at birth), and a father who was dead and no longer a rival.

We watched the funeral on TV and the deep sense of sadness pervaded everything for weeks. Having seen those images projected so many times, I have a hard time remembering what I saw then and what I saw later, but I remember from then the picture of Mrs. Kennedy being handed the flag from the coffin and John-John's salute.

Years later, when I was at Yale, I met JFK Jr. He'd come down to Yale from Brown for a football game. At a mutual friend's party after the game (Yale won), we ended up sitting in a window seat where we talked for twenty minutes or so. He then went off to another room to chat with his friends and I went to go talk to mine. One came over and asked me if I knew who that was. I responded, "Sure, John." He asked me again, not believing I could be so ignorant. I repeated, "I just told you: John."

"No, you fool," he corrected me, "it's John F. Kennedy Jr.!" When John came back into the room, he looked over and saw that I knew. He just grinned. That was his life. He appreciated that I didn't know who he was and that we could just have a normal conversation. It was clear it didn't happen often.

The assassination began a bad period in the 1960s, Robert Kennedy, Martin Luther King, the Vietnam War, and the Chicago Democratic convention. Around that time, we got a minivan school bus painted yellow with flashing red lights. Now that we had our own wheels, we could pile into the van and our counselors could drive us on outings. A factor in the Mohawks' love for the school bus was our secret service game. It was played as often as we could and we tried to keep it from the counselors, since we knew they would try to stop it. One kid was the president; the rest of us were secret service agents. When the counselor would drive up so we could get in, one of us would go BANG and the rest of us would grab the designated president, throw him into the back of the van, jump in following, slamming the door, and yell at our counselor to take off. We took turns being the president and the gunman. Looking back, I find it hard to believe that our counselors never caught on. On the other hand, they were preoccupied with traffic and the large responsibility of driving all of us. Maybe they weren't ignoring it.

One other big detail of that first year was the celebration of Christmas. As a Jew, I had never had much to do with the holiday. However, Christmas was such a huge national holiday that I couldn't help but know all about it. When I was little I figured that the reason that we didn't get Christmas presents was that we didn't have a chimney, so Santa couldn't fill up our stockings. When my parents finally bought a house with a fireplace, I was seven. I couldn't wait and didn't understand or want to believe my parents that Jews didn't celebrate Christmas. On Christmas Eve, I dutifully hung three stockings for me and my two brothers and went to bed. After a sleepless night, I finally ran downstairs early in the morning—maybe six-thirty or so. The stockings were empty. I concluded that there was no Santa Claus.

Being a Jew filled me with anxiety. I knew what happened to them. We all knew that Dr. B. had been in a concentration camp, which just added to my fears about being taken away in the middle of the night. Diana notes often my concerns about being Jewish. There was a time that I decided to be kosher, after my thirteenth birthday, when under old Jewish law a boy was considered a man. Feeling so inadequate, I had a lot of anxiety about entering the age of responsibility. I wouldn't eat pork or milk and meat together. On one of the first nights after I had started this, we were having pork chops. I wouldn't eat them and Dr. B. came over to the table. "Are you crazy?" he asked. I wasn't sure how to respond to that, but before I could say anything, he answered himself, "Of course you are. That's why you are here." He then patted me on the arm and walked away with his shoes squeaking. Although I continued my kosher phase for a couple of months until I tired of it (or decided that it no longer made sense in the modern era), Dr. B. didn't mention it again.

The concerns and fears about being a Jew had started even before I went to the School, which I didn't remember. The Becks, the people who gave me the Rorschach test, commented in their report that I had anxieties about being Jewish when I was seven. The need for protection and fear about being a Jew were continuing themes, which included the issue of circumcision (castration). Jews had to fight to protect themselves—or be destroyed. Once, after being told I was going home for the first time since going to the School, Diana reports the first thing I said was that I wanted to bring back my bazooka (a huge gun) from home, instead of my mezuzah (a Jewish prayer scroll often worn on a chain around the neck).[10]

Most of my life I have suffered frequent nightmares about being a child escaping from the Nazis. In the end of the dream, they would always capture me and often killed me by shooting me, although sometimes I was bayoneted. I have often heard the theory that you don't die in a dream, you wake up before you get killed. I can assure you that is wrong. You wake up *after* they kill you. Many years later, after I was finished with graduate school and was living in New York, a friend persuaded me to see a fortune-teller or channeler just to see what it was like. I figured why not—and found out that the *why not* was because I was scared out of my wits. The first thing this guy said to me was that in my most recent past life, I had been captured and killed as a child by the Nazis. My experience with that life was so terrible, I resisted being reborn far longer than usual, since I did not want to return. When I finally was reborn, I rebelled against this world from the moment I arrived. This fortune-teller guy, I must add, had never seen me before and knew nothing about me other than my name. Naturally, I was freaked out, but although I didn't believe him, his explanation for my troubles seemed as good as any. I had those nightmares for years, although they generally lessened over the course of my life. About five years ago, I started escaping the Nazis so they didn't succeed in killing me. Finally, after I started getting away from the Nazis, the dreams started to fade away. Then the next variation was that I could help other children escape with me—and when I couldn't save them all, I was profoundly saddened the next day, often without knowing why. Slowly, these dreams have become very rare for me, and I haven't had them in a long time, although I fully expect them to return when I am stressed.

Despite my Jewish concerns, at the School, Christmas was a huge holiday. The only problem was the letdown after it was over. The older kids who had families went home for visits, but the day before they left there was the Christmas party, which was a big event. The staff worked all night and day to decorate some room that was off limits. They would all play dumb and say, "What party?" when asked. For a child, even for me, this whole experience was magical. By the time I was twelve or thirteen, some of the glow had worn off, and by the time I was eighteen, I resented that all the staff got to go off and decorate while I had to stay with the little ones, helping them to enjoy the holiday in that limbo that the School was so good at creating with its older kids, no longer a kid, but not quite a grown-up. Such a suspension in time lasted for most of us older ones at the School for far longer that it would have in the outside world.

The day of the party we'd enter a room with huge paper hangings painted with trees and forests, a forest of small trees and a big decorated one, fake snow and icicles, cookies and punch, a pile of presents under the tree, and a visit from Santa, who called up each child and handed them their present. The small ones' faces glowed with excitement and even the most autistic child reacted in some degree to the festivity and attention. Later, as I got older, we played the game of guessing who was playing Santa. The staff would rope in ringers, getting some of their friends from the neighborhood to come in, so we older ones couldn't guess who was under that beard. We were also warned, in various subtle and unsubtle ways, what would happen to the one who tried to pull off Santa's beard. Given how important this day was, I was never jaded enough to want to spoil it, even when I was in the midst of a whole lot of tough stuff. And after the magic wore off for me, it was even better watching its effect on the small kids, most of whom had little enough joy in their lives the rest of the year.

Another of the customs I grew to enjoy was going to a special children's mass at Rockefeller Chapel. For vespers, there was a special service where each of us could pick one toy to bring to be given to underprivileged children. It was one of the parts of the holiday I liked best, sitting in the beautiful cathedral being part of the local community, all dressed up, and being able to give a present to someone, which was forbidden for us all the rest of the year. We couldn't give each other or the staff presents since some would feel obliged to buy attention and those who didn't might feel that they were being left out or not being prudent in trying to purchase favor. To avoid all the issues of apple polishing between and among us, all was forbidden. Even for vespers, if one child had trouble finding something to give away, the staff had presents for them to give. That first year I did not have a lot of toys by Christmas, so I was given a truck to take to vespers. I remember being a bit wistful when I placed it under the tree. I knew I was doing a good deed, but I had liked that truck.

Actual Christmas day dawned and each group followed a set of colored reindeer tracks cut out of construction paper down to the decorated room, where everyone's presents would be on chairs. Each group gathered together in one part of the room. Although Diana and Ugo wanted me to have toys, I was never much for them since it was hard for me to play with anyone else and I didn't like to be reminded of it. Also, my grandiosity didn't easily permit me to be a child. I once told Diana that what I really wanted for Christmas was my own dukedom, but if she couldn't arrange that, I would settle for a castle. Later I got a toy castle and soldiers for my birthday, so she granted me my wish as best she could, which she always tried to do.

Opening Christmas presents, everyone would be in pajamas and bathrobes, and afterward we would have breakfast in the dorms.

Luncheon would be our big meal, the cooks went all out, and to thank them, Dr. B. would invite them into the dining room where we would sing them some carols. Often they would join in with some amazingly good voices, since several sang in their church choirs. I had and still have such fond memories of those ladies who looked after me with so much patience and affection my entire stay at the School.

Dr. B. would serve each child coffee after the meal. That was his way of helping us celebrate, and he would ask each child how he wanted his coffee and serve the cup as a means of honoring each of us. It was an Old World custom, this serving of the coffee, and Dr. B. performed such services on each of the major holidays. To this day, in the morning, I have a bit of Christmas associated with my morning coffee, since for most of the years of my youth, the only time I had a cup was when Dr. B. poured me one on a celebration.

One year, one of the staff was from Sweden, so she orchestrated a Swedish Christmas for us, with Santa Lucia arriving with candles in her hair while bringing in a tray of Swedish coffee cakes in the morning for breakfast. We felt very exotic and sophisticated that year.

During my first Christmas there was a lot of discussion of its true meaning and stories about the birth of Christ. All of us were singing the Christmas carol "Noel" when Dr. B. walked in to talk to us—maybe it was a three o'clock meeting. What bothered Dr. B. was the refrain, "Born is the king of Israel." He took exception to the lyric, explaining severely it was absolutely wrong—and a historical misconception to refer to Jesus as a king, when what he had been was a prophet or wise man. He certainly never referred to himself that way. I can't remember his argument, but Dr. B. felt passionately about it and I figured he was mad at us for reasons that I didn't fully understand, which was not unusual. For years afterward, I lived in fear that whenever we sang "Noel," he might walk in and we would all get yelled at once again.

He also explained the historical concept of Immaculate Conception, which I had trouble grasping since, as usual, his conversation was directed at a more sophisticated level, so I interpreted what he said in my own fashion. My confusion over gender and parentage got all mixed up over the issue. A few days after my first Christmas, I acted all of this out with Diana by pretending to impregnate a beach ball. I asked Diana why a baby couldn't develop in the beach ball over the next nine months—somehow assuming that if Mary could have a virgin birth, why couldn't I?[11]

Whatever it all meant, clearly there were moments when I didn't suffer from a weakened ego.

6

The Stage

As I arrived, the School was in the final stages of being done over as Dr. B. had always wanted. He had received his Ph.D. in art esthetics and, as was typical in his era, had received a classical education. He put all of that knowledge to good use in the School, making it into a showplace, upper-class Viennese home. Finally, the School had achieved the reputation and had received enough funding to remake it to Dr. B.'s specifications. It had taken twenty years.

In his three o'clock meetings, Dr. B. would talk to us about a variety of subjects. The level of discussion was not too different from that of his undergraduate classes. When I was little, some of it went over my head, or I interpreted what he said in my own way, as I did the discussion about the Immaculate Conception, but a lot of it I understood or imbibed subliminally. Since certain themes were repeated, I comprehended more and more over time. I remember him telling us that in old Europe, the insane were often housed in the most beautiful building in the city, since they were mostly cared for by the church. This never squared in my mind with all the times they burned the insane at the stake as possessed by the devil, but maybe that was an earlier era. It may have been one of his ways to get us to feel that we were important. He said over and over that the best was just good enough for us, and his actions always backed up that statement. If the real world wasn't made an inviting and beautiful place, he would ask, why would his kids want to leave their own worlds to join it?

There was some irony in all this. After the building of the Adolescent Unit, Dr. B.'s ultimate creation, its beautifully decorated living room covered with gold-leaf wallpaper overlooking a courtyard with a center pool with jets of water surrounding a bronze statue of a girl caring for another smaller child, one of the older kids cracked, "He puts gold leaf on the walls and then yells at us for being spoiled." What more can I say? That pretty much sums it up.

The food was excellent, served on fine china, and, soon after I arrived, we got new glasses—blue crystal goblets with an etched seal of the University of Chicago. Then we got round tables, instead of square, because Dr. B. believed they facilitated better discussion. There were a dozen or so different new chairs that Dr. B. wanted everyone to try; later there was a vote on the ones we found most comfortable and liked best. When we finally voted, our selection was a chair he didn't particularly like, but since we had selected it after being given a choice, he got them for us anyway.

We had plain metal beds and wooden dressers in the Mohawks when I arrived. Soon Dr. B. came in and asked us each to choose which emblems we liked for our new beds. They arrived in blue wood carved into mini-castles, with heraldic lions on the dressers and the emblems we had chosen for our own headboard and footboard. I think I selected a knight rampant. Although it never occurred to me then, the choice of castles certainly fitted into my fascination with history, knights, and royalty—some of the other dorms had nautical or antique motifs, so there was variation. While the selection for the Mohawks was not due to my interests alone, it was by no means a coincidence, either.

Then it was new curtains, new bedspreads, a new rug (the one Francis peed on), and new custom-made chairs. The stairwell that went from the sunken ground floor up three stories to the boys' floor had a tiled mural of American legends, including Paul Bunyan, that Dr. B. had commissioned a painter to make years before I had come. There were good full-size copies of great paintings on the walls that each dorm could select—the Mohawks, in a closely contested vote, selected Van Gogh's "The Bridge."

Later a corridor was constructed linking the classrooms with the dorm building—with open latticed red brick with stained glass windows in each of the squares. Lining the wall of the corridor was a row of custom dark-stained, wooden lockers with bronze and enamel heraldic shields. Each of us got to select our symbol that was outlined in copper wire and filled with multicolored enamels by an artist Dr. B. found. Outside the door leading to the side yard, a new sandbox and a wading pool were built onto the porch of the corridor, and the side yard was redone with new sod and Japanese plum trees. We constantly got new wallpaper, new light fixtures (mostly from Italy), and new pieces of artwork kept popping up, particularly when Dr. B. got back from his summer European holidays.

The Adolescent Unit, which increased the number of kids at the School from fifty to sixty, was where I lived my last few years at the School. It had been designed by Ike Colburn, a famous Chicago architect, whose firm was I. W. Colburn and Associates. There was a custom mural by a Canadian artist, Jordi Bonet, under the arched colonnade in the front of the Adolescent Unit facing the street, linking the offices in front of the old dorms to the former church that housed the classrooms. Local visitors would often stop off to examine the mural.

During the late 1960s and 1970s, Hyde Park was surrounded by slums, which were patrolled by gangs. Dr. B. liked to tell us how everyone told him he was crazy to put his mural where it was certain to be vandalized. But it never was. Dr. B. took great pride in this, claiming that it proved his view that if you treated people with respect and gave them the best, they would, in turn, respect you back.

Soon after it was finished, Dr. B. had proposed a contest for the best essay on the meaning of the mural with the winner receiving two dollars. How I wanted to win that prize, not so much for the money (at a time when my allowance had been increased to eighty-five or ninety cents a week), but for the honor and the recognition from both Dr. B. as well as the body politic. I slaved for days over that essay, which was two typed pages. I went over it again and again trying to make it perfect so that I could win. In typical fashion, which still makes me smile, Dr. B. in the end said that he had received so many wonderful essays that he couldn't make up his mind which one was the best, so he had decided to award us all the two-dollar prize. I was both disappointed and relieved at the same time. I knew I couldn't win but hoped maybe I might, so I was pleased not to be a loser. Nonetheless, I had hoped for a miracle, which, as in the normal course of events, failed to appear. Now, in the course of editing this book, I found out by chance what happened to all those essays. I went to look up the spelling of Jordi Bonet in one of Dr. B.'s books, and there I found a photo of the mural—alongside an essay describing it. The essay is just the length (about two typed pages) and may be a composite of the many essays turned in, but after all this time, here were our essays after all. Now I know what he wanted them for![1]

In addition to the bright canary-yellow door in the front of the School that was famous on campus, there was a second door immediately behind it, Spanish, sixteenth-century I believe, with tiny carvings of polychromatic and gold-leafed figures all over it. Therapeutically placed, the door announced to all who entered that this was a special place of unusual beauty suspended in space and time. This was certainly true but, unfortunately, not the entire story.

When people now ask how I grew up, or even where I grew up, I am still not sure how to answer. Casual acquaintances get the response "Oh, boarding school"; it's not like I can really answer "On Mars," which is what it felt like. However, in the old days, I remember kids getting screamed at by Dr. B. for saying to outsiders that they went to boarding school, although how he found out, I never figured out. He didn't want any of us to be embarrassed about who we were or how we grew up. He wanted us to believe that we were as good as anyone else. There was no need to be embarrassed about being at the School. But it wasn't always so simple.

Often it was not the place to go into such things; some people were less open than others; a casual discussion didn't leave room to go into something that invariably led to questions like "Why are you there?" or more often, "Were you really nuts?" or worse, the unasked, "Are you still nuts?" Then, too, forty years ago, attitudes toward mental illness were considerably different than they are now. What passed for treatment was different. It was a hidden problem due to the embarrassment and social stigma associated with it. I understood that Dr. B. didn't want us to internalize these views—he had managed through his force of will to impose his view of the world upon it. I didn't have that strength and I was on the other side of the fence, so to speak, as a patient.

When I had job interviews years later, they always asked the stock question, "And what extraordinary life achievements have you done that separate you out?" I never supposed that "Well, I'm not drooling in a corner" constituted an appropriate response and would get me the job. Captain of the football team or debate team, editor of the newspaper, or working in a clinic in India, as many of my Yale classmates could answer, seemed simpler and more appropriate. Part of me always knew what I had achieved—true, with a lot of help—but I knew somewhere my own worth, despite my other anxieties. Diana always used to say that the kids who really made it had a streak of sanity somewhere. I think that is true.

But when I wanted a job at Lehman Brothers or Goldman Sachs, it was hard competing when I couldn't tell the truth. Especially when telling it meant for sure that I would not get the job. It was hard to sit there and be interrogated by someone who had a much easier time in life and had no understanding of what a life like mine had been like.

I would see other former Orthogenic School kids sometimes. Some were slightly different from most people. It is hard to describe exactly, but they and I had a certain limp in life. I was just glad to be able to finally walk at all, so in the beginning, when everything was new to me and just being out in the world or at Yale shouted at me "You did it!" that seemed enough. As the years went by, however, it was harder to have that limp separating me out. Eventually I went back into therapy to deal with the residues of my childhood, except that by now I have had two childhoods, the first with my parents and the second with Dr. B.

Sticking with my earlier promise to tell the truth, for a long time after I left the School, I still needed to work on myself. Just getting out of the School to me was such an achievement that other warning signs were ignored, because I felt fine. I still had a lot of anxieties—other people sensed them, but I didn't, which made me appear even more out of touch with myself. Physical limps are easily explainable. I do not mean to belittle physical infirmity. Stuff happens. Mental limps and anxieties, even in someone who is well meaning but a bit weird, make people uncomfortable. I think about that when I am not as patient as I should be with needy or anxious people. There is nothing wrong with them that years of therapy can't cure. But that is not really true. For some, they are always going to be different. I just like to think I won't be one of them. It has been harder to make the case in my life or to myself that mental limps are simply stuff that happens, too.

Even now, when I have lived so much more of my life that the School takes up a much smaller space proportionately, I still don't know what to say when people ask me casually where I grew up. Sometimes, when there just isn't time to go into detail, I still lie.

The right answer is that I grew up in a place I always imagined didn't really exist except for the powers of Dr. B.'s mind to create it. It was an island in space and time. I grew up in a pre–World War I Viennese home over half a century after the empire had ceased to exist. I didn't always think of it as a mental institution, except when times were bad and I wanted out, mostly toward the end. It was my home for a long time.

7

On Dr. B.

Before going too much further into my life and times at the School, it occurs to me that I need to discuss Dr. B. a bit more. Up to now, I have been writing about my beginnings at the School, and my image of him is based on my memories as an eight-year-old. There has been so much press about Dr. B., all coming into the public arena after his death, when he could no longer defend himself, that I am certain that I am going to be criticized by any number of people. He has been accused of falsifying his results on helping the kids, lying about his past, augmenting his résumé, using Gestapo tactics on his kids and staff, and hitting the kids. Mostly, he didn't correct the rumors that grew attached to his name. As an example, given he was a professor in the departments of psychiatry and psychology, it never occurred to me to wonder about his Ph.D., which was in art esthetics and not psychology. I am not sure it matters; he often made a lot more sense than some of his more classically trained colleagues.*

I lived with him and saw the results of his work. I read his

---

*While Dr. B.'s Ph.D. was in art esthetics in the philosophy department of the University of Vienna, the psychology faculty was also located in the philosophy department. His two examiners for his doctorate were Professors Reiniger and Bühler. Reiniger, although a philosopher, had done some work at the Psychology Institute while Bühler was a prominent psychologist of the day who ran the Psychology Institute with his wife. In fact, Dr. B. took more of his classes with Bühler and many of those classes were devoted to psychology. In addition, Dr. B. underwent

books and knew some of the children in them and the staff who worked with them. The case histories that I had some connection with personally were on the money. I never heard or saw any evidence to the contrary by the people involved. If his statistics were slanted in his favor, I don't know. I never paid much attention to them. As far as lying about one's past; as I said earlier, I've done it, too. It's been hard enough to live with the School on my back, so why do I need to explain it to everyone in the interest of full disclosure? He had Buchenwald and Dachau on his back, plus other stories that he never shared. I won't judge him on that. I did see what he could do with a child beyond hope. For that I am prepared to forgive much. If ever there was a gift given out to help those poor lost souls, it was his. He probably exaggerated his results or—more charitably—was sometimes overoptimistic about the achievements of his kids; not just to claim his own achievement—but to proclaim those of his kids. In the end, the only way for the School to exist was if it was bathed in an aura of success. Without that, none of us would have had anything. Severely disturbed children didn't have very many good other options—he knew that—so he did what he had to do to keep the School in business.

It is true that he slapped us, usually a whack across the side of the face. Sometimes two. A beating meant three or four. Once he asked me to take off my glasses, I imagine so he wouldn't really hurt me or send them flying. I was so stupefied at the request, I did it. He slapped me, and I put them back on. Later, as I thought about it, I realized that he gotten me to assist him in whacking me. God, was I a patsy or what?

It also is clear that he didn't discuss it publicly. I do not think he wanted a whole bunch of parents justifying hitting their children on his say-so. If anyone has the right to attack him for hitting the kids, it ought to be me, since I was on the other end, so to speak, of this discussion.

Being slapped was bad enough, but to be slapped in front of the

---

analysis at the time. The demarcation lines between departments so long ago were not as defined as they are currently—so it was perhaps not as misleading as might have been thought when people believed that Dr. B. was a psychologist. He had indeed studied the discipline in obtaining his degree. Given the complexity of the situation, not to mention the effect of the impending arrival of the Nazis in Vienna, correcting this particular misconception may have been more trouble than it was worth. (Nina Sutton, *The Other Side of Madness* [London: Gerald Duckworth & Co, 1995].)

entire School, as if you were outside the bounds of humanity or too stupid to understand an explanation, was worse. Seeing other kids slapped or yelled at in public was pretty horrible, too. I didn't want to watch because it might be me next time. If it was an older kid, that was especially tough, for they were being treated just like a little kid. Was this, then, what I had to look forward to?

The worst part was not knowing how to react. What do you do when your last shred of dignity is being stripped away? Do you get angry, respond meekly, yell back, or, worst of all, hit back? There were two or three times that someone did hit back: One of the girls once hit Jacqui back, and I was terribly unsettled by it. It was wrong and placed the girl outside the bounds of our society. It may be sexist, but a girl-girl fight somehow seemed less dangerous. When one of the boys took a swing at Dr. B., after Dr. B. had hit him, I felt worse. For one thing, Dr. B. was already an old man. But I had so wanted to hit back after all the times I was hit. Despite my horror, there was some sympathy or at least understanding.

In three o'clock meetings, in his classes, and in his writings, Dr. B. could be so reasoned and intelligent. He just didn't always practice what he preached. Nor did he always cloak his view of reality with human kindness.

> *Realistic views are always selfish. Already in Socrates, a realistic view is not a moral one. He refused to run away after an unfair trial because of his moral convictions. Would realism bring a mother to tell her baby that he is a shitty baby when he needs changing, even if it is realistic? There is a reason that the people who speak the truth are nailed to the cross. That's where they belong. People need human kindness to clothe the truth.*[1]

So he engendered a lot of anger. It was during one lunch, Dr. B. came over and felt that Fred was doing something bad to himself of which Dr. B. didn't approve. Fred was at the time thirteen or fourteen and had a somewhat unusual position at the School, since his family raised a lot of money for the School and his father, I believe, sat on the board of directors. Thus Fred had to live without the same separation of church and state that the rest of us enjoyed. While it is true that Dr. B. had no business slapping a teenager in the dining room, in front of the entire community, it is equally true that one does not punch an old man in the nuts. I was seated at the table a couple of seats away when it occurred and I immediately felt sick. Some holy law had been broken since always before Dr. B. had seemed invincible. Now, like primitive tribesmen who suddenly learn that the white conquistadors bleed, too, and are thus not gods, we all could clearly see that Dr. B. was mortal.

Many years afterward, I learned of the rumor that later the same day, Fred was held by two of the larger male staff so that Dr. B. could slap him back. I had chills when I heard this. If the kid had been expelled, he deserved it, but Dr. B. shouldn't have hit a teenager in the first place–and certainly shouldn't have employed Gestapo tactics later on with two ex–football players, whom I never truly respected again. However, this never happened. I ran into Fred recently and finally asked him. He said that not only did the incident never occur, but afterward, Dr. B. never hit him again. Yet I and many others believed this story—and it formed part of the lore of Dr. B. His reputation for viciousness was exaggerated, but his behavior made such exaggeration credible.

Even though I was never hit again after I was twelve, I lived with the terrible fear of what I would do if I were. Worse, how would I live with the humiliation? That fear of being humiliated and having no appropriate response left terrible scars.

This is a pretty loaded issue in this politically correct age. There are times, however, that I look around and see some outrageous behavior perpetrated by undisciplined children and I think about the old adage of sparing the rod and spoiling the child. One unintended consequence of Dr. B.'s hitting was it seemed to legitimize such conduct. As an older kid, I smacked one of the younger kids twice. The child in question, Michael, was a violent acter outer who spent his life in terror that the rest of us would take retribution on him for both actual and imagined activities. He wasn't always clear on the difference. In many ways, he sounds just like me when I was little, too, which is perhaps why I liked him so much, but, unfortunately, he was much worse off. The first time I hit Michael, he had just kicked me in the balls. It was an automatic response, not because I was hurt and angry, but because I knew that he would continue acting out and might really hurt himself until he felt that he had been punished sufficiently. I smacked him and that ended it (except for the ninny counselor who tried to interfere and often created trouble when she could). My smack, I knew, would not result in a trip to the emergency room; left to his own devices, I was concerned that Michael might end up there.

The second time was also Michael, who had gotten up in the middle of the night and peed on another kid's head. It was preferable that I smack him, get it over with to reassure Michael as well as keep peace in the dorm rather than risk an escalation of war among the younger kids. Also, I didn't want Michael thinking he could get away with such an act. It ended up that I was up most of the night, I had to slap him again and send him back to bed. I didn't sleep well, since if there was to be a new target, it might be me, and I didn't want to be woken by someone peeing on my head.

We had two new counselors at the time. Dr. B. had retired. I was nineteen, had been at the School for eleven years, and got stuck a lot of time picking up the pieces in the dorm. It seemed to me that our new counselors were not going to be able to do much except flap their hands impotently.

Looking back, I realize how important this experience was to me in fathoming out my life within this milieu. I was forced here to make a decision to smack a child, something that was against one of the highest laws of our community, to protect him. I didn't hit him out of anger even when I was angry but out of necessity and, perhaps, fear of what he might do unless this issue was immediately settled. I hadn't slapped him when he bit me once, which resulted in a trip to the emergency room for me to get a tetanus shot, because at that time I did not understand him well enough and wouldn't have dared. Also, I think, Dr. B. was still at the School. When Michael kicked me in the balls or peed on the other kid's head, Dr. B. had retired, so without the Big Bad Wolf around, I had to be the Little Bad Wolf. Not for me, but to reassure Michael that he was not going to be allowed to get out of control. In the back of my mind, too, was the knowledge that the stakes here were high: Michael's life and whether he could be controlled enough to stay at the School. I did not want Michael locked up for the rest of his life and was prepared to do whatever that was in my power not to lose him. Someday he might or might not forgive me for hitting him. I would never forgive myself if I had not done all that I could to help him.

The situation gave me a sense of what Dr. B.'s role was—and the pressures he faced, not just with one kid, but with sixty and a staff of thirty. Errors couldn't help but be made. In Dr. B.'s lexicon, errors were forgivable, inaction was not.

If I had been the person twenty-five years ago who I am now, I do not think Michael would have kicked me at all. In the end, we had a good relationship and he respected me. If I yelled at him, that was sufficient. Often a raised eyebrow was enough. That evolved as follows: There were dorm changes again; Michael and some of the smaller children were placed together in one dorm. Seven little boys like that were a lot of work. I would come over and visit Michael and the others sometimes after supper, just to say hi and see how they were doing. It was a privilege of being one of the older kids that I could roam around, and it was appreciated. The boys' counselor took the opportunity of my presence to go up front and take twenty minutes to go to the bathroom, regroup, and, maybe, have a cigarette. After spending all day with those kids, the miracle was that he wasn't up front shooting heroin.

As soon as his counselor was out of sight, Michael grinned and started jumping from one bed to the next. (It was strictly forbidden to sit, let alone jump, on another child's bed.) I started to get angry, realizing that unless I shut Michael down, I was very quickly going to have seven extremely anxious and giddy young boys on my hands, making my life miserable for the next half hour, all of whom would welcome their counselor back in a mini-riot. I started to get angry, stopped, sat down, and started to laugh. Michael didn't expect this. He came over immediately and demanded, "Why are you laughing?"

"Well," I said, "it strikes me as funny that here I am getting all worked up over this, when you should be the one who is angry."

"Why should *I* be angry?"

"Because look at yourself. You are behaving like a nut. You ought to be angry at yourself for letting yourself act this way. Is this the kind of person you want to be? Why should I have to be angry that you behave so badly?"

That shut him up good. (Maybe I had learned my lessons from Dr. B., after all.) Michael went to his bed and sat down to think, not saying a word for several minutes. When he got up, he behaved perfectly. There was peace in the dorm and his counselor never knew how much he had missed. Never again afterward, until I left the

School, did I have a problem with Michael. He certainly became no angel, but he didn't need to push my buttons and he could listen and let me help him control himself. He didn't need to test or provoke me any further. Why? I am not sure. But I think he witnessed my taking control of myself and my anger in a way he could comprehend. I chose not to get angry. I chose not to respond. I chose to be responsible for myself. If I could do it, then maybe he could, too. At any rate, Michael didn't need to worry I was going to lose control with him. He felt safe with me.

I discussed hitting kids with some friends recently. My friends, who are Danish, live in a society where it is against the law to hit your children. They firmly believe that there were other ways to handle things; it is never right to hit a kid; that if I had thought about it more, I could have come up with a better solution. I respect their views. They weren't at the School, however, and then, this kid needed to know that there was someone there bigger and stronger than he was to lay down the law for his own protection.

When I was little, I was always getting into trouble, but part of the reason that I got into so much trouble was that I had such a guilty conscience that I was always hurting myself. So Diana, Ugo, Luitgard, and Dr. B. or Jacqui would yell at me or smack me—well, Luitgard never hit that I remember, Diana maybe once (she says never), Ugo a couple of times, so mostly it was Dr. B. and occasionally Jacqui—to end whatever I was feeling guilty about, so I wouldn't hurt myself. Since I talked about throwing myself out the window and killing myself for several months after I first came to the School, they were not inclined to take any chances. This worked for me, although it also gave me a feeling of terror about Dr. B. I wonder, however, what my feelings of terror would have been had I felt at the time that there was no protection from my guilty conscience. In the end, it may very well have been worse.

If I felt so strongly about Michael, I am inclined to give Dr. B. the benefit of the doubt in many situations with the smallest and sickest children. He ran the School so the craziest children felt secure. For a time I was pretty crazy, too. Later, when older, the rest of us had to deal with the reign of terror. As for the weakest, most damaged kids, he did a great job. He vanquished their demons (and mine when I was one of them) enough to give them a few years of peace. We all acknowledged that in the case of the sickest kids, moving them from a back ward to a front ward was an immeasurable improvement in the quality of their lives.

Crazy as I sometimes was, I was never as far gone as many of the kids, not only the autistic ones, but also many others who suffered not only from extreme emotional immaturity, as I did, but also from an almost complete intellectual blockage. When push came to shove, I could understand many things. As for the ones who could not, most of us cannot imagine what their lives were like or the fears with which they lived daily. I thought I had problems, but I knew even back then that my life was a piece of cake compared to theirs. For a long time I have thought that if the cost for giving them security was the terror I lived with later, maybe it was an acceptable price. I survived and even prospered. I do wonder, however, if there was not a better way, where the sickest could have gotten what they needed without my feeling all the time this terror of being put down once I was older.

On the other hand, while Dr. B. created a reign of terror and sometimes slapped us, he never permitted anyone to drug us. (The sole exceptions were one or two times when a child was too far gone to remain at the School and was sedated for the plane trip home.) Dr. B. had a horror of drugs. I always presumed the strength of his views resulted from his experiences with the Nazis and Dr. B. had decided that physical incarceration may have been one thing, but imprisoning someone inside of his or her own body—he wasn't going to take part in that! I remember him saying once regarding behavior modification, "If you let a trained canary out of its cage into the woods, it will soon die." He elaborated on that later.

> *Plato described life as a chariot driven by two horses, the black and the white, which pull apart and the job of a man is to keep them together on the road. White is virtue; black is negative. If one could choose between the horses, one would unhitch the black. But two horses are needed to pull a chariot, not one, so each horse is too weak to keep going on its own, so one needs both. The reason the horses pull the chariot is similar, horses (forces) are not under our control. They are the vital forces, the forces of light and darkness.*
>
> *No view of man has stood up which had a monolistic explanation—only dualistic or more has stood up as an explanation of man.*

Freud tried for a long time to get along with a monolistic explanation, but it didn't work. They have never been able to explain phenomena of human nature, feelings, etc.

The horses are the id and superego; the charioteer is the ego. The ego balances between the id and superego—the ego has the energy to control the horses (superego and id).

A good charioteer must be familiar with the chariot, how it performs under certain conditions, and he must know the condition of the road. Plato says the charioteer must keep his eye on his star. But which one is a person's personal star? Only by knowing oneself can one know which star is one's own.

This is a very subtle image, for no one can know what another's star is, only the charioteer can know, himself, and perhaps he is in error.

Plato made it very clear that only each person can know which is his own star and can know his own life's path. The problem with behavior modification is that it is predicated that another can know what is best for you. One of the tenets of psychoanalysis is that no one else can know and determine another's goals or purpose in life. One can erroneously select the wrong star by not knowing himself or one can believe what others have told one which is his star. Or one can try to go too fast to one's star and the psychic chariot can break—a psychotic break, coronary, ulcers, etc.—because one does not adjust his speed to his particular chariot. . . . One cannot compare one's road with another's or one's speed because we don't know another's road or star.[2]

He felt the same way about drugs. Within the School, tranquilizers or other psychopharmacology didn't exist. Just getting an aspirin for a headache was a major undertaking. I seldom had headaches, but I remember one or two times when the only way I got an aspirin was to go find Dr. B. and ask him. Otherwise, the staff never would have given me one. But pills did present a certain magic as a cure-all. Once when I was little I asked Diana what it meant to get better. She responded by asking me what did I think. I responded, "Taking an aspirin." And my first day at the School, when I was sad on my bed, I had asked for an aspirin, then, too, since that's what grown-ups always took in commercials to feel better. Aspirin had another meaning for me because when I was three, I had eaten an entire bottle of flavored children's aspirin. I had to have my stomach pumped. Later Dr. Perkins, the consulting psychiatrist, said that he had thought it was a suicide attempt. I was curious that so much was already wrong with me that at three I wanted to kill myself. It was also curious that I would think of aspirin as the magic pill for a long time.

Much later, when I was seventeen (although I suspect the same thing went on when I was little, too, by older kids unbeknownst to me), we would smuggle in aspirin to the school since it was so hard to get. One case that brings a smile to my face was, after visits, the staff would go through kids' luggage like customs agents searching for drugs. I wasn't bothered much, but some kids got put through the wringer. One of them knew he was about to be searched, so he palmed off a bottle of aspirin to a dorm mate who hid it in the School's youngest child's toy box—in a place the little one would never find. Later, after the boy emerged from customs, the bottle was removed and placed in a more secure hiding space. In times of desperation, one knew how to get an aspirin, but various black market favors would be called, and you always knew you had to pay.

Looking at the rampant drug use of kids today, it is a good illustration of what our world was like back then: For us aspirin, not pot or coke, was the drug of choice and the one that we smuggled. In the long run, if you were stuck in a group with an autistic kid who screamed for hours, aspirin was far more vital than anything except a gag, and none of us was really prepared to do that, even if we thought about it. Besides, people who lived in glass houses, since I was not one of the more silent types, had to be careful pushing that route.

Part of the dread of drugs resulted from the overall barbaric attitude to any sort of treatment in those days. Prozac and Paxil didn't exist. The drugs that did exist left you like a zombie. It was an era that still believed in electroshock therapy, but back then, unlike now, it did a lot more actual brain damage. I mean, they just ran a current into your head until you had convulsions and passed out. By the 1960s lobotomies were out of favor, but for a time they had been an accepted treatment. Rumor had it that even the Kennedy family had given their daughter Rosemary a lobotomy in the hope she could be helped.

Anxiety of what would happen to one outside the School was not unjustified. Getting thrown out of the School was a big worry, particularly since I wasn't really sure how "one got well." I just managed the best I could. Every now and then, one of the kids would suddenly leave, and those departures had the sense of a funeral. Dr. B. was up front about it with us, and we would be told when a child was drugged for the plane trip when being sent to an institution. Thus, drugs for me were connected with institutions, failure, and all the other anxieties associated with being turned loose in a society that often treated mental illness with medieval barbarity.

For me, when a child left the School suddenly, frequently to go to a "real" mental institution, those sudden leavings were akin to the knock on the door in the middle of the night by the Nazis as they dragged you off to the concentration camps. Once you were in their clutches, you were finished. Every time a child left the school in this fashion, it confirmed my sense of anxiety and worked to continue the reign of terror that I felt living under such conditions. I didn't know when it might be my turn to get thrown out. Indeed, Dr. B. was known to threaten to throw me out of the School. Since at that point in time, a rather long point in time, I wasn't sure I could survive on my own, that put the fear of God in me. Dr. B. would reiterate time and again to all of us that if I didn't do what I needed to do in the School, I wasn't going to be able to do it outside later. This was, as he would say, the last stop. Years later, toward the end of my stay, such warnings, although they may have been helpful when I was little, worked to rob me of any confidence that I could manage on my own in the outside world.

The stakes were high. Even so, I think Dr. B. sometimes stepped over the line. It wasn't the hitting in the end that bothered me most but the humiliation. He was tough on parents, too. Once, when my father asked him about my Jewish education, Dr. B. snapped, "If you are so concerned about your children's Jewishness, move to Israel!" He never provided much support to my parents after I came to the School, or suggested that they might want to investigate treatment for themselves to deal with my being sent away and to assist them in helping my brothers cope with my sudden disappearance.

Dear Mr. and Mrs. Eliot:

After your last telephone call, in which you requested a visit with Steve, I carefully surveyed the situation with our staff. It appears that the last visit set him back considerably. Of course it might have to do with the fact that it was the first time Steve saw his baby brother; but it took him more than six weeks to recover from the visit, from which he returned with as bad a feminine identification as he first came to us with. While the July visit had no such bad effects, the October visit had such far reaching consequences that only during the last month did he begin to recover from it.

After your call we took occasion to talk with Steve about a visit and he himself realized that the last was not good for him and does not want any right now. I therefore feel that there should be no visits for quite a long time. I realize that this is very hard for you to accept, particularly after I told you on the phone that you might call me about a visit in about six weeks; but this was before I examined the situation carefully. I hope that you can accept this long postponement, in view of that fact that this is what's best for Steve.[3]

It is possible that Dr. B. felt that he had to guard my interests most of all and that my parents were smart enough that, if so inclined, they could seek out treatment on their own. (Indeed in his book *Home for the Heart* he makes that exact point about his treatment of parents; he waited for them to ask since, if they wanted help, it was clearly available. However, he also felt that for him to suggest it would be resented and would not do any good, because the parents needed to desire it for themselves, and not undertake it at his suggestion.) My parents were so deeply offended by Dr. B.'s conduct that my father usually referred to him as "Brutal Bruno." Since many of us at the School referred to him the same way among ourselves, out of the hearing of the staff, I never thought that this was so unusual.

It is pretty easy to attack Dr. B. for his failings—by being so tough and so arrogant, he made it easy. I felt most of my terror with him as a child; by the time I was sixteen or so, it was far easier for me to make sense of the world and, with it, him. What people forget is that serious illness requires serious treatment. We accept poisoning ourselves by chemo as appropriate treatment for cancer. We amputate when necessary. For me, there may have been an easier way, but it would not have been easier, I don't think, by much.

If I think about what I have had to do on my own, after I left the School, it was pretty tough, too. I do not think I can blame Dr. B. for that. During the bad times it is easier to look for someone to blame, and he made an easy target.

Too, we forget that he was, as all of us are, a creature of his time. Autocratic father figures were not unusual in prewar Vienna. He would remind us of this often, when he discussed Freud, by pointing out that Freud's theory on sexuality was due to being raised in the Victorian era.

> *Freud emphasized sexual aspects of behavior to the detriment of others, but that was due to Victorian repression.* Interpretation of Dreams *is Freud's major work and appeared in 1900. Each society represses some things and flaunts others. Victorians showed great morality and repressed sex. Now it could be said the reverse is true.*[4]

He did not suffer fools, worried about the big picture, had enormous concerns about society and its apathy, and spent his life fighting enemies, both real and perceived. His concentration camp days worked to remove normal consideration from his concerns, and his work with such severally disturbed children most of his professional life forced him to spend his time on life-and-death issues, since I considered being locked up in a ward for the rest of one's life to be a death sentence.

I do not forget that he created the School; its ethos, drive, and conception were all out of his head. He pulled together an exceptional staff who were dedicated to us and put up with us and with him and yet somehow managed to find within themselves the wherewithal to take care of us. He began this process in 1944 when there was no true treatment for severely disturbed children, just holding tanks, heavy drugs, lobotomies, and electroshock. Compared to that, whatever he did doesn't look so bad.

Maybe his problem was that while he had to fight everyone to make his vision come true initially, he continued battling long beyond when he needed to. The psychiatric establishment didn't like him, and he thought they were fools. I tend to side with him in this. The question is whether he had to continue fighting beyond a certain point, when it became counterproductive. In the end, he was winning the war without needing to fight. He just couldn't stop himself. In one of his classes, he said: "Reading exams is the only thing that gives me insomnia."[5] There was no reason to make the class feel bad about their work. They did not share his vision, passion, or intelligence. He couldn't stop himself from letting them know that he found many of the class beneath his contempt, since they would never be able to truly understand what he was trying to teach. So he insulted them, mildly this time, but there were other times when the insults were more difficult to bear and were remembered.

Nonetheless, nothing takes away from his gift for seeing and understanding in the times of the most duress whatever the craziest children were capable of communicating. I, too, have a gift with children in that I can almost always understand them and, for the most part, they like and trust me. But my gift is nothing like his was. One small example of how he operated. It again involves Michael. I spent a fair amount of time with him since he was in my group for a year, and later, too, because as difficult as he was, he had his charm and I loved him. And, as I mentioned before, there were similarities between us, which I didn't recognize at the time. Michael's mother had lost a finger in an accident, and Michael's castration concerns spilled over onto a multitude of daily issues. He was not shy about much. We could not have hotdogs for supper without his calling out "Fried dicks for dinner!"

One day, leaving the dining hall, Michael grabbed my arm and yanked it, smacking my elbow into the exposed brick corner of a column, which hurt. "Damn it, Michael," I yelled at him. "Cut it out!"

Instantly, as always, Dr. B., who was sixty-nine at the time and just about to retire, appeared in the hall, having gotten up from the dining room table. He looked at me and said, "Exactly what and with what is he supposed to cut it out?" Then he turned around (his shoes squeaking) and went back to the table.

And I thought, "My God, he's right again. How could I be so stupid!" He wasn't mad at me, but he was criticizing my word choice. Here, with Michael, I had used the very words that would most terrify him, which meant greater anxiety for him and perhaps more work for me later to deal with him. Dr. B. understood this; he also understood that I had made my word choice because I was angry at having my elbow smashed. I could have made my anger known directly, however, as opposed to acting it out subconsciously by provoking Michael. Moreover, by pointing this out to me, Dr. B. was holding me to the same standards as his staff in my work with Michael, which was giving me a great honor. He didn't bother to stick around after making what to an outsider must have sounded like a pronouncement from on high because he trusted I could figure it out and was perfectly capable of dealing with whatever repercussions arose with Michael on my own. He was right on all counts. How could I be angry? The remark sounded severe, but behind it was great honor and respect for both Michael and me.

There was one additional thing. If I had done something like smashing another kid's arm into a wall when I was little, Dr. B. would have had a fit and I would have ended up getting hit. With Michael, Dr. B. didn't say a word about it; in the grand scheme, he was not concerned and it was not something over which to make an issue. I was trusted to keep things in sufficient control so that any additional intervention was unnecessary—beyond pointing out my failings. Dr. B. also had faith that Michael would be able to listen to me and allow things to calm down. On the surface it almost appeared that I was being taken to task, but I think it was more an example of *to whom much is given, much is required.* By then I had been given a lot.

In various ways, this sort of thing went on all the time every day. It is a small glimpse of his genius and why his staff stayed with him, despite his occasional brutality. He was a genius, and his particular genius was not only to champion the craziest of children but also to instantaneously see the world as they did.

When I see all of the attacks on him now, after he is dead, as if everyone waited to come forward when he could no longer defend himself, I am irritated: Not one of these issues reached the media prior to his death. I understand where these complaints come from: Brutal Bruno could be brusque, abusive, and high-handed. My own anger has lasted almost forty years, and I am still processing all the conflicts that I feel. Yet I know what he did for me, too, and can see both sides of the coin. The ones you should really ask whether or not he did what he said are the very ones you cannot: the kids he moved from the back wards to the front ones.

Once, in a three o'clock meeting, after a particularly harrowing week with one or another of the really whacked-out kids, someone complained to Dr. B. that what was the point about taking in someone so crazy, when it was clear from the start they could never live outside an institution. His response was simply "Because you learn the most from the sickest kids."

I watched this man seesaw back and forth from viciousness to empathy for those who could not speak on their own behalf. The viciousness was directed at those who could fight back, not at those with no defenses. I could fight back and clearly so could those who did so in the media. At least, no one has accused him of mistreating his craziest kids. He never, ever attacked Michael or put him down, as he frequently did to me. As a matter of fact, he had a sense of benign amusement at Michael's frequent transgressions.

As the saying goes, there is no such thing as a free lunch. I am forced to ask all those who complained about what Dr. B. did and did not do the following: Given everything, including the fact that his flaws were part of who he was, would we/me/us-as-a-society be better off with him or without him and his work? Make your choice and take the consequences. I did.

8

The Middle Period with Diana

The center of my world from the time I arrived at the School until the day she left to get married, six years later, was Diana. I fought with her day and night from the beginning, trying to argue that I was a better grown-up or a better mother than she was so I didn't need to listen to her and she should go away. Fortunately for me, she never did. Reading and rereading her notes, I realized how much I had forgotten. What I came away with from her most of all was the fact that I felt truly loved for who I was inside. I had forgotten how similar I was to many of the younger kids who came after me. I couldn't admit that I had once been that crazy or so crazily raw in my behavior, with all of my numerous anxieties constantly coming to the fore.

The issue for me with Diana was how I could get what I needed from her while keeping myself a separate person. For a while, in my mind, I merged us, and Diana notes how at one period of my life, I would refer to us as me. Later I needed to get some separation and figure out how to be a male. Part of that was fighting Diana off, so while I desperately needed her, in the iconography of my world, she was at times as much monster as mother to me.

Initially when I wrote this, I had assumed that it took a while for me to become close to her. From the beginning, I started out being involved with her and started to cuddle with her those first few days. I was far more babylike when I first came to the School than I remembered. Later I used to play a game with her: the Diana milkshake, where I would pretend she had been in a blender and I had to put her back together. I would pretend to take her arm and reattach it at her shoulder, remove her breast, now on top of her head, back on her chest, and so forth and so on. The other kids used to be amused. Diana was a good sport—whatever this game meant to me, she allowed me to play it. Originally it had started with my asking her if she could be a malted. Her reply, sensing my thoughts, was that she had no milk inside of her, since only ladies who had babies had milk and she was not even pregnant. At that conversation, I poured her a glass of milk, handed it to her, and said, "Now you will have milk inside you." We just started laughing.

She was a smart, articulate modern woman from New York. I thought of her as really old; in reality, she was twenty-four when I met her and had been at the School for about a year and a half, really at the beginning of her time there. As I knew her, she grew into one of the senior counselors, but at the time I was unaware of all of that. Her approach to life was passionate, not cerebral. As I thought of myself as only one large brain with no feelings, it was probably an ideal match. And she was clearly fascinated by me and liked me. Not always my behavior, however, which often drove her to her wits' end. I now surmise that the reason Dr. B. and Jacqui used to interfere and come in the dorm to yell or slap me so often was not just to demonstrate power but to protect one of the young, developing counselors and keep the lid on. It was clear to me even then that Diana resented Jacqui's interference. As for Dr. B., I got into trouble all the time, but Diana told me years later she considered it a failure on her part, too, when I got into trouble with Dr. B., that she hadn't been able to prevent it.

Once Lilly la-la kicked a ball into Paul. Paul was upset and kept walking around repeating "Lilly kicked the ball! Lilly kicked the ball!" When Dr. B. came in during rounds, Diana told him what had happened, since it was unusual for Paul to be vocal about what was upsetting him—and I think she wanted Paul to know that she took his talking so seriously that she would tell Dr. B. But Dr. B. initially misheard, thinking Diana had said me, not Paul. He replied, "Oh well, Steve probably deserved it."

Diana corrected him, but I went into the bathroom, where no one could see, and cried. For once, I hadn't done anything, and still I got insulted. It was too much.

Life moved along. In September, we got a new kid in the dorm, Winston. He was quiet and didn't start talking until he had been in the School for four or five years. I can't decide if part of the plan was to balance me out, since I talked enough for two people, or whether the gods were punishing Winston for past transgressions by putting him, who couldn't say more than a word or two, next to me, who ran over him verbally without even meaning to. For me, each new kid who came into our dorm was traumatic. It was like getting another brother and reminded me of my former life at home. I was insanely jealous of the new child and feared that Diana might like him better or that he would be her new favorite. Underneath it all, I had egotistically assumed in my heart that I had the favored status already to be able to risk losing it. And indeed, whatever the reasons were that I needed to act out my considerable anger and resentment about my condition to Diana, such action could only have happened because I was fundamentally convinced that I was not going to lose my place in her heart. In other words, my doubts were legion, but not about the fact that Diana loved my soul.

Diana used to call me on my shortcomings, which I hated. In particular, she would point out how I would avoid the things that I had difficulty with rather than work at developing new skills, which was too frustrating for me. Despite my voracious reading, where I could read two 300-page children's books a day, I could not write. My thoughts were so far more advanced than my literary abilities that any writing I did turned into an immensely frustrating experience. Although my parents would send me weekly letters—sometimes more than that, since it was the only communication permitted between us—I had a difficult time answering them. All I could manage was a few times per year. All of our mail was read by the staff before we got it, which didn't bother me so much when I was little but got progressively more annoying as I got older. Finally, years later, I got my request honored that at least my responses to my college applications were not to be opened by anyone but me. The censorship office did succeed in stopping some upsetting missives from reaching their destinations. From my case files, there are a number of letters from my parents and other relatives that Dr. B. sent back, each with a note explaining why. It protected us but must have been frustrating to my parents, who couldn't always understand the rationale.

My mother started out writing often, long descriptions of life at home so I could keep up with my family. Unbeknownst to me, after several of these letters, she received a call from Dr. B. asking her to stop. He said that I was at the School now and it was too hard on me to constantly be reminded of what I was missing and how my brothers were still at home. Thereafter, I received a series of postcards from both parents, which didn't say a lot but did let me know that I hadn't been forgotten. My mother has a twin sister, and she wrote me every other day as soon as I arrived at the School. It was overwhelming to me, since I didn't know her that well (she had always lived a thousand miles away) and I felt bad, since I couldn't write back. It was too difficult for me, and it was too much.

My aunt felt terrible I had been sent away to this place, and I think some of her horror and guilt seeped through her letters. She and my mother had had a difficult relationship. Dr. B. just called my mother and asked her to see that her sister turned down the volume. My aunt's letters slowed down to a few times a year.

I, on the other hand, knew I had eventually to respond to some of the letters I received. We were allowed one letter to ask for things that we had forgotten, after which we were not allowed to ask for anything. Our wishes for what we wanted for our birthdays or what the staff thought we should have were communicated by Dr. B. to our parents. After thinking over carefully what I wanted sent from home, I asked my parents to send some plastic patching material and glue to fix a blow-up beach ball that I liked—an atypically modest request to be sure.

I finally solved my enormous trouble writing by finding a small address book with little sheets of note paper in it. The pages remain the smallest I have ever seen—2.5 by 4 inches—and I would fill up one, feeling happy I had written an entire page. My child's handwriting was okay, but large, so my parents got their two sentences that let them know that I was still alive and hadn't forgotten them, either.

My grandmother over the years earned a certain amount of fame in my dorm. She was a great baker and every now and then would send airmail special delivery a huge box of cookies, brownies, and cakes. I came to treasure those packages, and, although I wasn't supposed to share them with the other kids, I did in a somewhat miserly way hand over some of the goods.

With all the battles, yelling, and smacks, life settled into a normal blur. A year and half passed and then the boat got rocked when Ugo announced he was leaving. He either passed his boards and was going to work with patients or hadn't passed them and was leaving to focus full time on studying. I can't remember. He went on to establish a successful psychiatric practice, marrying one of the girls' counselors shortly after he left. Losing a counselor was a bit like having someone die on you. Here they were one day, responsible for your life, taking care of you, and all of a sudden they were gone. Dr. B. wanted our energy focused within the School, so there was virtually no contact with departed staff. We were able to write them, but that was a laborious practice. And, as previously noted, I wasn't much of a letter writer.

Ugo came back to visit two or three times in the next ten years and I saw him much later at a symposium celebrating Dr. B.'s work, which was in 1986, and again at Dr. B.'s memorial service after his death in 1990. I was always fond of Ugo, but Diana was the one who went on to teach me how to be close to someone else. Still, Ugo was with me when I first arrived at the School and did me many good deeds. I had overexaggerated my importance to him in my mind so that when he came back to visit the first time, he seemed much more interested in talking to Daniel and seemed as if he had forgotten me. At the time I was hurt, but years later when I mentioned it to him, he was surprised and said that he hadn't forgotten me at all. Since a year and half with me the way I was then certainly would have been unforgettable (and probably not because someone wouldn't try), I was still much too sensitive and jealous of Daniel to gauge reality accurately.

I was very worried about Ugo's leaving—did it prove that I was a "bad" person and did it presage Diana's leaving? I was consumed by the leaving and alternatively would blame Diana for making him leave and accuse her of not doing enough to make him stay.

Our new counselor was Julie. She had gone to New Trier High School with the actress Ann-Margret, which was a constant source of amusement for us, and I am sure that she regretted telling us. While Diana was warm and from the heart, Julie was colder and more cerebral. You couldn't have found two more different people. I slowly warmed up to Julie, but her distance drove me crazy and my verbal attacks and snide remarks distanced her. As long as I had Diana, it was manageable, but after Diana left, I began to feel like I was banging my head against an icy wall to get the attention I needed. Julie had a hard time coping with my alternating neediness and rage. Fundamentally, our problem was that I knew that I never had the special meaning to her that I did to Diana. While Julie did more than her duty to me, a large part of what occurred was out of her sense of duty. For me that was like waving a red flag in front of a bull. I wanted or needed to have meaning for someone else, and I never felt that I made a crucial difference to her. I think I distanced myself from her, as well, at times and tried to make her pay for not finding me more important.

At times even Diana had difficulty with me due to my behavior. I had rejected her for months following one of her vacations, since I had been so upset at being deserted. My fury sometimes would cause her to pull back, which made things worse.[1]

Despite her occasional ambivalence, which only proved she was human, Diana would try hard to make me feel at peace. Shopping was difficult for me. I was always a clotheshorse, but I didn't think I looked good in very many things because my body image was so bad. And I had to be special. One time I needed a suit or sports jacket for something because I had outgrown everything. Diana took me shopping to Sears. Even at age nine, I didn't want to go there, which I considered down-market, and I couldn't find anything I liked. In the end, I got nothing. Diana details numerous shopping trips in her notes. Mostly they were difficult affairs about which I always had such high expectations and was always disappointed. Invariably, I had to try on rack after rack before I found something that I thought looked good on me. If I think back about my life then, it occurs to me that I was already an insecure New Yorker trapped in a child's body. Being taken out shopping was also a treat since it meant that I could have Diana to myself and spend extra time with her. I constantly needed to have it proved to me that I was special. Maybe it was easier when I was little, but Diana could make me feel special and enjoyed doing so, whereas I always felt that Julie resented it.

Birthdays were another travail. I was notoriously fussy. I had no interest in toys and trucks but understood early on that expensive cameras, country houses, titles, and private planes were to be preferred, so I was doomed to be disappointed. I could be distracted from time to time with other presents, but I always knew I couldn't have what I wanted. Perhaps what I could have I didn't want. For our birthdays, both counselors would come to the dorm in the morning carrying the birthday child's loot. It was often hard on all the other nonbirthday kids to watch someone get a pile of presents. The birthday child could pick an activity for the entire dorm—going to the movies, playland, the park, or the zoo, whatever was within reason and appropriate. Sometimes a kid would just have a party in the dorm with presents for everyone, but I considered that a waste, since a birthday was almost a get-out-of-jail-free card.

There would be a birthday dinner, which the birthday child chose, and his or her cake, decorated with a design of his or her choosing and ordered from a local bakery. Once during a huge Chicago snowstorm, the bakery couldn't deliver, so the cooks made a homemade cake and decorated it home-style. We all agreed that the birthday child lucked out—it was the best birthday cake ever. When all the kids had come into the dining hall, the counselors carried out the cake, lit the candles, and we all sang "Happy Birthday." The birthday child would blow out the candles and carry the cake around to each table to show the design he or she had picked. For the small or really sick kids, this was a big deal. By the time I was twelve, I hated it. How stupid to have to carry around a cake with a design by some bakery! But I did and didn't dream of making a scene—not so much because of dealing later with Dr. B., but because I wouldn't want to demean a custom that meant a lot to so many of the little ones. There were times I was tempted to take this cake, which was enough to serve seventy people, and chuck it in a variety of people's faces.

On at least one day a year two kids had their birthday on the same day, so we had cake and singing at both lunch and dinner. As Murphy's Law worked, we once had three birthdays on the same day (out of sixty kids)—that time we had three o'clock snacks at the handoff in the dining room with the entire school singing "Happy Birthday."

You were encouraged to ask a grown-up guest to sit with you at your table for your birthday. When Diana was on, that was easy, because I could choose her and Margaret, who became my therapist and almost as important to me as Diana. However, if Julie was on, and I had to choose between Diana and Margaret, I was almost paralyzed and would have gladly forgone my birthday to avoid having to make a decision (and not making one announced to the world that I couldn't decide, too, which was almost as bad). Did I say that these customs didn't serve a purpose?

When I was little, Diana reports that the way she finally got me to concentrate and learn the months of the year was so that I could figure out how far away my birthday was. My first one at the School I enjoyed, but subsequent ones got harder. In the end, I hated the fuss.

For one birthday, Diana offered me the opportunity to sleep late, spend the day in bed, and basically have her spend it with me. I was terribly tempted but felt it was too babyish. In addition, I didn't want to waste my get-out-of-jail-free card, although I am sure that I never described it that way. I can just imagine what Diana or Dr. B. would have said on hearing that one!

It was a most generous offer, particularly since she would have had to spend all day with me. She put my needs first the entire time I knew her, which I accepted as totally normal and reasonable. In fact, there were times when she couldn't, but that wasn't the image she left me with. The first time that she really put herself first was when she decided to get married, which meant she had to leave, since her fiancé was a professor at an out-of-state college. By then even I couldn't fault her for making such a choice, but losing her was one of the saddest experiences in my life. Once during the few weeks before she left, she told me casually, "Well, Steve, you aren't gonna have another six years here," meaning that I had more than completed half of what I had to do for myself. I had come a long way by fourteen. Neither of us contemplated that she might be wrong and that it would be another long seven years without her. I am glad now that I didn't know that when she left. I never would have survived.

Somewhere during this early Cro-Magnon period, I began seeing Margaret in session. I had gotten to know and like her as she walked around the School. She was one of the two therapists there who saw their kids twice a week. In addition, some of her kids after they left would continue to see her twice a week, as well. We would see them from time to time in the halls as they walked over to her session room. The School (or Margaret, for that matter) never charged anyone who continued with their therapists after they had left.

Another reason I got to know Margaret was because her session room was next door to Luitgard's class. She would leave her door open for her kids to let themselves in to see her. If someone forgot, she would just sit there quietly waiting: it was their time, after all, to do what they wished. There were times that I forgot or was badly late—the guilt and chagrin I well remember for standing her up.

An open door with a grown-up alone was an invitation I could not resist. I would wander in to talk to Margaret and get some candy from her candy dish, which was always full. She never seemed to mind, although I knew I had to leave when her next kid arrived. I am sure she must have shooed me out on occasion, but she did it so gracefully that I never noticed.

When children had been at the School a year or two, it was time for them to start sessions but not always with one of the therapists. Depending on their fragility, they often would see their counselor or teacher, someone with whom they had already established a relationship and who wanted to see them, not only to use the relationship to further help them but also because the staff member really liked them. While Diana was a logical choice for me, I was very vocal about wanting to see Margaret. Since I was in the process of establishing a close relationship with Diana, given the fighting, it was felt that it would be a good idea for me to have someone else to talk with. I am sure that part of the reason I initially wanted to see Margaret was because a lot of the bigger kids saw her and I wanted to be one, too. For whatever reason, I made a good choice, for Margaret stuck with me and, along with Diana, was responsible for much that I achieved. My life at the School can be divided into two main sections: Diana and Margaret.

I began seeing Margaret two days shy of my eleventh birthday. I don't remember what I talked about with her in the beginning. It was mostly a time for me to get to know her and make her part of my world. As I got older, I found a sense of sanctuary in Margaret's room, the one place where I could get away from Dr. B. or whomever, and feel secure. We had an understanding: Whatever we discussed in session remained between us. Margaret, I knew, had to dictate notes, as did all the staff after being with us. She knew how not to engage Dr. B. when necessary and what not to tell him so that he wouldn't misuse it by yelling at someone. I needed some protection where I could talk without fear of repercussion. I needed space from everyone, especially Dr. B., and Margaret gave it to me.

From her notes, Margaret often seemed overwhelmed by me and more uncertain of how to help me than she ever let on. This evidently began on our first day together, when she noted that I made so many references that she could barely take notes because there was so much there.[2]

Margaret had been a nurse at one point and then had started working at the Jewish Children's Bureau overseeing adoptions and foster children. She would talk about her experiences there. She used to tell me there would be a baby in one family that would be colicky, losing weight, and crying all the time. She would take him out of the family and give him to a new foster family, and instantly the baby would stop crying and start putting on weight. I wanted to know why this happened—had the first family been at fault? Not necessarily, because the first family had raised other babies that had done fine with them. It was a question of fit. Some babies fitted better with some families and some with others. Outside of obvious mistreatment, dumb luck figured into things about where a baby got placed. When dumb luck didn't work, Margaret used to pick up the pieces.

Later on in life but before I met her, Margaret became interested in painting, took a number of classes, and became quite good. I have a watercolor of hers that hangs over the sofa in my living room. It used to be in her bedroom and I always loved it. When Margaret got too old to live on her own, after suffering several strokes, she gave it to me when her apartment was sold. It is of an elongated, nude Modigliani-ish woman wrapped in a red shawl. She was very good indeed.

She taught us about painting during her turn taking the three o'clock meeting. It was one of the meetings that I liked. She would bring in copies and slides of paintings. The only one that I can remember now was of Duchamp's "Nude Descending a Staircase." I never could find the staircase.

Margaret was Canadian, the only daughter of a good Presbyterian banker, with two older brothers, who were also bankers and/or businessman. When I once told her that I had inherited a streak of good old Scotch Presbyterianism from her, she was horrified. "I had no intention of imposing *that* on you," she kept saying. It was part of her charm. Even when she was in her seventies, she liked to walk to work in the middle of a Chicago winter, "Because it was good for you." From the time I started seeing her, there was barely a month that went by that I didn't speak with her until her death, talking with her from wherever I was in the world. She delighted in getting calls from me when I was in Tokyo or Hong Kong. The last three or four years of her life, she was in a nursing home, unable to walk and, finally, unable to talk. Then I would call and ask the nurses to put the phone next to her ear, so she could hear my voice and know I hadn't forgotten her.

From the beginning of her stay at the nursing home, I visited Chicago whenever I could, three or four times a year. I would go and wheel her over to the Lincoln Park Zoo, where we would look at the animals and have lunch, or take her to RJ Grunts, a fashionable hamburger place, for dinner. Once we were sitting there, Margaret in her wheelchair with an oxygen tank behind her, and the couple next to us started to light up cigarettes. Concerned, I pointed out the oxygen tank and asked them to put their cigarettes out before they blew us all up. They were very nice about it and Margaret toasted them with her mug of beer. Later all I could do when I visited was feed her ice cream.

A few years before Margaret's death, I asked Jacqui, who was minding Margaret's financial affairs, to get someone to come in a couple of times a week to help her paint or conduct art therapy. Jacqui did, and for the next two years until her death, this wonderful young man came and helped Margaret draw and paint. After she died, there was a memorial service for her with an exhibition of her amazing paintings. In our eulogies, I was struck when the young man who taught Margaret painting and had only known her for the last two years of her life, when she couldn't talk, got up and talked about what she had meant to him. What he said was exactly what the rest of us did: how unique and understanding she was and what a good sense of humor she had. I thought that despite her strokes and being unable to talk, her indomitable spirit shone through. That was Margaret all right.

In her session room there were several paintings—full-size copies. One was of Munch's "The Scream," eventually later another was Van Gogh's "The Bridge," which had once hung in the Mohawks' dorm, and one was of a Cossack with a bright red hat, whose artist I cannot remember but I think was Delacroix. There was also a dollhouse, typical for a children's therapy room, that I made good use of in the beginning.

In much of my play with the dolls, the mother doll was vain and preoccupied, fed her children with a bottle of glue, and often chopped their heads off with a room divider in the dollhouse that was loose on one side, so I could swing it up and down, thus making it a guillotine. The father doll could use the guillotine, too, and the children every now then would break free, imprison their parents, and escape. I can't say that such play was enormously illuminating, but over the first few years, I used the dollhouse less and talked more. I was slowly, much to my horror, growing up and starting to behave.[3]

Margaret had a mirror image at the end of the hall, another white-haired lady who was the second of the School's two therapists. Florence White was gracious and stately and glided down the hall. She was a great friend of Margaret and I always thought of them as two pillars of the School, since they were the only full-time therapists on the staff and, to my child's mind, each one was a member of a pair, like two knights or two rooks on our living chessboard. They seemed to provide some sort of balance for our side, the inside world against the outside one. They both had white hair, both were in their sixties, and their session rooms were at opposite ends of the same corridor. In the middle was my classroom, so I would see them and their kids all day long coming and going. I have this image of the two of them which persists that is not based on any facts or observations but more on a sense of stability provided by these two old ladies whom I knew as symbols before I got to know them.

Like many of the staff, Florence had a certain sangfroid when working with her kids; even so, hers was legendary. One story concerned a session with a young boy with numerous anxieties (from that description, he could have been any one of us, as long as he had a penis) and during session, a mouse ran across Florence's back. It started to climb down the back of her blouse, but she attempted to quietly maneuver it out and away without alerting the boy and scaring him. She was startled, to say the least, but the boy never noticed there was a mouse in the session room. With many, one would doubt the story, but not about Florence. I watched her calmly insert the sash of her dress into the mouth of one girl who had a grand mal seizure in class. Since Florence's session room was across the hall, someone had gone to fetch her. Later, when she had cancer, she worked every day until a month before she died and none of the kids ever knew she was ill. In fact, Dr. B. told us that she was planning to return as soon as she could. She was scared, he said, of what she would do after she left the School. She couldn't imagine not working and not working with the kids. Perhaps she got her wish, since she died before she could find out.

Both Margaret and Florence would do intake interviews with parents of kids coming to the School, each taking one parent. They would write up their findings, discussing them with Dr. B. and the other staff, including the outside consultants who often saw potential kids to see if they could benefit from the School. In addition, something that Dr. B. spoke about only rarely with us, was the fact that unless at least one member of the staff bonded to a kid and felt he or she wanted to work with that child, Dr. B. would not take a kid. He felt that the School could not help a child unless there was at least one person rooting for him or her. I think he was right, for there were several kids whose primary staff left and no one wanted to "take" them over, and then they floundered. It was subtle, everyone was polite and did what was expected of them, but I think in their hearts, each of those kids knew that they were not special. Given how hard it was even knowing I was special to Diana and then Margaret, I do not know how someone could have managed without that. Many didn't, so Dr. B. was wise in his policy.

For my parents, Florence interviewed my mother and Margaret, my father. Only a few years before I left, Margaret mentioned something about those interviews to me. Clearly, she had compared notes with Florence to try to assess what made me tick and how to approach some of my issues. In contrast to most "nice" ladies, who are sweet but eminently forgettable, my mother clearly remembered Florence's understanding ten years later. Since they had only met once or twice, I thought it typical that Florence would leave a strong impression.

The third of the trio of white-haired ladies, either graces or fates depending on your point of view, was one of the more original of the cast of characters: Miss Lukes, who was eldest of all the staff. She must have been already near seventy when I first met her, but she was old school and she never told anyone, not even Dr. B., how old she really was. Other than Dr. B., she was the only staff member who was not called by her first name, and she never had to sit on the floor in meetings like the rest of us, including the staff. I remember her as always wearing a gingham cotton dress, cinched in with a matching belt, high-heeled black oxfords, with wavy white hair and blue veins that showed through the backs of her hands. She was thin with perfect posture. Looking at her, I always imagined she had stepped out of *Little House on the Prairie*, that this was what Middle America had been like at the turn of the century. True to form, she taught an all-girls' class, the only single-sex class at the school as far as I know. Her classroom was next to Luitgard's but as opposed to the unruliness of our class, with Jim, Lilly, Benji, Humphrey, and me running around, hers was orderly and organized. Miss Lukes brooked no nonsense from anyone, and it is amazing to me now to think back that this frail lady had such presence and so much self-assurance that everyone obeyed and felt reassured by her.

Even the little kids who with anyone else might need some sort of physical restraining fell under her spell. I was too little to understand how exactly she did it, but after some thirty years, she had so much experience, there was very little that could surprise her. She had a number of older girls in her class, plus one or two younger ones who were a lot of work. She could hardly run after them at her age in high-heeled oxfords, but she never had to. If ever there was an example of mind over matter, it was Miss Lukes.

At first for me, the three old ladies of the School, Margaret, Florence, and Miss Lukes, formed their own cabal, and trying to keep them separate was difficult. After a month or so, the differences were so obvious that I wondered how I could have lumped them together. There were similarities, however. All were old maids, all had worked for a living all of their lives, all had a magic with crazy children, and all had, in varying degrees, white hair.

Miss Lukes struck me as being played by Katharine Hepburn on *The African Queen*. Proper, ladylike, and far tougher than she looked, she was the only staff member who had been at the School longer than Dr. B.—it was as if she had been present for Genesis, when Dr. B. separated the heavens from the earth. I think I was too scared of her to talk to her much, but those times that I did, she always had a twinkle in her eye, as if she was trying to figure out what mischief I was going to do next. I, like most everyone else, liked her. And I liked watching her, too, because I wanted to know what she was going to do next.

Eventually she had a three o'clock meeting where she would talk to us about the old days. These were my favorite ones. Miss Lukes sat on a high-back chair, perfectly ladylike with her back straight and her high-heeled oxfords crossed genteelly at the ankles, answering our questions and telling stories.

When she had first come to the School, it had been a mix of disturbed and retarded children. There was an odor of urine in the halls, and it was gray and depressing. Her first interaction with a kid that gave her an inkling that she had a talent working with children and permitted her to stay was with a young man, maybe sixteen or seventeen, who stayed at the School during the week and then went home on weekends. It was so long ago and I was so little that I do not know the entire import of the story other than she reached out to this boy and nothing happened. She had noticed, however, that he didn't eat. She was worried about his lack of nourishment, so she started making him bacon sandwiches, which she would leave on a plate for him at night. In the morning, the sandwich would be gone, so she was pleased he had eaten. In her characteristic understated way, I remember her saying "I was a pretty bad cook, but I could manage a bacon sandwich and I understood that the salt in the bacon encourages the appetite." Even then I marveled that she was so self-effacing and didn't allow that her concern had made any difference to the young man. In time, those sandwiches led to conversation, so that by the time the young man left, he had someone to talk to who cared about him. I gathered that such a relationship was unusual then.

When Dr. B. arrived, he eventually fired all the staff except Miss Lukes. She said, "He thought I was good with children for some reason, so he kept me. I was surprised, since he had fired everyone else, but pleased, since I was learning to like working with the kids and now had some hope that we might be able to help them." Over the next few months after Dr. B.'s arrival, he weeded out the retarded and the kids kept for "holding" and began seeking staff who could assist him with the kind of children he thought he could help.

What an adventure. This was 1944, there was no child analysis per se, disturbed children were looked on as bad kids, and barbarity often passed for treatment. The worst thing was nobody thought it was shocking and nobody cared. Pushed out of sight and out of mind, the truly disturbed kids, as opposed to delinquents or troubled youth, had no hope. Even now, thinking about what would have happened to most of the kids I grew up with if we were all back in the 1940s still makes me shudder.

I know that Dr. B. discussed his original experiences at the School with us, but since he also wrote about them in his books, it is difficult for me to separate out what I heard from him and what I read later. I did find in my lecture notes from one of his university classes a fascinating story of how he used anything he could to learn more about running the School and making it attentive to children's internal needs. This story takes place shortly after he came to the School. These notes are, except for a few edited words, as I originally took them down twenty-five years ago, when I took the class.

A murder was committed on the South Side of Chicago in the parking lot of an ice cream place that was a hangout for young people. This was thirty years ago [1945] when Dr. B. was just starting as director of the Orthogenic School. The South Side was a mostly white community then, who were outraged by the brutal murder. The girl had been cut to pieces. The murderer was a young man in his early 20s who had killed his so-called girlfriend. He had been at the Orthogenic School many years before [prior to Dr. B.] *and in the course of the preparations for the trial, the School had been asked to contribute some information about the young man. There wasn't much; he had been adopted and had come to the School because of delinquency. Before his adoption, he had been in several foster homes and it had been no good with the adoptive parents, either, which was why they sent him away. He was only at the School for six months to a year, not very much time for such serious problems. Afterward, he had been called into juvenile court and given a stern talking to by the judge. He went back to the court and again was talked to by the judge. He was sent to St. Charles, released, and sent back again. The murder occurred some time (not too long) after his release. In the course of gathering the information together, Dr. B. became interested in the boy and obtained permission to talk with him. He won the boy's confidence by telling him why he came.*

"I'm the head of the Orthogenic School and am reorganizing it so it can better help children. Since the School obviously failed to help

you, could you tell me what was wrong so that I can in my reorganization try to correct it?" The young man began to talk to Dr. B. and very bitterly told him ("I can still hear the bitterness in his voice after all these years") that in all the time he was called up before the court, no one had ever asked him what was wrong and what could be done about it. Never. Only now, after murder, everyone asked him why did he do it. Only after murder. And he would be damned if he was going to tell any of them.

But Dr. B. was not part of the courts and because he was from the School and had asked this man's advice, he told him. Dr. B. had said, "But I am not from the courts, could you tell me?" And the man consented. He had liked this girl—he had, in fact, been in love with her, and she with him, and after she got off work at the ice cream place, she had come out to his car. She had wanted to have sex with him, but he did not want to. But she made him so excited that he couldn't control himself. At the moment of intercourse, he had a vision: This was how he was created, perhaps. His mother, thinking only of her own pleasure, had had sex in a car and conceived him. And with that thought, he grabbed his knife and began cutting the girl. He wasn't going to be party to bringing forth a child who would have to go through the living hell he had.

Dr. B. talked with the judge and persuaded him to hear the case without a jury. The sentence was second-degree murder with mitigating circumstances. He was paroled after twelve years and now is leading a decent life.[4]

In addition to his intellectual inquiries, Dr. B. mucked out the stable to get rid of the urine smell. Bedwetters' sheets were to be changed every morning, children were not to be humiliated, and the staff was picked carefully to find those who would try to understand what was going on in a child's mind. In those days, the candy was locked up, although the kitchen knives were not. Dr. B. realized that he needed to switch the locks the day there was a note pinned to the door of the locked candy cupboard with a butcher knife, reading "Next time it will be your heart." Thus, the open candy closet began, and it kept growing bigger and better. When I first arrived at the School, it was already normal closet size, with shelves stacked with Hershey bars, sours, suckers, licorice, M&M's, peanut butter cups, mints, Pez, and twenty other items. When the Adolescent

Unit was completed so that there was more storage space, the candy closet moved to a double-door closet—one side was candy, the other, cookies.

Every evening after dinner, there was a trip to the candy closet. I and anyone else could take as much as we could carry. During the school day, it was not unheard of for a class to march over to the candy closet once a day. Luitgard had put limits on how much candy we could have during the day to avoid fighting over who got to hoard more and so that people could concentrate a bit on studies. But she was the exception.

Now I am seldom tempted by sweets since the entire time I grew up I could have them as often and as much as I liked. Instead, even as a child I held out for the really special stuff, such as homemade cookies or Swiss chocolates, because I had so much of the garbage available for free all of my childhood and I didn't want to waste the calories unless they were worth it.

There are so many questions now that I would like to ask Miss Lukes. I missed my opportunity. She left after I had been at the School for two or three years and moved to spend her retirement in California. One day, about five years after she left, Dr. B. had a three o'clock meeting in which he told us that he had just heard that Miss Lukes had died. It was Jacqui, I think, who mentioned it in passing to him in a letter (by then she had left to get married and she, too, was living in California) assuming that he had already heard of her death. He was upset that she could have died and he hadn't heard about it. I felt sad that after a lifetime of working with others, she would die, if not alone, then without the knowledge at least of those who should have known about it. But it wasn't so surprising. Dr. B. lived in the moment and focused on his work. Aging, illness, and death were assumed to be facts of life, but he didn't want to be reminded of it, for it hit too close to home. He was, by then, approaching seventy himself.

The end of the beginning was marked by one event that showed that I was making progress, if in a self-centered way. I had been given by my parents an enormous building set. I had spent all day building a skyscraper that by bedtime was almost as tall as I was. It was time for evening snacks and Diana asked me to put away my building, but I wanted to continue working on it. She yelled at me that she wasn't going to have it falling down in the middle of the night, waking everyone up and scaring them. Enraged, I grabbed the building's base, picked it up, and tossed it on the floor, whereupon it broke apart and a thousand pieces skidded across the floor. I looked at her defiantly and said, "Now you pick it up." I went to my bed, grabbed a book, curled up my knees, and started reading.

Diana didn't say anything but fled to the small kitchenette in the hall to get snacks. I finally went out to see what was up and to get being screamed at over. To my complete surprise, she was crying. Suddenly I wasn't very proud of myself. It had never occurred to me that I was important enough to make Diana cry. I knew somewhere, of course, that she loved me, but I did not know that I was important to her. I just couldn't believe it. Here she was crying because I had been misbehaving over nothing, really. I truly was sorry and felt terrible. The only thing I could do was go clean up, which I did as fast as possible, trying to erase the evidence of my misdeed before Diana got back into the dormitory with bedtime snacks.* I had to start growing up sometime and learn to compromise and control myself so that I wouldn't make someone I loved cry. I realized how important Diana was to me, how much she did for me, and she had just demonstrated that I was important enough to her to make her cry. I had to start figuring out a way to stop being such a self-centered brat.

I was emerging as a person who could recognize that others had feelings, too. From this point on, my memories started to improve.

---

*We had snacks twice a day, at the three o'clock handoff and before bed. They consisted usually of cookies, milk, and Hawaiian Punch (to this day, I cannot bear its odor or sight). There was a period when we had mugs and then paper cups were discovered, which made the counselors' lives easier. One day, Dr. B. noticed that we were being served snacks in paper cups. He thought that paper cups were tacky, whereupon the staff went back to using mugs—and having to wash them themselves or lug them up and down the stairs. Given how hard they already worked, they could not have been happy about this, but as reported earlier, food was a big deal at the School. And making the School like a home for us was important to Dr. B. Whatever the staff said among themselves, we never heard a word of complaint about this.

9

The New, Improved Mohawks

With Ugo gone, the Mohawks underwent some major changes. Some of the older boys, including my chief rival, Daniel, moved down the hall into the older boys' group. The rest of us stayed with Diana and Julie. We also got three or four new kids in a short period of time. This gang became my first true friends and ushered in the middle period of my stay at the School. It was to prove to be the golden years of companionship for me, where we grew old enough to understand our lives and situations yet not old enough to resent constantly being watched and controlled.

Before this happened, both Paul, who had once complained about my dressing him, and Francis, of flupping fame, left. Julie had begun to see Paul in session, but while the attention and the time may have been good for him, he was incapable of discussing or, probably, reflecting on his life, himself, or others. He was entering puberty, and for some reason I remember Dr. B.'s comment, unrelated to Paul, I think, that "puberty is a perilous time for our autistic kids." It was one thing to have a five-year-old screaming, throwing tantrums, wetting his pants, or trying to run around naked. For an adolescent, it is sad and scary, indeed. Paul began acting out more and more bizarrely even before Ugo had left: One time he didn't go to the bathroom for days, so that when he finally moved his bowels, what resulted was too big to be flushed. Another time, after Ugo had dressed him in the morning for school, he smeared his clothes with shit. Ugo just left him soaking in the bathtub with his clothes on and took the rest of us down to breakfast. I didn't bother going upstairs to find out what happened later.

Eventually Paul, who could only echo back phrases and had no means of interacting in the real world, would masturbate in public, because, without any sense of a social world outside of himself, he didn't feel any embarrassment or have any idea that this might be better done privately. The staff certainly wasn't going to object, but it made the rest of us uncomfortable—I was about ten. One day Dr. B. called us all together and told us Paul's parents had come for a visit and decided to take him out of the School. They had had a frank discussion with Dr. B., who told them that Paul had gone as far as he could at the School and it was unlikely the staff could get him ready even for high school.

I felt terribly sad and remember Diana and Julie went out to lunch together to deal with this loss and failure. It was unusual for us to know this, since the staff seldom told us anything about their private lives, even something as minor as this, but they were so shell-shocked after losing one of their kids that they told us as a way of letting us know how overwhelmed they felt, too. In a strange way, Paul's leaving was a relief: We all had known it was coming. It was just a question of when. While I had bossed him around from time to time, we had some gentle moments together. Pretty disturbed myself back then, I was fond of him and felt bad that I hadn't always behaved better with him. He deserved more from life than he got, and there was no way for us to give it to him. That was what scared me most, I think, that sometimes things were just unfair and there was nothing that could be done about it. For me, I wanted to do whatever I could, but feared that there might be a bigger gap than I thought between what I wanted and what I could achieve.

Francis left, too, but I barely remember it. He left before Paul although I do not remember it as being as sad as Paul's leaving. He went back to his parents, who had found a school where he could work on his reading and learn some technical skills. He was able to make as good a life for himself as he could. He had charm, liked others, and knew how to engage us all. No question that he was strange by any standard, but true originality has a certain leeway. To this day, whenever I stub a toe, if I am not jumping up and down from pain, I am certainly calling out "Oucha poucha oo!" The cry was a Francis trademark that I have always remembered as well as his flupping. For Francis, the staff held a formal leaving, where the entire School gathered in the biggest classroom. There were rows of chairs set in a semicircle, with the child who was leaving at the far end, next to Dr. B.'s chair. Dr. B. would give a small talk to introduce whoever was leaving, who then would say a few words. The School would give a parting gift of some symbolic meaning to the child and we would all have punch and canapés. Finally, with a finality that still brings tears to my eyes as I remember it, there would be one last moment when Dr. B. would escort whoever was leaving out the classroom door. There would be a wave, a loud chorus of good-byes, and then he or she would be gone forever. Although Francis was strong enough to have a formal leaving, as opposed to Paul's disappearance, where none of us got to say good-bye, he was not considered a great success by any of us. But his years at the School had allowed him a much better existence in the outside world than he would ever have had otherwise.

In short succession, we got Toby, Roger, and Sean in the dorm. Roger became my best friend and compatriot in crime; Sean and I were close, too, but not as close as Roger and I—although Roger was as close to Sean as I was to him, which would create petty jealousies every now and again. Toby had arrived a couple of years before either of them, but he always seemed to me to be one of the younger ones. Later he became more a part of the group, and, since he was closer in age to Roger and Sean, he formed part of their inner circle. For me, however, I found him a pest for a long time. He ran around and was even more uncontrolled than I. He also, in his early days with us, liked to imitate whatever I did, so when I did something wrong that I might have gotten away with, when he followed it up, I invariably got caught. Since I got into a lot of trouble already, I didn't appreciate any additional confrontations with Dr. B. For a long time, I hated Toby. Eventually we were able to make a bridge.

Diana always pointed out to me that Toby was acting as I did when I first came, but that remark always enraged me. I didn't like being reminded of how I had previously behaved. Moreover, when Toby first came, he was another little rival for Diana's attention. He was one more little brother in a long list of them. Even though I never got anything less from Diana, you never would have convinced me of that back then.

Roger, however, was as articulate as I, so we could talk about many things and get the gist instantly. Toby, however, was a bit thick, which was why we considered him one of the younger ones. Studying was difficult for him; somehow whatever problems he had affected his ability to use his intellect. I thanked God every night such a thing had not happened to me. Where someone's symptoms pop out has to do with his or her experience and internal world, but some problems are far more debilitating than others. The kids who didn't talk or couldn't do well in school had a far harder time after leaving the school. The staff tried to make our world a level playing field, but even then, Roger and I knew that that attempt was as big a fantasy as any of those of the craziest kids. Eventually there would be a wall, we would all hit it; it was called back then "the outside world."

Diana and I were not the only ones who argued. Of all the things the Mohawks were accused of, being quiet and keeping things hidden were never among them. On rare occasions, I could blend in, for once no longer the loudest.

And there was Sean. Despite all of the time I spent with him, he was a cipher to me. Good-looking, with blond hair, a kind of athletic grace, and cheekbones that we accounted for by his Norwegian ancestry, he held everything inside himself. When Roger or I was upset, it was not a subtle thing. With Sean, we'd never know until often too late. Prior to coming to the School, he had been placed in a typical institution and given electroshock treatment. Fortunately, it did not seem to have left any permanent brain damage, but there were residues from the horror he had experienced. He knew in a way the rest of us did not what the alternatives to the School were and he never wanted to rock the boat idly. That didn't mean that he didn't get as irritated with some of our restrictions as Roger or I; he just kept it to himself, as he did many things. It took a long time for him to feel safe enough to believe he wasn't going to lose the School and permit himself to be angry at it and the staff.

This quiet self-control, which he saw as necessary for survival, left him in our midst like a seemingly gleaming snow-covered mountain hiding a volcano beneath. To continue the cliché, somewhere, unconsciously, I was always concerned about the force of that volcano, should it ever erupt. With most of the kids, like my buddy Roger, I knew what lurked underneath. In fact, often those problems weren't hidden at all but were on display in the living room where we could go on in, sit down, and take a good look around. Sean was a friend, for sure, but there was a distance that I never overcame. His struggle to stop hiding and integrate his interior world with the rest of our worlds continued for as long as I knew him. He took a long time to come out from hiding; his intense privacy made him somewhat alien to me for all the time I knew him.

I was still pretty isolated, reading all the time. I was probably in my Louis period, where I read everything about Louis XIV that I could get my hands on. Then I moved on to Louis XV and eventually Louis XVI. When he got his head cut off, I had to start over: I think with English history, which I began with William the Conqueror and a history of his family, the Plantagenets.

By this time, I was grappling more with who I was and what I needed. Margaret tried to get me to focus on what was going on inside of me. We would talk about this now in sessions, discussing exactly what was their purpose for me.[1]

When I was twelve, I went home to my parents for the month of August. By now it was 1967, and this was the first time I had spent the night at home since I had left when I was eight. My brothers knew who I was, but only David, who had been six when I left, really remembered me: Mitchell had been three when I left and the baby hadn't even been born. There was a lot of adjusting for us to do. I remember that both my parents tried hard to give me a good time. I had no friends from before—except Ilene across the street, who had been my friend since I was seven. Two years younger than she, I would fight with her in the morning before school every day for a year to prove I wasn't going to be beaten by a girl. Every morning she won.

Now I was too old to fight her, and she always seemed, like an older sister, no matter how much older I got, still ahead of me. She was in high school and part of a social group that I couldn't imagine, let alone fit in. She included me with her friends, however, and I would hang out with her or, more accurately, tag along. It was a taste of normalcy for which I was starved. I still was pretty odd, but Ilene always accepted me for who I was. There were few enough people who did. I returned after the visit in a bit of shellshock. Being home was never easy for me. Diana felt that it was good that I get a glimpse of reality after all this time at the School. But it had been so difficult for me that I didn't return home again for another year, until the next summer.

I returned back to the School that fall the Tuesday after Labor Day, along with all the other kids who had visits. I don't really remember what happened that summer specifically at home that made Diana so concerned, but I remember Dr. B. yelling at me about something, then adding "Whatever did they do to you?" referring to my parents.

Evidently in the aftermath of that visit, I began to be less isolated.[2] As my isolation continued to decrease, I presume so did my overbearingness, since my dorm mates increasingly let me join in. Roger was a merciless tease who could coax me out of a book or, failing that, provoke me so that I had to respond. We got into trouble a lot, with Diana and Julie knowing that they nailed us only for about half of the crimes we committed because there were simply too many. Crimes were a relative thing: We worked out a deal where one of us subscribed to *Newsweek* and the other *Time*, so we could trade. But trading was not allowed. We traded all kinds of stuff, moving on to aspirin only much later. The really over-the-top stuff, Roger didn't include me in: I was too much of a prig. We also made constant cracks about the cast of characters around us, including the staff, a number of whom were even stranger than we were.

Life in the dorm continued with its ups and downs. Despite all of our problems, the Mohawks coalesced into one of the best-functioning groups in the School. Our counselors—Diana, Julie, and, later, Mary Margaret, who became our counselor after Diana left—should get a lot of credit for this.

We still, however, had our antics: At one point, American Airlines as a marketing ploy had blank tickets on the counter so people could write their own tickets and then just pay for them at the airport. It never did travelers any good, but I got my hands on a stack of blanks and became known as the travel agent. Leslie, who was a counselor down the hall, had a couple of kids in her group who were a lot of trouble. I was constantly sending her, via Roger, who loved this kind of thing, tickets for Hawaii or Paris. First class, of course. This was the time when the Boeing 747 first came out with their lounges in the sky, long before they started packing us in like sardines. Flying still had some mystery, particularly for me, who felt locked away from a huge world out there that I couldn't see. Given all the personal worlds to which so many of us traveled, we made visits to a variety of twilight zones that even Shirley MacLaine hasn't seen.

We'd set up the chairs like an airliner, had a tray of snacks, and got the counselors to be the stewardesses. Every now and again we would crash, but that would get us into trouble, since we were not supposed to play games where we got killed. We settled on cops and robbers, where prison was permissible. We just didn't tell Diana or Julie about the electric chair. The real fight was over who got to throw the switch. Diana was always a good sport. One time she asked to be released from prison so she could go get snacks and put away the laundry. It was so ludicrous that we couldn't stop laughing.

Julie wasn't always as good a sport. Once we arrested her but she got upset that after all she did for us, we still wanted to arrest her. She walked out of the dorm to get snacks and sulk. Roger, Sean, and I just looked at one another, flabbergasted.

Sometimes in the afternoon, I liked to take naps. I would throw a sweater over my head to block out the lights and sleep on my back with my hands folded across my chest. To get me up, when he wanted to play, Roger would come over to my bed and begin the funeral oration: "We are gathered here to say good-bye to our dearly beloved. . . ." There were lots of variations on this theme, including my arising from the dead and scaring the little ones. After a while, Diana and Julie gave up trying to stop this, as did Diana's successor, Mary Margaret. One variation was the auction of my worldly belongings. By the time we had evolved that version, the funeral game was well known and the kids from next door used to come over to bid on my property in the auction that Roger would run after the service.

One item of enormous value that reached great heights in the auction was my red button sweater. I wore it all the time—and would hand wash it so that I would have it back the next morning to take with me wherever I went. It was like Linus's blanket in *Peanuts*, an association that nobody missed. The sweater had pockets, which I really liked, since I could stuff them with Kleenex, particularly at hay fever season. At any rate, I wore it all the time. Roger spent hours figuring out how to steal it, would hide it, and generally found that jokes about the sweater made life sweet. In time, he got everyone else, including the guys from the dorm next door, in on the act. If I lost a button, it was headline news. It truly was one of the stupider things we ever did, but it was amusing at the time.

A few years later, after I had moved to the Adolescent Unit, while Roger remained in the Mohawks, I made a red sweater centerpiece for Roger's birthday table out of red construction paper to celebrate the famed mania throughout the School; I even created pockets stuffed with Kleenex. I ran into Mary Margaret in the kitchen, just before dinner, when she was getting the "real" centerpiece—and we ended up putting both on the table. It might not have been much, but you have no idea of how much freedom I felt that I could make a centerpiece for another kid, even my best friend in the School, go set it up in the kitchen by myself, and have that be taken as normal. By then I was beginning to feel freer—it was only a couple of years before I left, so I was probably nineteen.

Roger and I used to create scenarios on the lives of the staff. We thought that Julie liked Al, the older boys' counselor from down the hall. Once at dinner Julie whacked me when I made some crack about either her or Al speaking to the other one with "burning passion." Afterward, unknown to Julie, burning passion became a code word for us. Depending on usage, it meant being over the top, Julie's arbitrariness, and a symbol that we had to watch out, as in "don't pull a burning passion."

All of us in the Mohawks loved the movies. We used them to illustrate our lives and would often create our own screenplays and spent endless hours trying to figure out which actors ought to play which characters from our daily lives. With natural comedic abilities, some of our scenarios were very funny, if not vicious, which would get us into trouble. But since it seemed that we were always getting into trouble over something, it might as well be for something we enjoyed.

At one point, we decided that we would cast a film on the School. We had Telly Savalas as Dr. B., Ethel Merman as Diana, Cloris Leachman as Julie, Diane Keaton as Mary Margaret, Pearl Bailey as Theresa, and Stockard Channing as Leslie. Sean wanted Paul Newman to play him and Roger then wanted Woody Allen to play me. At that point I quit and went on strike. We settled on someone else for me, but I didn't get Sean Connery.

Films were a big deal for us—opening a window in the prison wall—and since we had an entire School to view them, we got to see one or two major movies every month, in addition to the weekly Monday afternoon educational films. Sometimes for birthdays, one kid or another would select a movie. After a screening for the birthday group, the rest of us would get to see it, too.

Getting a film in this era before video meant that someone had to go to the rental place and come back with a huge metal case containing the actual film reels. Often the older kids were the couriers. We'd all get together in the big classroom, pull the shades, find a seat, and wait for the whir of the projector to start. I still remember the joy of seeing life outside the walls of the School and finally seeing on screen all those periods and places that I read about so avidly. Life at the School was luxurious, to be sure, but for me, since I was not convinced that I could survive outside, it often was Alcatraz. Needless to say, *Birdman of Alcatraz* with Burt Lancaster had a bizarre fascination for all of us, and we pestered our counselors for days to let us have some birds—or at least a goldfish, which were forbidden on the theory that if they died, it would be too much for some in the dorm. There was also an issue of treating the animal fairly, when there were certain of our denizens who would clearly pull the wings off flies, since something so small might be safe enough to use to express anger, if they were permitted to do so. The staff didn't want to have to interpose themselves between an expression of rage or a symptom now finally expressing itself or to protect the rest of us from witnessing such torture or to protect the kid from us preventing such acting out, so it was easier all around to have stuffed animals, which didn't create such obvious problems.

From *Casablanca*, to *The Guns of Navarone*, to *My Fair Lady*, which Diana took us to see in a big Chicago movie palace with its ormolu fittings of gold leaf, grand balconies, and massive crimson curtains that glided up at the beginning of the show, we saw almost all of the great American films from the start of the motion picture era, including those of Charlie Chaplin and Buster Keaton. The great musicals were considered perfect for us with dancing, singing, great scenery, and sensible plots (meaning not too much violence and not too much sex).

At the School, however, whatever came up in films was considered grist for the analytic mill, which always ran in high gear. If someone was upset by a film's immediacy, it would not necessarily be considered a bad thing. Except for me, since what came up was another new means of escape, which Diana definitely did not encourage.

As a child, when I was four or five, my mother had sent me to take dance and tap lessons, which I enjoyed. I had a couple of performances, one where I was a toy soldier in *Babes in Toyland*. My role was limited to being one of a pair of soldiers who roll out a wagon carrying one of the leads onto the center of the stage. Later, in my last year of grade school before I left my parents, I was given a lead role in our class play, I think because I had so many difficulties that my teacher, a decent women who later would have my brothers in her second grade class, wanted to give me something special, since it was clear to her that I wasn't making it.

Thus, I had been bitten early on by the acting bug and liked the idea of being a star, which I later, not always successfully, tried to forget. Movies would bring it all back. My wish to be an actor was something we discussed and not something that Diana encouraged, since I had enough trouble just living on earth.

> *Steve has often stated that he is going to be an actor when he grows up. After seeing a movie, Steve lives the roles in fantasy for quite some time. One morning at breakfast he spontaneously mused that he thought he might be a doctor or a teacher instead of an actor, "because they are more useful; an actor just stands in front of people and makes money."*[3]

At the School, some of this search for stardom continued, since we had ballet class once or twice a week with Miss Cody, who would come to teach us for the first five or six years I was there. Each fall we would draw outlines of our feet for her and she would come back with ballet shoes that fit us perfectly. In her class, we worked on stretching, leaping, and coordination, which was something many of us had difficulty with. She would bring in records and I learned the word *syncopation* from her when she was explaining why certain records were good to dance to. Miss Cody had long black hair that fell below her waist and legs longer than most people's, which is why she was a good dancer. I both loved and hated those classes. I loved them because I could imagine I was in training to become a Gene Kelly, although his position in the firmament was never threatened by anything I ever did. Later I would resent these classes because I liked them but felt with my trying to become more of a man, ballet was not supposed to be something that interested me. Still, Miss Cody managed to teach me a lot about dance and music, and I appreciated her patience and indulgence in my somewhat bizarre view of the world. Although I had moments when I could do well in her class, bottom line, I always knew I looked like a plowhorse trying to waltz.

Dr. B. was pretty liberal about culture—he once even let a group of the older boys attend a Rolling Stones concert. Those of us in the Mohawks who understood what was going on were deeply jealous. I later wondered if he had any idea of how much drug use went on in those concerts. He wanted us to know more about the world and would insist that we go to concerts and the symphony. However, we were pretty cut off from popular culture, which was not considered nearly as important, and we needed to pester the staff just to find out what was happening. Even as cut off as we were, when the Beatles appeared suddenly in 1964, we heard of them, as indeed they were virtually impossible to miss. We didn't often get newspapers until we were older, never listened to the radio, and seldom saw television, but some of the older kids did, so we learned about "Love Love Me Do" from them. I often felt that we learned of the outside world like long-term prisoners of war struggling to obtain pieces of information over the grapevine. I was living in my own World War II movie, but it was hardly glamorous. By the time we were getting *Newsweek* and *Time*—we were teenagers.

Although television was very restricted, we usually got to see the Academy Awards, which was a big deal for us. In those days of black-and-white television—I think I didn't see my first color TV show until I was ten or twelve—we saw the old Academy Award shows on old televisions filled with glowing glass tubes. I would have a lump in my throat watching as someone came up to the podium, clutching his or her statuette, thinking that someday maybe that might be me. Maybe not an Academy Award, but the idea of finally being recognized for making a great achievement, to be for once a success, and be lifted out of my dreary life.

Looking back at that period of my life, I felt more alive watching movies or reading my books than I did in my own life. That was not a good sign. When the last reel of film spluttered out of the sprockets and began clacking against the projector, I was always sad. We had to go back to the dorm, and while for the past two hours my life had been in color, now it returned to black and white.

Our lives began to finally settle in after a few years. While I can't say we had peace, we had rhythm. Diana began seeing Roger and Sean in session. By that time, she was already seeing Winston. I still felt that I had my special position with her, but it was hard on me to know that others might become as special as I was to her. However, Diana never made me feel second to anyone.

Then our lives changed again. Timothy, who was five, arrived in our dorm. He was the youngest child up to then that the School had ever taken. His arrival was life wrenching. We had finally gotten to the point where we could go out to movies, museums, the parks, the public library, and pretty much had the run of the neighborhood. We had our favorite shops, the storekeepers knew us, and it was part of the good public relations of the School that we were liked and accepted throughout the community, despite some obvious strangeness. By now my mother's friend Ruth and Diana would wave at each other when they ran into each other without us. I wish I had a picture of all of us waving back to Ruth when we would see her.

Timothy really was little. He just couldn't keep up with us, so either we had to leave him behind or we had to stay behind with him and not go. There was a lot of grumbling. Timothy essentially was a little boy who had the lungs of Aretha Franklin. When upset—a frequent occurrence—he could fuss at the top of his voice for hours. We didn't know how to shut him up and we quickly learned to live in terror of upsetting him. Timothy loved toys and loved even more understanding how they worked. He would often take them apart and then scream for hours when he couldn't put them back together again. Of course, if we didn't let him take them apart, he would also scream for hours. There was no winning. At one point, he had received a toy washing machine, which began to stick and slow down as the parts inside began to rust, since Timothy liked to put in water and soap—something for which it was not designed. To fix it, Timothy took it apart. Since he couldn't fix it or put it back together, he began fussing. At some point, I yelled out, "Damn it, this is enough. From now on, he needs to get two of everything, one to keep and one to take apart!" Timothy fell silent. He thought about this for a minute and then began laughing. This was a great idea. It became a standing joke with us, but the staff never did it. I would have forgotten the remark, except that later on, when Timothy would fuss about his toys, he now would throw in, at the top of his lungs: "Steve is right. I need to get two of everything. One to keep and one to take apart."

The fussing could be over anything. Once Timothy scratched his finger on a closet door. We had a substitute taking a shift (a medical resident doing his psychiatric rotation, I think). We all looked at the scratch to try to calm Timothy down, but we had a two-hour litany about the "shitty closet doors" until someone got Julie. He continued over and over, "If my skin was made of metal, this never would have happened. How come my skin isn't made of metal?"

After Diana left, Mary Margaret became very close to Timothy and was his primary person for the rest of his time at the School and indeed after, since they stayed in touch. Mary Margaret had begun with us as our substitute, taking a shift a week with us and then working when Diana or Julie went on vacation, so we knew her fairly well. Timothy always liked her, and she did some amazing things with him. Often Roger, Sean, and I would take her to task for spoiling him. When she would sympathize with him in some of his more outrageous demands that the world should be changed as he saw fit, such as changing the weather, we would get mad, particularly when it occurred while Timothy fussed for hours. I mean, this went on for years, so our patience had begun to wear very thin.

Our objections, however, were not necessarily based on our lack of patience but our concern that how was Timothy going to learn to live with even the smallest amount of frustration without fussing for hours if Mary Margaret encouraged him, rather than trying to push him toward a saner view of the world. Despite the anger sometimes, we all truly cared for Timothy and wanted him to have a successful life. This battle over Timothy with Mary Margaret went on until I left. The rest of us tried to push Timothy and suffered the consequences, since he didn't like it. I hope, in the end, we did him some good.

I became particularly close to Timothy and he relied on me. I couldn't always calm him down, but after Diana left, when Mary Margaret or Julie wasn't there, I was the next best thing. Timothy

At the period of his greatest fame on January 11, 1970, Dr. B. was featured on the cover of *The New York Times Magazine*. Courtesy of *The New York Times*

Holding my brother David when he is one and I am three. Despite our battles, he was both my best friend and best enemy for all of my childhood at home. It is impossible for me to imagine it without him.

My first visit home in October 1964, age nine, after being at the School for fifteen months.

Working in my small garden plot, where I conducted my biology experiments as well as raised tomatoes, corn, and peppers every summer. I am ten.

Diana in the Mohawks dormitory after I had been at the School for several years. Behind her, in the left corner, is my bed, where I had copies of antique maps and other items that interested me on the wall.

Margaret in the late sixties, her hair frizzy, as I often remember it, before she traded in her glasses for the fire-red pair that would become her trademark.

The cover of one of Dr. B.'s often "therapeutic" postcards to me. Before I started going home for visits, he would send me several while on his summer vacation.

> "Dear Steve, Can you imagine a baby sleeping in this cradle made out of pure gold and inlaid with the most precious stones? The coverlet is sewn full of pearls, which must have been most uncomfortable for the poor infant. With my very best, Your Dr. B."

The original Mohawks dormitory. My area is in the top left corner with the maps and a ship on the wall. Dr. B.'s taste is evident in the furniture, with its heraldic motifs, the Italian light fixtures, and the bedspreads covered with stuffed animals. There was no doubt that this was a room for children.

The large formal classroom where we painted the radiators different colors, while dipping Oreos into the paint to match. This was the room where I learned that President Kennedy had been shot—and the room where we held the formal leaving ceremonies, including mine.

Margaret's session room. In the foreground is the dollhouse that I played with when I was little, including the trapdoor I used as a guillotine. With the paintings, stuffed animals, candy box, and Play-Doh, it was an inviting place for a child.

The playroom where we held three o'clock meetings and would watch television on rare occasions. This is the room where Teddy first sought me out to play hide-and-seek. The full-size rocking horse is the one on which Anna Freud wished to sit when she visited.

A view of the Adolescent Unit living room, where I studied every night once I started going to the University of Chicago High School.

My parents, my late brother Paul, and me at my graduation from Yale in 1980.

had a cuddle blanket, a small piece of fabric that he needed to go to sleep. When he would wake up in the middle of the night and couldn't find it, we all woke up to a major tantrum. There was a night counselor who slept on the girls' floor whom we were supposed to get in times of trouble. But it meant walking downstairs, which was a pain. The night counselor, whom Timothy didn't know, could do little to restore calm unless they got Mary Margaret, who eventually needed to sleep. Knowing this, I at one point wrote a step-by-step checklist on where to look in the middle of the night when Timothy lost his cuddle blanket. Timothy enjoyed and appreciated my efforts, especially the part about looking in his pajama bottoms, where the cuddle blanket often ended up. These efforts were not entirely altruistic, since by that time the person everyone got when Timothy woke up was me.

Even as a small child, Timothy, who lived in his own world, was not cut off entirely from ours, except when he was fussing. Even he learned eventually that his fussing was too much, but for years he couldn't stop himself. He had perfect pitch—we used to like to test him on toy xylophones and pianos. Someone would hit a note and Timothy would interrupt what he was doing, turn his head on one side for a second, and answer A-flat or whatever. We never could stump him, though we tried. He was also a perfect speller. Even when I was sixteen and working on a paper, if I asked him how to spell something, he almost always knew. And he liked being able to help.

Slowly, slowly we integrated him into our lives and began to take him with us on outings. We would still leave him behind with another group from time to time, when we did something we were sure he wouldn't like or if he was fussing so much we needed a break. By and large, though, we managed together.

I was the one who still was off a lot on my own, buried in my books. I had my bed in a corner, so I was a bit separated from the others. We traded dorms with another group, since we were one more person and needed the extra space—and they stuck my bed out from the wall, next to Roger's. I complained that I was the only person in the School who had a therapeutically placed bed. Julie and Mary Margaret—even Dr. B.—thought that this was funny for some reason. As for me, it made it harder for me to read. I hated it.

Around this time, Roger achieved his ultimate prank. In the winter, the radiators ran full blast to counteract the Chicago cold. By the middle of the night, the dorms were as dry as the Sahara since humidifiers were not then yet well known. Every night I would wake up and go into the bathroom for a drink of water. Each of us had a cubbyhole, where we kept our toothbrush and stuff plus a mug. Knowing my habits, Roger filled up my cup with ice and then Scotch-taped it to the bottom of the cubbyhole. The plot was brilliant. Sleepy, in the middle of the night, I would go to my cubbyhole, which was level with my head, think my cup was stuck, give it a yank, and splash myself in the face with the melting icewater. Unfortunately for Roger, I went to get a drink before going to bed and figured out the plot without splashing myself in the face. I think I waited for him to go to sleep and then dumped the cup of ice down his back. For us, this was a Nobel Prize–winning creation, and Roger basked in its glory for a long time.

I went on my second summer visit home when I was thirteen, seeing my family for the first time after a year's absence. Dr. B. had felt that the first summer visit had been so hard on me, he hadn't wanted me to go home for the following Christmas. It was unusual for someone who had gone for the entire summer visit not to go home for Christmas, but Dr. B. was worried and wanted to make a point. I needed to be stronger, so that being at home did not make me revert so much to being a brain acting out without understanding my feelings again.

During that second summer home, my father had a business trip to Martha's Vineyard. Since my mother's brother went there with his family every August, my father took me with him. I had been close to my uncle since birth. When he was finishing college, I was a toddler, and often, on weekends, he would take me to Kiddy Land or out to eat. He had started dating his future wife, Liz, then, and I always looked forward to seeing them.

I was so excited to be able to take a real plane ride somewhere, anywhere, without a counselor playing a stewardess. We changed to a little prop plane in Boston and then arrived at the Vineyard. I had no way of knowing how chic it was, even then, but for me it was an adventure. For the next seven years, I would go by myself to visit my uncle. The years and memories run together, but for five or six days every year, I had freedom. I would live for those days on the Vineyard all the rest of the year. It was the high point of my life until I was twenty. I could pretend, if just for a while, that I was like everybody else. My uncle, Seymour Hersh, was a well-known journalist, who had won a Pulitzer Prize and was plugged into the island intelligentsia. Some of his neighbors' children and a cousin of my aunt's were my age, so there were people to hang out with who hadn't grown up in an institution. I was not part of their world and they put up with me, but I didn't care. I was free—with no Dr. B. to pop out from behind the corner and no parents, either. However, underneath everything, my dislike of myself was palpable, if not to myself then certainly to others, who found it off-putting and difficult to be around me. My intensity sometimes masked my self-loathing but not my awkwardness, and held me a prisoner away from the rest of the world. There was one more aspect to this equation, which, in the end, equaled loneliness. At times I could easily read people, almost getting inside of them. When this was combined with all my other baggage, most people didn't appreciate my observations or even the look in my eye when I understood far more than they wanted me to. Over my years on the Vineyard, I would become very close to a number of people—my aunt Liz, her cousin, and my little cousins—but the relationships could exist only in that special time and place for a few days—I was not ready yet for the rough and tumble of daily nonvacation life.

I remember one summer sitting on the beach talking to Richard Dreyfuss, whom I had never heard of, as he was making some movie called *Jaws*, which I had never heard of, directed by some director, Steven Spielberg, whom I also never heard of. Dreyfuss was on a picnic with Uncle Sy and Richard Goodwin and Doris Kearns Goodwin, who were married. Goodwin had been a member of the inner circle of the Kennedy administration and his wife was a well-known intellectual and historian. Sy, of course, knew all of these people. He would hang out with them, and then pretend that he didn't care that they were famous or well connected. As for me, this was pretty heady stuff and certainly beat looking for Timothy's cuddle blanket in the middle of the night.

I remember asking Richard Dreyfuss about *Jaws* and have always remembered him telling me that he didn't think it would be very good. I mean, it had a mechanical shark, for Christ's sake. I was vastly amused much later to think of that remark, because the movie made his career, as it did Spielberg's.

Never an early riser, I would get up early on the Vineyard because

I did not want to miss a minute. One morning, in the early New England mist, I heard clopping on the pavement. As I slowly made it back into consciousness, I realized that there were clopping sounds on all the roads surrounding me: horses' hooves striking the pavement, since it was the morning of the horse contest at the West Tisbury country fair. It was the nicest sound to which I have ever awoken, unless it was a certain little boy sticking his hands in my face, asking for pancakes, an event that took place many years after the events of this story.

Back in Chicago, one of the passions in my father's life was horse racing. He and two of his best friends formed a stable to buy trotters and pacers, which all the kids loved. Those horses brought us a lot of fun.

Every year we'd go to the Illinois State Fair, where my father would have a horse racing. I spent a lot of time with Alfred, the son of one of my father's horse partners, who was a couple of years older and already an accomplished photographer. George Smallsreed, the photographer at *Hoofbeats*, the magazine of the United States Trotting Association, kept an eye on us. With his deeply tanned face from standing in the sun taking pictures all summer and with his snow-white hair, we could recognize him from across the track. He always had some good stories to make us laugh. The three families had ten kids between them in three groups: older, middle, and babies. We created all kinds of havoc and the hotel staff hated us, since we would use the elevators for races or try to break into the pool at night. Once when we were driving back from Springfield to Chicago, my little brother had to go pee. We used to joke with him that he was writing a guidebook on every gas station toilet from Chicago to Springfield. It was on one of these trips, when he was five or so and talking, that the subject of the differences between boys and girls came up. When informed with great superiority by the number-three son, who was his elder by three years, that girls didn't have penises, he responded with "Oh yes they do!" not wanting to be taken in one more time. When we all started laughing, he was most upset. This was his introduction to the birds and the bees.

One other trip I always remembered was the one when I discovered James Bond. One of my father's brothers lived near Springfield and often invited us to visit. My parents stayed in a local hotel with the two younger kids and my brother David and I stayed with my aunt and uncle. My aunt, an immaculate housekeeper, had just gotten new white carpeting. David came down with violent stomach flu that night and, just after we had gone to bed, threw up all over the brand-new white carpet. My uncle heard the commotion and came in. He took one look at the floor, looked at my brother, and said, "My God, don't you ever chew when you eat?" That priceless remark made up for the fact that my brother was so sick I was scared to sleep next to him on the trundle bed, because I didn't want him to puke on me, which, after a lot of Pepto-Bismol, was now coming up pink. I got up and went into the living room to sleep on the sofa. Instead, I found a bunch of James Bond books and spent the rest of the night reading.

Returning from visits became tougher. I didn't want to live at home, but it became progressively harder to be at the School. As long as Diana was there, it was easier for me. I trusted her and she didn't seem to have a problem with my growing older and taking on more responsibility. I was still pretty isolated, had many anxieties about whether anyone could like me, and needed to be the center of attention. Since there were so many kids at the School who needed to be center stage all of the time, the staff somehow made it possible for all of us to share the stage at the same time. Such a life seemed normal to me. When I finally left the School, however, or even on those days on Martha's Vineyard, my implicit demand that I be the center of attention and my neediness, which did not stand out at the School, since there were so many who were even worse about it than I, created a lot of trouble for me and caused me to be often alone.

By then, I was an older kid with some responsibility for Timothy. In the School, I was an upstanding citizen. But I didn't want to be an upstanding citizen of a nut house, even one as good as the School; I wanted to be a fully participating citizen of the world. Even then I dreamed of going to Harvard or Yale. The staff, who were willing to push one to feel and understand one's feelings, were not so good at helping one fit into the real world. As I got older, it got worse. After spending an afternoon on the beach with Richard Dreyfuss, Doris Kearns Goodwin, and Dick Goodwin, I wasn't prepared to give up the bright lights.

Diana had fought with me a lot about this. She didn't care about what I did so much but how I felt. She didn't want me to fill myself up with the trappings of success to hide that I really felt insecure and a failure inside. To her, I was this growing boy who still had enormous difficulties maintaining friendships and even a good grasp of reality, since I had to cover over all my inadequacies by being the center of attention. For her, the biggest thing I needed to learn was how to be less anxious and not to act out my neediness so that it drove away those who might otherwise have been my friends. Without that, even with a Yale degree, I would just be a misfit who had gone to Yale. She was right to be concerned. In looking over her notes, she was also concerned about my depression, which underlay a lot of my problems, my dislike of my body, and my feminine characteristics, which had become far less pronounced in our years together.

Diana always acted independently to try to meet what she thought were my underlying needs, which she viewed as more important than my intellectual ones. She infuriated me when she would call my attention to my hidden emotions and was unconcerned about whether she embarrassed me. Once, when I was thirteen, she took me to the doctor and told him I was worried about cancer of the penis—resulting in my spending the rest of the afternoon not speaking to her, since I was totally embarrassed.[4]

Many of the issues started coming up in the aftermath of those few summer visits home and continued for the rest of my stay at the School. As for the wish to be more independent, the School never gave it much consideration, at least to me. To go back to living in a dorm with seven others with no privacy ever and with everyone constantly reporting back to Dr. B., who came around four times a day, was agonizing. One lived in a closed society with secret police. By this time the setup had gotten old. Puberty just made it worse.

The underlying basis, or the focus of the lenses I used to see the world, was changing in front of my eyes. I could see from my visit home and the trip to the Vineyard that other people my age were different than I was. They seemed more comfortable in their skins, they had real friendships, and they could juggle home, school, and their internal lives, while I could not. In short, I was scared. I could see that all the information from the past that I had processed to interpret the world had to change. I just didn't know to what. Deep down I felt there was something wrong with me: I was always surprised that someone liked me, and somewhat distrustful—there had to be something that I was missing.

It's true that I had faith in Diana, but even I knew then that there was no possibility of my finding someone else who would have lived through all we had to live through in order for me to be convinced of her trustworthiness. For one, I was no longer a child. For another, I didn't really need to go through that degree of testing again, for either myself or others. But running the gauntlet to get through to me, so I could really hear another person's voice, especially when they disagreed with me—most people who were not staff of the School just wouldn't put up with. I still made a lot of people's lives difficult.

While there were others who involved themselves in my life at the School, my relationships with them never had the same depth as my relationship with Diana. Finding a bond with a small child, as I had been when I first arrived, is far easier than establishing one with an adolescent, which I was at that point becoming.

10

Back to Class

After Luitgard left, we got a new teacher who took over her class. Marsha was sweet, patient, and left after a year. In the five pages of notes that I have from her, she was concerned about getting my inner world out, particularly on paper, where I could write my ideas down and where they could be examined and made substantial as opposed to the ethereal fears endlessly whirling around inside my head. As I have stated, I hated writing because, in contrast to my verbal skill, my writing was childlike, backward, and a source of endless frustration. Particularly when what I wrote on the page was compared to what was in my mind or came out of my mouth. Marsha made a lot of effort to get me to write.

Then Len came. He was much more interesting than Marsha and fit into our wacky world better. Initially I looked at him as a rival and resented him as another man who could boss me around. We met him as a substitute teacher who got the amazing privilege of taking our class while Marsha went on vacation. Most of us had a hard time with staff vacations. In addition to having someone new who didn't know us or understand often what was going on, there was a lot of anger at the vacationing staff member for deserting us. A lot of that anger was directed at the poor substitute, who was almost always new to the School, which is why he or she was a substitute. Thus, the substitute had to cope with outraged children in addition to trying to understand us and the School. We had Lilly la-la running around, and Jim and I were still fighting it out most of the day to see who got to be top dog. Jim often won, since it was easier for me to pick up a book than continue to argue. Given the choice, I preferred any number of European royal houses to being with him.

Len had been born in South Africa, which started my interest in that country and some deeply seated feelings about apartheid. Alan Paton's *Cry the Beloved Country* touched me, and I would later read everything I could about Steve Biko. Len had a number of stories about his homeland: One concerned his making such a mess eating a mango that afterward his nanny used to give him one to eat in the bath. I loved that image. But I didn't know what a mango was. Back then, none of us had ever seen one. Or, for that matter, a kiwi. When the Mohawks saw our first kiwi, we called them furry testicles. Even avocados were rare and unusual. I was fourteen the first time I tasted yogurt. Julia Child first came onto the scene in the early 1960s, so America was still discovering food that wasn't burgers or steaks.

After growing up in South Africa as a Jew, Len moved to Israel, where he lived on a kibbutz, until he decided to come teach at the School. He had met Dr. B. when Dr. B. had spent time researching his book *Children of the Dream* about the education of kibbutzim children. Dr. B. invited him to come teach us and he arrived shortly thereafter. In his mid-thirties, he was relatively old for a new staff member. His Israeli connection was more than just historical for us: During the Six Day War in 1967, Len, who was part of the Israeli army's reserve, was on standby for a flight back to Israel to fight for his country. I never knew anyone going off to war before and I was scared of what might happen to him. As it was, there was not a free airline seat, and the war was over so quickly that Len never had to go. But I remember his calmness and his bravery as well as his willingness to bear arms for his country, which was a side that I had never seen before in this decidedly nonviolent man.

He was this cheerful guy with a wacky sense of humor. He was famous for his corny one-liners, such as once when we leaving on a trip somewhere, he announced, "Speak now or forever hold your piss." We just winced. Another time, when I asked if he considered me a megalomaniac, he thought for a second and then answered, "Absolutely not, your majesty."

He'd come into a preexisting class and he was an outsider. Not only was he from Israel, but also he held different attitudes and beliefs from those adults I knew. The only city I knew was Chicago, and here was a man who had moved from South Africa to Israel to live on a kibbutz before arriving in Chicago to teach. During the month that he was our substitute teacher, he gave us lessons on how the English language changed after the Normans came to England in 1066. He also tried once to teach me deep relaxation technique, a big mistake, since he wanted me to take off my belt and shoes and lie on my back with my eyes closed. I thought he was trying to hypnotize me. So did the rest of the class. It freaked us out, and we never let Len forget it.

Marsha returned from her vacation and left shortly thereafter. Our classroom was restructured—we moved next door to another room and got some different kids while others went to other teachers. We still would see our old classmates every day when we went out to the side yard to play and had recess with the entire school. Often we'd play kickball or jump rope or do whatever we were permitted to do, such as play in the sandbox or play tag or fool around on the jungle gym or monkey bars. Len, however, tried to put some discipline in the class and organize us into proper lessons. I was eleven, so I was old enough. But studying came easily to me, and Len prepared lessons so that much of the class could participate. Easily bored, I paid attention when I wanted, but that wasn't often. Otherwise, I disrupted class.

Diana's notes state that I had a lot of trouble with Len because I distrusted him because he was a man. Conflicted, I wanted his care yet looked on him as a potential rival. I had a complete aversion to being controlled in any fashion. I felt that I was being destroyed and so the harder someone tried to make me do something, the harder I resisted. In the end, trying to control me was totally counterproductive. Diana and Dr. B. were the only people from whom I could accept any discipline.

Finally, we worked out a deal. Instead of following the class or Len's lessons, I could read the *World Book Encyclopedia* when I got bored. So I did. In the next couple of years, I read the entire series cover to cover, from A to Z. Reading an encyclopedia caused me to amass a great quantity of trivia, some of which has stuck with me even to this day. As an example, I remembered the other day that black silk is weighted with lead salts to make it stiff, although if it is weighted too much, eventually it will crack and tear. Such weighting is also done to hats, which is where the expression "mad as a hatter" comes from: lead, as we know, is poisonous, and it was not an unusual occupational hazard for hatters to go mad after using it for years to stiffen their hats.

I also had special projects that caught my fancy. Biology I'd always loved from the beginning, and Luitgard had encouraged my interests. Since there wasn't really anyone on the teaching staff who could teach it, I taught myself. I read up on cells, mitochondria, mitosis, meiosis, and pheno- versus genotypes. One citation would lead to another: silkworms versus moths to chrysalis versus cocoons. I kept myself busy and Len kept the peace.

While special lessons were sometimes prepared for me, although Len was available to answer any questions I had and made it clear he was prepared to assist me in learning whatever I wished, the thing considered most important for me was to join in with the class and be less isolated. No one was particularly concerned about my intellect—what bothered them was my depression and how hard it was for me to join others in a mutual world without my commandeering the common ground. My boredom in lessons, which were geared for the entire class and often too easy for me, was considered an opportunity to examine why I was bored, which the staff (and Dr. B.) always thought to be a sure sign of something else, generally anger. To me then, however, I was just bored and needed more distraction to interest me.

Some new kids joined from other classes. Janet was one. She was awkward and goody-goody, which we referred to as being too "orthogenic"—not a compliment. She also suffered from grand mal seizures from time to time, which terrified us, but we learned that she would recover and that we needed to place something in her mouth so she wouldn't bite her tongue. Fortunately, I was never called upon to minister to her. I found it too scary that someone's body could be so out of control.

I spent more time than I should have provoking Janet to watch her over-the-top reactions. Anything I did with the slightest hint of rebellion or irreverence, which was pretty much everything, horrified her. How could anyone be so bad all the time? she wondered. The answer, as I told her all the time, "It's easy!" For her, being bad meant challenging, questioning, demanding. Dr. B. used to say often that he preferred children who were fighters, because they had a better chance of getting well, once they could direct their energies appropriately. This statement always reassured me that maybe there was hope for me: I sure knew how to fight. Janet was no fighter.

Then there was Georgina. I have met many Georginas in my life and have disliked them all. She was passive aggressive, always wanting to play with us, never any fun, good at making us feel guilty for not including her, but if she played, no one could enjoy themselves. While I too was pushy and often oblivious to others, I was very different from her. My inability to get along with others was up front and loudly proclaimed—there was nothing passive about me. I never bothered to hide anything and certainly never pretended to be nice while stabbing someone in the back. I probably should have hidden more; it would have been preferable to alienating so many so often.

Georgina in the end refused to do anything about herself. She was too thick to understand anything complicated, not because she was stupid, but because she was lazy. But she wanted to be acknowledged as smart and part of the action, anyway. She pretended to be nice but was often quite nasty and, when confronted, would always deny it. She also had little personal vanity and sometimes smelled bad, but it never occurred to her she might do anything to make herself more pleasing to others. I quickly found that there was no hope for her and she was just a waste of time. When I pointed this out, the staff defended her, but I could see that even they didn't mean it. It was sad that Georgina succeeded in making everyone dislike her. Underneath the pretense of liking us all, she really was a bitch. I was grateful that whatever my problems were, they hadn't made me a Georgina. I was sorry about her life and what was going to happen to her, but it was clearly inevitable, and I didn't want to watch.

Her modus operandi was always like this: once, in Dr. B.'s three o'clock meeting, he was talking about something and referred to it "as a pain in a three-letter word for a part of human anatomy." Georgina raised her hand and said proudly, "I know, shoulder." With anyone else, Dr. B. would have yelled at them for making such a public fool of themselves. He just rolled his eyes. It was then that I understood he had no patience or interest in her, either. I turned to Roger and whispered a little too loudly, "Well, I guess we just found out who's class valedictorian." Julie heard it, too, and we sat there trying not to laugh. Fortunately for me, Dr. B. either didn't hear us or ignored me. Otherwise, making fun of another kid was a good way to get yelled at. Since I did that kind of thing way too much, he would not have shown me much mercy.

Somehow, I got an education. It was unorthodox but I put together the pieces here and there and managed to get some classical background. In fact, I had little formal education from the second to eleventh grades outside of a few classes some years later. When I first came to the School, as I indicated, I didn't know how to write. Despite my second teacher Marsha's work with me, I still did not know how to write an organized letter of any serious length or a proper paper since my thoughts were too unstructured. This was interesting because my father was an editor and later a publisher and my uncle a well-known journalist. And here I was, almost unable to write at all. Over the years, I finally achieved the necessary self-restraint to endure the frustration of doing something at which I wasn't good, so I could become better. In plain English, what this really meant was that I had to practice—and write a lot of really bad stuff to improve. However, for years my sense of self was so fragile that I couldn't bear to do anything at which I couldn't succeed. I stuck with what I knew, which was reading and fighting. As Diana slowly was able to give me some confidence in myself, I could begin learning to do those things that I didn't know, such as playing with others and, eventually, writing. It was she who got me to write down stories and my imaginings in the dorm. Only later could I do so in the classroom. Diana encouraged me to write to teach me and because it was something I could do on my own; since I was still not capable of really playing with others, there wasn't much else I could do left to my own devices, other than read.

In Len's class, however, at first I was too uncontrolled to do much organized with the others, but over the years he got me to be part of the class. He started me with math, which Len originally taught, and then moved me on to algebra and fractions with Ellen. Ellen was an older girl, about eighteen, I think, who was a math whiz, and she started to teach us. I loved her. She was patient, kind, and spent the time with me so I could understand what I was studying. She also understood my idiosyncrasies and adjusted for them.

Ellen had come to the School as a ward of the Jewish Children's

Bureau, which I assumed paid for her to stay. Back then I never paid attention to such things as tuition fees, but the School was vastly expensive. Tuition, when I first arrived, was $1,550 a quarter, which was just less than tuition for a full year of college at the time. When I left, I think tuition was $15,000 a year, still more than double a year's college tuition.

In current dollars, this was over $60,000 a year. The last time I asked, current tuition for the School was $70,000 per child. In the end, my thirteen years at the School would cost close to a million dollars today. My father was not a wealthy man; he was still a magazine editor and would not start his business for some years yet. And he had three other children. Keeping me at the School required some real sacrifices by my parents. Initially I paid no attention to what things cost and just assumed we were rich, which also fitted into my fantasy life much better than reality. Again, Diana intruded by pointing out that the state was paying a portion of my tuition, because she wanted me to come back to Earth and stop thinking I was the Prince of Wales. (Curiously, my father's nickname for me has always been *the dauphin*, the title of the heir to the throne of France, equivalent to the Prince of Wales.)

Later, when my father had started his own publishing company, Saks was down the street from his office, where I would stop on my way to shop, since it was a place I couldn't go at the School, as the School did not have an account there. I also think they thought it was inappropriate. My father, however, used to refer to Saks as my local discount store and was mostly amused that "the dauphin" liked to go and stock up before going back to the School after Labor Day.

After Diana had gotten me to see my family's financial situation realistically, I tried not to burden them with all of the unhappiness I felt about being locked away. For the first several years, local state government contributed several thousand dollars a year for me, since there was not a school in my parents' district that could provide the education I required. My father's older brother, a wealthy man, would from time to time help out with my tuition. My uncle was tough but never said a word to me about paying for me to be at the School. I only found out when my father told me after I had left. When I visited my uncle in his house in Florida during my first college spring break, I thanked him. He just responded that he was pleased to help. It was one of the more generous gifts that I ever received, since he did it without asking for anything, not even a thank you. This same uncle, who was in the automobile business, also used to make sure that I always had a car available to use whenever I was home—or visited him in Florida.

Later, when I went out to high school, the University of Chicago Laboratory High School, which was one of the top three private schools in Chicago along with The Latin School and Francis Parker, my father paid tuition for that as well. By then he was doing fairly well, but it was a hardship to pay full tuition for both Lab School and the Orthogenic School at the same time, since I lived at the School while attending Lab School. When I protested once to Jacqui, who by then was director of the School after Dr. B.'s retirement, that since the School was part of the University of Chicago, my father shouldn't be double billed for two tuitions, since I could only go to one set of classes, she just about took my head off. As far as costs went, by the time I got to college, tuition seemed like a relative bargain to my parents.

So, Ellen lived at the School. She had no family to go home to on visits. Her view of the world was shaped only by what she could observe from the School and from the staff. I knew how lucky I was to have supportive parents who could look out for me in the real world and send me to places like Martha's Vineyard. The idea of seeing the world as fed to us by the staff was a terrifying thought. While I needed to do a lot of work to understand my inside world, I was never so gone as to think that would ever be enough. Even with a family, it was a major fight for me to fit in after I left. And not only did I have a family but also one that was relatively well off.

Ellen did not have those advantages, and she was not particularly attractive and suffered from acne, for which she used to lie in the sun. Looking back, I realize time and circumstance allowed us to be friends. She was sweet and patient with me and taught me very well. When she left the School, it was a blow. Julie found me in the big classroom after the final wave good-bye with tears in my eyes—something she hardly ever saw, because I was damned if anyone was going to see me cry. I was fourteen or fifteen, I think. I was also saddened for Ellen.

That leaving ceremony was one I long remembered. Dr. B. got a lot of grief over it, too, all of it deserved. Ellen and two other girls were leaving together, sharing an apartment and going to college. In his narrative speech, Dr. B. praised one of the girls on how well she had done, was mild to the second, and then blasted Ellen for how little work she had done on herself. Ellen's counselor and therapist, Nonnie, had died a year and half previously in a car accident while on vacation, a true tragedy, since she had been one of those rare people: kind, smart, beautiful, and modest. She worked harder than anyone and I would see her taking Ellen to lie in the sun; Nonnie with her golden beauty and tall lithe figure while Ellen was stout and not nearly as pretty. Just looking at the two of them, you knew that life was unfair.

One of Dr. B.'s comments has burned in my mind ever since, as it no doubt has in Ellen's as well: "I really thought that Nonnie's death would shake you up and get you to do something about yourself. But no," he continued, "you wasted your time here." It was neither the place nor the time for a brutal speech. At the time, I didn't understand exactly how one got "better" and was unsure what would happen to me. I certainly didn't want Dr. B. to say something similar to me when I left. To have that comment ricocheting in my mind as my last memory of the School would have been unbearable. Ellen was going off with two other girls who by Dr. B.'s standard had done better than she. If Dr. B. had failed to change the situation earlier, he should have at least had the grace to keep his mouth shut. Margaret, who saw Ellen in session and who would continue to do so after Ellen left, was outraged and told Dr. B. off later. I was always pleased to see Ellen when I ran into her when she came back to see Margaret. I never asked her how she felt about Dr. B.'s send-off, but it was the kind of thing that accomplished nothing but make him enemies. When the rest of the pack came forward to attack him after he died, Ellen was too much of a lady to say anything, although surely she had been given cause. She became a teacher, and, judging by how much she helped me, I hope has had an exemplary career.

In Len's class we got a new girl who had come to the School at the relatively old age of fourteen. Her name was Allison and we became good pals, despite our frequent arguments. She was one of the few kids, it seemed, whose parents were able to reach inside the School, like Carrie's hand reaching out from the grave, to harass her. Starting fairly soon after she arrived, Allison would report that her parents were thinking of yanking her out because it was so expensive.[1] Worried about being thrown out of the School myself, I found the thought of anyone leaving before he or she was ready unsettling. I didn't feel ready to live in the outside world. And, given what we had heard, ending up at another place seemed a death sentence. So when Allison talked about being threatened to leave, it left a strong impression.

It is hard for me now to know what were the actual effects she suffered from the hands of her parents and what was due to her interpretation of events. For me, I lived my middle years at the School in terror of Dr. B., a terror that receded finally as I got older. I am not sure now how much of the terror was my own interpretation of life at the School and what was actually being done to me by Dr. B. Certainly some of the reaction then came from my adolescent interpretations; on the other hand, I can see now that the reign of terror inflicted on me was not totally uncalculated.

I liked Allison; she was tough, unsentimental, extremely smart and verbal, a quick study, and, ultimately, sad and angry. She was the original pessimist, and if there was any means of pulling out of a situation an explanation that derived from the basest of human motives, she would find it. There were also so many petty jealousies and such bizarre behavior in our lives, including some of the staff's, that finding opportunities to laugh at people was easy. Allison was a bit older than I was and knew a lot more about many things. She was happy to help me learn and was patient in explaining what I wanted to know. Through her, I first heard the expression "It is better to remain silent and be thought a fool than open one's mouth and remove all doubt." That saying has been most useful to me in a variety of settings, including the writing of this book.

Allison and I both came to distrust those who keep most of their thoughts to themselves. Either they had no thoughts, which is why they never said anything, or they only wanted to come forward to gain the advantage, lurking in the background like a scorpion under a rock, waiting for their chance to sting. Even my less verbal friends could make their thoughts known by a roll of their eyes, a grin, or another gesture. As for the veiled ones, we learned to beware.

Dr. B. always used to warn us "Beware of those whom everybody likes." He was right. The only way people can be liked by everyone is if they don't have firmly held standards and shift their arguments and what they believe from person to person. Ultimately, they are undependable, since they care more about presenting themselves so that everyone can like them than standing up for what is right. At a time of war, they are dangerous. In times of peace, ultimately boring.

Dr. B. made numerous warnings like this. Yael Dayan, daughter of the famed Israeli general, had written a book one of whose main characters was a man who couldn't feel his feelings and thus destroyed the lives of those around him. Dr. B. called him a rock. For a long time, "Don't be a rock" was a mantra about those of us who weren't allowing themselves to feel. The discussion about the book started off, as usual, with a long harangue in a three o'clock meeting, but this one seemed to continue for days. As a result, I never read the book—I had had more than enough of it. As a concentration camp survivor, Dr. B. was always concerned about the issues of trust, responsibility, guilt, and honesty, and not just about us. His public pronouncements also generated controversy. We, on the other hand, just had to live with it as did the others who came to know him.

> *People who cannot feel guilty about what they do: one should avoid them. They are dangerous people.*[2]

All of this fitted neatly into my view of the world. How much came from Dr. B. I can't tell, but many of my concerns predated meeting him. I still divide the world up into two groups, those who want my piano and those who don't. This theory, strange as it sounds, is based on the actual experiences of John, my father's Harvard roommate. I have found out that parts of the story had been confused, but that doesn't make it any less meaningful to me.

John was born into a wealthy German Jewish family in 1927. When things got really bad for Jews in Germany, John's parents had the foresight to send him to safety in England, where he lived out the war with an English family. Their chauffeur denounced the parents. It turned out that what he had wanted was their grand piano. After the war, when Germany was bombed by the Allies and food was in short supply, the chauffeur wrote his former employers, who were by then in New York, asking them for assistance and telling them he hadn't meant to harm them. I thought if ever there was a good example of chutzpah, this was it. John's parents declined to assist.

After hearing that story, I divided up the world, which ends up forming a traditional bell curve, as follows: I don't expect my friends to save me at the risk of their lives or the lives of their families, but I do expect them not to sell me out for the equivalent of my grand piano. Unfortunately, there are not many in that class of whom I can be absolutely sure. Then there are those who would clearly sell you down the river for your piano without a second thought. Determining them may be harder than you imagine, since the ones you need to worry about most tend to be smart enough to keep their motives hidden. The majority you will never know until the time comes—maybe because they themselves do not know what they will do when faced with intense pressure or opportunity.

Allison and I would debate these kinds of issues and try to arrive at some philosophic understanding of the world. She understood that my fascination with history, including various leaders, many of whom suffered from severe personality defects, was part of my desire to find a working explanation for what I observed in life. I had focused on the French and English. Allison knew the Italians, many of whom raised depravity to an entirely new level when compared to their French and English brethren. Cesare Borgia and his sister, Lucrezia, both children of a Renaissance pope, fascinated me with their misdeeds. While many of the stories may have been apocryphal (a word that I also learned from Allison), many were not. Between poisons, daggers, and ambushes, life on a sixteenth-century Roman sidewalk made a midnight stroll through Central Park look like a ride in Disneyland.

We were also fascinated by cavemen. Since so many of our dorm mates behaved like them, it was not a study unrelated to our daily lives. I think we got away with that one, since we never suggested where anyone could overhear what our associations to cavemen were. However, we always assumed Georgina would not have made it for long before being hit on the head with a large boulder. Once Allison got a leather skirt—something avant-garde in those days, unlike now, when leather everything is common. I was jealous, since she now had the couture of a cavewoman. How she loved that skirt, which was a rare luxury for her.

Over time, Allison softened and seemingly became less bitter. In the end, her parents finally made good on their threats, and she left before I did. I think by the time she left, she was ready to go. When the pack came forward to attack Dr. B. after his death, she was one of them. She accused him of dragging her out of the shower to hit her when she was fifteen. Clearly, this was monstrously inappropriate. Whatever occurred was never discussed between us, either at the time or afterward, so I have no personal knowledge of what happened. It does not seem out of the realm of possibility, and I have never known Allison to lie. Hitting anyone that age, let alone dragging an adolescent girl out of the shower, seemed unforgivable to me, too.

The main difference was in the staff—if you had a good senior counselor who was on your side, you were lucky. I had Diana and Margaret. If Dr. B. had done something like that to me, they would have intervened—if not at the time, at least later. I don't know if any of the staff stood up for Allison and were willing to take on Dr. B. Allison did not have the same relationships with the staff as I had, but coming to the School as an older child was difficult. I don't believe that she confronted Dr. B. while he was alive and for that I am sorry, if for no other reason than she might have had an explanation or apology.

11

Beginning Adolescence

As often happens in group therapy, the Mohawks made a lot of advances together. We of course had our individual issues and families, but our ability to pull together and form a cohesive whole moved to the point that we could look after ourselves when Diana or Julie went up front or was called in to help a more junior counselor. For me at thirteen, being part of a group was an enormous achievement. The staff had worked hard to force me out of my books and cynicism. (They failed about some of the cynicism.) I had some friends among the kids, and I trusted Diana and Margaret. Dr. B. was still a major factor in my life since he seemed omnipresent and was still our absolute ruler, but I was getting into trouble much less. Now when I did, it was not always because I was being difficult but because I was starting to grow up.

We also looked after Diana by now. We'd tell her that she had to go do her hair or that she needed to take a nap when she was exhausted. She was studying for her master's degree and we'd yell at her to go study. I think she even went once or twice. Before she left, we were quite capable of looking after ourselves for several hours. It didn't happen very often, but we could manage. One of us would look after Timothy, who felt safe with the rest of us around. In full tantrum, he would scream for someone to go get the counselor, but even then, unless someone was actually bleeding, which almost never happened, we could get him to manage. Also, there was the Wednesday night staff meeting for all of the staff that usually started at 10 P.M. or so and went on for an hour. Sometimes, after lights-out and reading us a story with a flashlight, Diana would fall asleep waiting for us to fall asleep. Now we'd wake her and tell her to go to staff meeting. Diana used to tell the other staff about that with a mixture of embarrassment and pride. One of Diana's good friends was Joan, the boys' counselor down the hall. When the two of them were on at the same time, there was a lot of back and forth between the two dorms. Joan had started out as our substitute counselor when she first arrived at the School. She thus had her indoctrination by fire.

The boys' group next to Joan's group was the big boys, who had Steve as their counselor. He was Hungarian, about six two or something, and weighed at least 220 pounds. We used to tease him all the time about his size. Once we were discussing how much babies normally weighed at birth and Joan cracked, "Unless it was Steve, who must have weighed at least forty pounds!" This remark later came back to haunt her, for eventually, some years later, she married Steve. She must have gotten tired of our asking if their first child was going to weigh forty pounds, too.

At this time, I started to go for haircuts by myself. While the barbershop was only a few blocks away, the idea that for the first time I was given permission to go into the neighborhood by myself, without a counselor or the other kids, was huge. I could be trusted, I was no longer a little kid, and I had gotten to the point that Diana wasn't worried that I would have a fit, hurt myself, or mouth off at someone, requiring her to pick up the pieces. I pushed all the time to do things that I knew Diana wouldn't let me, since she felt I couldn't manage it. Diana reported in the notes that I was shocked once when she responded to me "in a year or two" when I had asked about going off on my own. As much as a revolutionary as I was, I also thought, or hoped, I would never grow up. I was scared by getting older. Going outside was a sign that I was getting closer to leaving the School, and I still felt so desperately angry and empty. Even after all this time, there seemed like so much was still wrong, how was I ever going to manage?

As part of growing up, we even got to watch TV by ourselves, something that we had never been permitted before, no matter how much we had begged. During this period, John Galsworthy's *The*

Forsyte Saga was made into a long-running TV series, so Sunday nights after supper were organized around the show for us older ones. It wasn't a huge deal, but it was a tangible sign that we were no longer considered little ones.

We were also old enough to understand our place in the cosmos—we knew about Dr. B.'s fame and took an interest in what was happening politically. There were a string of famous visitors to the School. We enjoyed our place in the firmament—I mean, if we had to put up with all the inconveniences of our lives at the School, we sure were going to enjoy the pieces of fame that came our way. When Dr. B. was on TV, we watched him, pleased that we knew more about him and his work than the interviewer, so we were the insiders.

One of the more famous visitors, and one of the nicest, was Anna Freud. She was Sigmund Freud's youngest child and one of the founders of child analysis, spending her life applying psychoanalytic principles to children. She was based at the Hampstead Clinic outside London and was already venerable when she came to see us—in her late seventies—so she traveled with a lady companion to assist her. We walked into the three o'clock meeting and Dr. B. introduced her to us. As usual, Dr. B. sat on a chair facing us, while we sat on the floor. Miss Freud was seated next to him. In the corner we had a life-size rocking horse, covered with an actual horsehide, mane, tail, and a saddle and bridle. All I remember of her remarks was that she was sorry she was too old to sit on the rocking horse. She had such a twinkle in her eyes and smiled so nicely that I liked her instantly. I was not alone in that view. Dr. B. took her on rounds, giving me another chance to size her up and make a direct connection to her and, through her, to Sigmund Freud.

In a remark attributed to her (I don't remember if she herself wrote of this or someone else did), Anna Freud, when asked what she did when she saw in session a child she didn't like, responded that she saw him again. If she still didn't like him, she saw him one more time. And if she still didn't like him? Her final response: It never happens. What do you mean? asked the interviewer. "Well," said the founder of child analysis, "I can always find something to like about a child in three sessions." The other major founder of child analysis was our very own Dr. B.

After I had been at the school for six years and was fourteen,

Diana announced that she was leaving to get married. We had a month to get used to the idea and say good-bye. Diana was apologetic. She hadn't planned on getting married and had turned him down once before. This time she couldn't say no again. She felt particularly bad because she had started seeing Sean and Roger in session about a year earlier, which she never would have done if she had thought there was any possibility of her leaving. I was devastated, but I am sure that I blocked out a lot of my terror of having no Diana in my life. My only consolation was that at least I had Margaret so that I wasn't losing both my counselor and therapist in one fell swoop, as were Roger, Sean, and Winston.

By now I was capable of thinking of someone else. I tried to be pleased for Diana, but I was in despair. Life without her was impossible to contemplate. I was proud of what I had achieved with Diana's help, and losing her felt like losing a parent at an early age, when there is still so much more to be shared, learned, and taught. I was scared that I might not ever make it—or make it to an acceptable level of living, as far as I was concerned.

I had loved Diana from the very start, unless I was in the middle of a fight with her, in which case I hated her, didn't understand why I had ever liked or trusted her, and wanted to know why she was so stupid as to disagree with me. Toward the end, before she left, while we had a number of disagreements, such fights were only a few times a month as opposed to a few times a day, much to both of our relief, not to mention the relief of the rest of the dorm and others caught in my crossfire. Again, there were still plenty of times when I genuinely didn't understand what I had done even when it was explained to me: My judgment and memory of a situation was so different from what I was hearing that I necessarily assumed that Diana, Julie, or Dr. B. was wrong. My lack of vision occurred with lessening frequency, but, unfortunately, it took me a long time to start seeing things from other people's point of view and to have it finally dawn on me that I might have something to do with the problem. The day that thought entered into my head was a bad day; I was depressed for a long time, realizing that I had created so much trouble for others and myself.

Those realizations came in steps over time. Each time I would think "Now I have finally got it." Then, a couple of years later, I'd get hit with it again and realize "Now I finally got it." After having now-I-got-it epiphanies every few years, I finally realized it was an ongoing process. Even now, much as I dislike admitting it, I am still acclimatizing myself to the fact that there is stuff I am missing about myself that others around me figure out almost instantly. This ability to face frustration and to take responsibility started with Diana. I could admit my failings because she had proved to me over and over that her love for me was unconditional and I believed her.

While I was in too much shock to totally take in all of my feelings about losing Diana, I was clear then on how much emotion had been unleashed. I ran into her once in the afternoon, walking Winston back from session. We only had a week or so to go: She just put her arm around me as we crossed Dr. B.'s beautiful new corridor with its stained glass bricks. I was too choked up to say a word. It was a shared moment that I saved up in memory to warm me later. I was appreciative of all Diana had done for me, sad that she was going, and almost capable of being happy for her. I hope at one point or another that I thanked her for all that she had done for me. But if I didn't, she understood. That walk down the corridor seemed like an acknowledgment of all we had done together. It had taken six years to get there, and I never would have been able to do so without her.

Diana brought over her fiancé, so we could meet him briefly. It was like rounds, in a way; he came in, said hello to us, and then left. At least we learned he was real. The final day arrived and all I remember was Diana coming in soon after three and walking around to give each of us a hug to say good-bye. She then stepped out of my life for thirty years.

We would trade a letter or two a year, and she came back to visit once or twice. Unlike with Ugo, I always picked up with her and felt the old connection return. I invited her to my high school graduation a week before I left the School, and we visited then for a bit. The next time I saw her was when I was still in college, I spent an afternoon with her, her husband and daughter. However, those were "visits" as opposed to seeing old friends whom you don't see very often but are still part of your life. It is only in the past year or two that I have started seeing Diana from time to time for lunch or dinner, when she comes to New York where her daughter lives. Now we have been able to pick our friendship again in the present as opposed to having something that was a memory of the past. Those memories are still there, of course, but I now feel that Diana is back as part of my current world. But it may give you some idea of how strongly I felt for her and how big a blow her leaving was to me that it took thirty years for me to be able to contemplate resuming our friendship or, I suppose more accurately, create a new one. I am glad that we both lived long enough.

After Diana left, the School was never the same for me, and the next several months were a blur. I got through them, but every day without Diana was tough and everywhere I turned, I had memories of her and our lives together. Roger and Sean were also pretty shattered, so it was nice not to be alone in my grief. We all knew Mary Margaret and it was no surprise when Dr. B. named her as Julie's co-counselor. There were some struggles as we got comfortable with each other, but that was to be expected.

I had a much different relationship with Mary Margaret. I could see her as a person sometimes, I wasn't a child depending on her, and my primary relationship was now with Margaret. Moreover, Julie had been with us several years. While she was important to me, there would never be the intimacy that Diana and I had shared. Mary Margaret for me, and I think for some of the others, could be our counselor and also our friend. We enjoyed each other's company for the most part. (There were also a couple of knock-down scream-outs, but nobody's perfect.) The Mohawks made it a project to take her and make her into our image of a sophisticate. Mary Margaret was as low key and casual as you could get, which was part of her considerable charm, but she used to eat with her fingers, not like a slob, but delicately picking. Roger and I got tired of pointing out that she wasn't going to be able to do that at Mrs. Onassis's next dinner. Since Mary Margaret was less concerned about her appearance there than worrying about Timothy's next fussing attack, we never managed to make her over into a New York society matron.

Memory works strangely sometimes. All of us in the Mohawks had a lot of serious problems, and yet in discussions what most of us remember are the laughter and the jokes. Mary Margaret was a full member of our society of humor, since she appreciated our jokes, especially when they were not directed at her. I always thought that Roger was the ringleader, but there was by no means universal agreement about that. I was often accused (or honored, as the case may be) of being the instigator.

Due to my cheerful disposition prior to ten o'clock in the A.M. Roger dubbed me initially Groucho and then Groucho-in-the-Morning. It took about five minutes before everyone on the boys' floor had seemingly forgotten my real name. Although names were considered serious business in the School and heretofore the giving another kid a nickname was strictly verboten, no one said anything about this. It was too true. For the most part, it was amusing, but after months of being Groucho, particularly when I really was very grouchy about something, Roger and I had some big fights. I was such a prig at times that he enjoyed poking holes in my bubble to prove that I was not, in fact, that much older and wiser than the rest of the dorm. I was, however, the oldest member and had been at the School longer, which I thought gave me some privileges, and as you know by now, I had long had a problem with grandiosity. I was less of a boss but still unable to be just one among equals. However, before Diana left, she had managed through her complete and unconditional faith in me to install me as an integral part of the dorm. As difficult as it was for me, I could endure the frustration of learning how to live with others because I knew she supported me. I was no longer an outcast of society.

By then some of the Mohawks were working in the kitchen—each of us had to work one meal a week. It was considered good for us, we got an increased allowance, $10 a month, and it allowed some time out of the dorm. Roger, Sean, Toby, and I frequently worked together in some combination, although we also worked with numerous other of the older kids. Once, Roger was doing something stupid—I think trying to figure out how to lock Toby in the pantry by blocking the door—and I told him he ought to deal with it instead of getting us all into trouble. He later complained to Mary Margaret, "I can work with a grouch, but working with Sigmund Freud is too much!" Toby, as was typical, never figured out how close he had come to being locked in. A few months later Toby got into trouble for hiding in the same cupboard, allegedly to dip into the cooking sherry. His behavior made the accusation plausible; however, anybody who had tasted the cooking sherry would have known that nobody in his right mind would have drunk it unless at gunpoint. Not even Toby.

Money and the operations of the School had never been something I had thought about or something we would have been permitted to discuss. Dr. B.'s attitude was that if something was a good idea, then he would find the money. If not, then we weren't going to do it anyway. The cooks and maids did not like to work Sunday nights; they wanted to have dinner with their families. We always had had our big meal on Sundays at lunch and then a light supper that didn't require a full service staff and could be easily cleaned up. Finally it was decided that Sunday supper would be served in the dorms—and the counselors would go downstairs and bring up cold cuts and salads for dinner. Somebody came up with the idea that maybe we could make dinner, and Katherine, one of the counselors, volunteered to do it with us.

We divided into teams, which presaged a competition that eventually would doom this enterprise. Each team did dinner once a month or so. At the first general meeting for all hands, Katherine stated that she wanted each of us to pick one dish that we wanted to make. I complained vociferously that we had an opportunity to do some really good work and why should we waste our opportunity because one of the less enlightened members of our community wanted mashed potatoes, as one of the goodies-goodies just had requested. Katherine felt strongly that everyone's wishes should be included, thus enfranchising the less vocal among us, which I didn't mind, as well as the Georgina types, which I did. There was a lot of argument, but fortunately I lost, since she was right. I just couldn't see it then and, worst of all, wasn't capable of seeing her point of view. I wanted to learn how to do a complete meal and, more than that, do something spectacular that would do honor to the best tables in the world.

And that, both because of and despite Katherine, was where we ended up. Not because of me, since I lacked the political ability or following to pull everyone in such a direction. Having four teams did the trick, since the competition started immediately. Each group wanted their dinner to beat the other guys'. We started out with a few simple meals and ended combing through Henri Paul Pellaprat and *Larousse Gastronomique* while complaining that we couldn't find a copy of *Escouffier* in translation.

I learned a lot. We did Bordelaise sauces, cooking down marrow bones to mix with the wine sauce; we did hollandaises; someone found an Imperial Russian menu for chicken breasts in Russian walnut sauce; I found a recipe for a double chocolate sour cream cake and our prep time kept increasing. Roger, a few others, and I would pretend we were making dinner for the king or queen and everything had to be perfect. We would then decide who got to be the reigning monarch but wouldn't tell them. They just thought we were acting weird as always. We used to get back in the kitchen and roar with laughter. Generally, the most imperious of our denizens received such a dubious honor. It was in these weekly endeavors that Toby got accused and nailed for allegedly getting into the cooking sherry.

We finally broke the bank. The coup de grace was steak stuffed with shellfish—extravagant to be sure—but we thought it worth every penny. Not everyone agreed and we went back to cold cuts and canned ravioli. We were saddened to end our sojourn through the realm of haute cuisine. Looking back, I also think it ended because our ever more elaborate dinners became much more work for Katherine than she had ever envisioned when she took this project on. We did, however, gain an appreciation for haute cuisine and the subtleties of flavor. After cooking so many meals for seventy, I have no fear whatsoever about making dinner.

Food remained a central part of our lives. As mentioned earlier, my grandmother gained fame when she airmailed me her care packages. Once I returned home from my summer visit and forgot most of my underwear. My mom mailed them back in a large box, which was sitting on my bed when we got back from class. Seeing the box when we walked into the dorm, we all assumed that it was more brownies from my grandmother, but lo and behold, it was my underwear. Roger developed this comedy routine about my opening the package, biting into it, and getting snapped in the head from the elastic band in my shorts. He went on about this for months. And the next time my grandmother actually sent a package, he wanted to know if there were any shorts hidden in the middle layer. By that time, most of the School knew about the underwear joke and people would make snapping gestures at me, imitating Roger imitating me.

Roger himself had a few issues with food and, like many of us, gained some weight after a while at the School. He finally decided to go on a diet—which I think he wrote his parents, so they wouldn't send him any candy, which they liked to do periodically. His grandmother, who was a serious diabetic, loved to send him huge boxes of chocolate that she wasn't supposed to eat. This was unfair to poor Roger, who was desperately trying to drop some weight, so I suggested he send the candy back with a note "Enjoy in good health." I think a box of that stuff would have killed the old lady, and no matter how much Julie yelled at us, "Enjoy in good health" became as much one of our slogans as any remarks about Groucho.

While all of this was going on, we finally changed dorms and moved to the bigger room at the end of the hall where I got my therapeutically placed bed next to Jon. We were now the older, more stable group on the floor. The older boys, including Daniel, had moved to the newly constructed Adolescent Unit, which was not connected to the main dorm building, something that was later to prove a big mistake. Mary Margaret's good friend Leslie was the counselor next door. After Diana left, Roger and I would invite Leslie into the dorm to yell at us like Diana did. Leslie, being a good actress, would camp it up with us and pretend to yell at us, imitating Diana. After a good performance, we would all applaud and she would go back to her kids.

When the Mohawks moved down the hall to the bigger dorm, not only were we right next door to Leslie's dorm but also we had more closets and two bathtubs/showers, which made getting ready in the morning or at bed twice as fast. In many ways, it was easier to be in a dorm that was not associated with Diana and where I didn't keep imagining her in every corner.

Leslie had Cole, who behaved as Toby had when he first came, but somehow never seemed to stop. He was seven when he came, large for his age, with a mop of blond curls. As cute as he was, he was an agent provocateur and essentially created trouble from the moment he got up until he fell asleep at night. The kind of trouble he got into was different from mine: I had spent so much time involved with Diana that I didn't have much time or energy to deliberately provoke the other kids; I just did it naturally. Cole, on the other hand, delighted in it, and since he was aggressive and big for his age, he was usually successful. Later, when he got even bigger, there were a number of punches thrown. Sam, another of Leslie's kids, did not like all of this provocation and hated Cole's fighting. He wanted to be in our group and would run in like a madman yelling "Mohawks, Mohawks, Mohawks" and run out again, like a verbal flasher. He used to do his "hit and runs," as we called them, several times a night until we got tired of them or he got told it was time to go to bed. Then he would just write Mohawks-Mohawks-Mohawks on a piece of paper and shove it under the door.

Leslie used to come in laughing to collect Sam, who had a privileged position in our dorm and was very good friends with one of my dorm mates. Robbie was another frequent visitor—he was one of the first geniuses that I had met next to Dr. B. Socially geekie, he was smart as a whip and could read anything, including the most difficult text on gravitation, filled with differential equations, and do all of the math in his head. I liked him a lot but he was in a class by himself. Nobody was as smart as he or could do what he could do in his head. It was good evidence that being smart didn't make you happy. Given his problems, I remembered Dr. B. yelling at someone, not me this time, that "the state institutions are filled with brilliant people. Stupid ones don't usually need to be locked up." When he was young, right after he first came to the School, Robbie would get upset about something and have a fit. It was different from mine in the sense that he would get so angry that he would be screaming, but it was almost incidental, because what came across was immense frustration and unhappiness. The intellectual rigor that he could bring to bear on any cerebral issue did not work in solving problems of everyday living.

One of the things guaranteed to make him throw a fit was Cole. Cole was a pest. His great skill was driving someone crazy just by looking at him—whatever were the worst things he had ever done to that person could be summoned in that one look—and the race would begin. I never understood how someone so skilled at such a subtle art could have so few skills in other areas, particularly academics, since he did badly in his schoolwork. He had to be smart or else he couldn't have created so much trouble. But his skills and abilities somehow seemed diametrically opposed to having a useful, normal life. I sometimes thought about it like a career criminal: Even if someone is the most brilliant criminal ever, such skills were not going to provide any of the abilities that would enable one to live in normal society. Cole had a brilliant career living outside of society in the School and probably outside of it later.

As it was, Leslie could usually contain him and repair the damage created with the other kids. But as Cole grew into a strong and big kid, he got more and more intimidating. He seldom bullied me, but when he did, I never knew how much self-restraint was possible until I kept myself from slugging him.

With my bed sticking out from the wall, I was more exposed than I had been previously—Timothy was now in the corner, maybe in the vain hope he would have less to upset him and we would have more peace from his tantrums. Neither occurred. I still got up, if not every night, then most nights, to find his cuddle blanket and put him back to bed. The responsibility made me feel worthwhile.

As Daniel had developed in time into a good big brother for me, I did the same with Timothy. By now Daniel had been out of my dorm for years but still kept an eye on me, and we were still close. The difference was that Daniel had some responsibilities for me the moment I walked in the door of the School, since he was three and a half (not four!) years older, after he had been at the school for only three months, while I had been at the School for over six years when I started being responsible for Timothy.

I tried to keep up contact with Daniel, which I did in class, because he was in Len's class with me. Since he was the big kid in my life, he was the one I turned to for questions I didn't want to ask the grown-ups. It never occurred to me that he had his own difficulties and that he may not have needed the additional pressure I placed on him to be my big brother.

There were questions, later, about sex I preferred to ask Daniel and not the grown-ups. For all the supposed freedom, I felt like there were a lot of things that I didn't know and had no one to ask. It was not something that I wanted to discuss with Diana when she was there; after I reached a certain age, I felt funny talking about sex with her. Too, in a feeling that must be genetic, affecting mostly males of the species, I didn't want anybody to know what I didn't know. I knew about the birds and the bees, but there were other more specific questions that one wants to ask at fourteen that don't occur to someone who is eight.

For example, I thought that when one grew up, every time a boy had an erection, sperm would come out. Since that didn't happen to me, I assumed that there was something else wrong with me, since I frequently thought my body didn't work. Thinking that I had something wrong with me in such a sensitive area was an unnecessary burden, but I felt there was no one around to ask. (Ugo had been gone for years and Len was relatively new to me.) Daniel did not want to discuss those issues with me, and when I asked him something once, he told Len, who then wanted to analyze me to find out why I was asking Daniel. Following that discussion, I just shut up and didn't say anything. It took a long time for me to feel comfortable discussing anything about sex.

One summer before I left the School, I worked for my father's brother who had assisted with my tuition. At lunchtime, we'd all sit on the roof of my uncle's office building and eat lunch. The mechanics would come upstairs, and their discussions were colorful to say the least. This was new to me. The idea that people could discuss sex and make jokes about it was something I had never seen before, living in the Freudian-oriented, analytic environment that I did. I had so many other things to think about that sex, while certainly something I thought about, was not uppermost in my mind. I was still worried about ending up in a loony bin. When finally I became convinced that I would not, I was still worried that I might be a failure. Sex was an issue that I avoided for a long time in part because I was still depressed and, with high school eventually approaching and my survival at stake, it was further down on my list of priorities than most people's.

Four or five months after Diana left, one weekend evening I started feeling sick to my stomach. I was concerned about it; although I had had stomach aches before, this one was different. I had trouble not only eating but in keeping down what I ate. Because I was in such discomfort, I worried that I might throw up in public. The idea of embarrassing myself filled me with terror, and there would be times that I would throw up before going out just so I wouldn't have to worry about it later. Eventually most of my life revolved around this anxiety and my considerable discomfort. This would go on for the next two years.

In going through the historical records of my stay at the School, I found something that made me think that this was even more directly connected with Diana's leaving than I had thought. When I was eight or nine, I had asked her once what would happen if I ate her up. The fantasy's origin was that I would thus be able to keep her with me forever. Once or twice I even bit off a small piece of her fingernail to act this out. Responding to my original question, however, Diana told me that I would probably get a huge stomach ache if I ate her all up since she was so big and I was so little. Instead, years later, I got the stomach ache because I hadn't found a satisfactory way of keeping her with me.

It was a classic Freudian neurotic symptom. Initially, the staff assumed that it was psychological. Finally, there was concern that I might have an ulcer, so I got taken to the clinic, but the doctors couldn't find anything wrong. If there was any medicine that I could have taken to make me feel better, I never got it. The staff seemed to feel this was just more grist for the mill and figured that when I had dealt with things, it would go away. I was more than irritated that there was so little help in the immediate present. I just suffered.

Julie noticed that I was having a problem and pushed me to do something about it. But I never had the warmness or closeness with her that I had with Diana. I felt like a prisoner, and my body was torturing me for some reason that I was powerless to stop. Everyone's telling me that I was doing it to myself just made matters feel worse. There were times that I was concerned that I would starve to death and would figure with each mouthful of food, this was thirty calories from death, now it's another thirty calories. There would be times I could relax, but I felt this overwhelming pressure about making a fool of myself in public. I was completely paralyzed, except for two things. One was the time I spent with Margaret, which offered me sanctuary; I may have felt discomfort, but it was manageable. The other was the time I spent with the smaller kids; since they were dependent on me, I had to worry about them, not myself, so caring for them helped me to survive.

All my doubts, feelings of self-worth or lack of it, my ability to interact with others, my feelings about being nurtured, my ability to interact socially, and whatever closeness I felt to the staff were all tied up in this one symptom. I felt fairly sure at the time that Diana's leaving had set it off—I felt abandoned and sad and yet did not feel there was anything I could do about it. Once more I felt cornered by life and didn't know what to do.

There was one positive side to all this: Because I felt ill most of the time and constantly worried about how I would function in the outside world, I wasn't fighting so hard to reject the School. Without Diana, my main anchor had been lost and I was floundering and wanted out. The weight of supervision and the feeling that I was being closed in upon somehow became less pressing when faced with constant pain. I don't know if the symptom arrived to save me from myself, since it weakened me enough so that I could listen to others. I even did not like leaving the School's grounds since my fear of throwing up exceeded my wish to escape. My focus changed 180 degrees. This lasted several years. Eventually, slowly the stomach trouble faded. At the time, enduring a two-year stomach ache combined with the fear I would starve to death seemed to be forever.

I survived this with great difficulty. Margaret was key in making some shape out of my world. She would bring me roast beef or French cheeses that I liked during session because I felt more comfortable eating there with her. By now, I hadn't used the kids' dolls to play with in session in years and had begun Freudian-based psychotherapy, as it was more widely known.

Meeting Margaret twice a week and sometimes at other times whenever I asked covers a lot of time and ground. I wish I could give a better description of what we talked about, but I don't remember well our numerous discussions. The general themes I remember—the universal human ones of how to deal with anger, whether it was possible to feel loved, why I had such a difficult time getting close to others, the enormous frustrations I felt about being at the School and losing the experiences that everyone else my age was having, as well as the anxiety over my seemingly never-ending stomachache. Most of all, we discussed that talking about all of this didn't automatically change me. Much of the changes I had to live through took time. Time, however, was the one thing I felt I didn't have.

Dr. B. was patient about my stomach trouble; he made reference to it once or twice but didn't see fit to say any more about it. Many of his remarks were as ironic and mysterious as ever.

A year or so after Diana's departure, Len left after spending four or five years with us. We had had a good run of it and he taught me a lot at a time when I was mostly unteachable. I missed his good humor and maturity of judgment.

After Len, I went to Sue's class. Sue had been a counselor with the older boys and a co-counselor with Steve, the forty-pound baby. After getting married and finding the hours of a counselor a bit too onerous for maintaining a relationship, she decided to become a teacher. She made a valiant effort to teach us, organizing classes. I found with her that I was behaving better. She was a senior staff member, I liked her, and she wasn't full of herself, so we got along and I was able to apply myself a bit more to suffering organized classes.

Our class was upstairs behind the gym where a few multigroup classes were taught. One of the kids from Joan's dorm was Big Barry, who was aggressive, obnoxious, and fat. He had a way of using his girth as an extension of his anger to try to bully those around him, physically pushing forward, using all of his blubber to do so. It was the summer of the Carole King song "I Feel the Earth Move." Since the stairs creaked up to the classroom, we started singing that song whenever Big Barry was on his way. Initially Sue didn't get it (we did keep some secrets, after all), but one did not need to be Einstein to figure out why we were suddenly singing this song so often just before Big Barry arrived. We had a discussion with Sue about making fun of another kid. In the end, we got off, since Big Barry was so obnoxious even the staff wasn't going to defend a losing cause. I had disliked him after a couple of needless run-ins. Life was too short. Sue did yell at me, however, when I suggested we should harpoon him and use him to fuel an Eskimo village for winter, but I didn't mind. My rule at the time, and for quite some time to follow, was that it was okay to be rude, provided you were funny. Life is not a talk show, however, so I paid for that view years later.

A couple of the older girls were in my class, and, other than Allison, it was the first time I had been in class with them. Prior to this, the older, cooler girls never had much interest in me and vice versa. They all hung out together, seemed to giggle all the time about stuff that I never could figure out, mostly had a lot of eating disorders, and were much too cool for me. They all liked Jim, of course, who seemed to do much better with them. While I never liked being considered uncool, the cool crowd didn't seem to see what I saw in people like Timothy, and I figured one Timothy was worth all of them put together. I figured fuck 'em. My attitude didn't do much to improve relations, so I remained one of the outsiders. I wore it as a badge of honor, but inside I felt really bad about it once I had burned my bridges. I wasn't yet smart enough to leave myself with an escape hatch.

If backing myself in a corner socially had only been a one-time thing, it might not have been so bad. At the time, I figured, honorary membership in the Orthogenic School Cool Club wasn't a long-term life goal. It would take me a bit too long to recognize that I made it difficult to have any honorary membership in any club, if you call waiting until I was forty too long.

Some of the cool-crowd attitudes struck me as really stupid. Once I was home on a visit and got together with Daniel and a few other kids who had recently left the School. We were discussing college, and one girl who had formerly been at the School and was going at the time to a small college downstate asked where I had thought about going to college. I told her that I wanted to go to Harvard or Yale. She was genuinely horrified. Her response: Why do you want to put so much pressure on yourself—why not go to a small college like mine? I was stunned. What bothered me so much was that she had invested so much in being a good patient that even after leaving, she carried that attitude with her and could not even imagine life other than her own. If an Ivy League school wasn't what she wanted or needed that was one thing, but what scared me was that she was incapable of at least imagining the advantages. Is this what ten years at the School was going to do? Teach you to be a good patient and parrot back what you thought you should say without being capable of challenging, questioning, and striking out on your own? At the time, I supposed there must have been some happy medium between being a revolutionary like me and a brainwashed sap like that coed from the college downstate, but I wasn't sure where the boundaries were and, if I was going to err, it was going to be on the side of the revolutionaries.

My teacher Sue had a lot of patience for my revolutionary tendencies and since she wasn't bothered, I had less to prove and could calm down. I made friends with one of the cool girls in my class, Jennifer, the daughter of a wealthy New York family. I would feel some envy at the time when we would talk about our visits home. She got to see a world that I wanted to join, knew the difference between Central and Gramercy parks, which were the chic stores on Madison Avenue, and who was who in Manhattan. At Christmas she'd go to Switzerland to ski or her grandparents would pick her up in their limousine and take her shopping. I thought she had the door open to a life that I wanted that seemed out of my grasp. I felt then that almost everything I knew about the outside world was learned secondhand from books and movies. Here I was, shut away, when I wanted to be outside, exploring.

Even with my jealousies, I knew that I would never trade lives. In the end, she was just ordinary with a privileged background. That I didn't strike her as cool said more about her than it did about me. Adolescent doubts, however, made being an outsider a lot more difficult.

With Sue's help I slowly felt less of an outsider, but there was a lot of stuff that went on that I either never heard about or was the last to know, since I was not a player. I also didn't like to feel forced to keep secrets to be cool. I didn't want to encourage anybody to be self-destructive and I didn't want to go down for something so dumb—so maybe I was brainwashed, after all. There were limits about how much I could be integrated in that inner School society. I never admired them enough to want to shut down my thoughts or admiration for the unusual, including those people who didn't measure up to their standards, to join. To be honest, even if I had wanted to join in, they never would have let me. They didn't want me. I was still too overbearing and still living partially in my own world.

Sue became pregnant after I had been in her class about a year. After all of my jealousies and concerns about pregnancy, I had advanced enough that it was not insurmountable. As much as I liked Sue, she was not a crucial person in my life.

Post Sue, I entered the class of John, who was now in the big classroom, where we had the Monday movies, where the good-bye ceremonies took place, and where I heard that President Kennedy had died. We had enough room to have desks, sofas, and tables. Despite having calmed down a lot with Sue, I gave John a lot more trouble. The conflict I had suffered with Len—between wanting to be cared for by a man and finding him a competitive rival—surfaced again. Since my anxieties were not that well contained, I was a nuisance. Too, for some reason, Jim and I were rejoined in class plus one of Leslie's kids, Jack. We were, if not the Three Stooges, close enough, and poor John was slowly driven mad by us. He thought he was well adjusted and in control of his temper. That self-image didn't even last a week.

We joined his class and soon he was observed jumping up and down and screaming. This was a new trick and, since he was pretty big, over six feet and 200 pounds with a tendency to portliness, when he jumped up and down, you really noticed it. I am afraid we used to get him to do it at least once a week. In fairness, I made him suffer the least of the three of us, but I was no angel. Dr. B. used to get really irritated at us, but since it was John who let himself get provoked, Dr. B. said less about it than he might have otherwise. However, that did not mean he ignored the issue. A couple of times he threatened us with staying alone in the dorms, although I suspect he was more concerned about leaving us alone to our own devices than about anything we might do in class to John.

John had gone to Harvard. He was smart, no question, articulate, and truly decent. After a few months of torturing him, we settled in. Then he mostly acted as a referee among the power plays and battles of the classroom and hoped that any resulting all-out wars would not be directed his way. Timothy was in class with us, which was a good thing, and we had a number of other kids, as well. Timothy used to chuckle after some of the mini-riots, like the time we got our hands on water balloons. (John ended up hitting Jack over the head with one, whereupon it burst, much to everyone's amusement, except Jack's, of course, and John's, who figured that now Jack might really make him suffer.) There were other times, though, when Timothy had enough and then he'd start fussing, just to show the rest of us how a professional did it. We may not have been scared of John, but we were careful not to provoke Timothy. He could be more trouble than even we wanted to cope with.

Johanna was there, too, shy, unassuming, and, on the surface, completely boring. At first I didn't know what to make of her, since she was so concerned about always doing the right thing. She had a lot of trouble getting angry and felt that she had to hide, as somehow she wasn't entitled to be human like the rest of us. It was her overarching humility that enabled me to like her. Goodie-goodies I always disliked, but Johanna wasn't one. Instead, she was too scared to feel that she had the same rights as anyone else. Eventually most of the class, me included, tried to force her out of her shell so she could learn that she not only had the same rights as the rest of us but also would not be destroyed for using them. She became more forceful in her quiet way than I think she ever imagined. She was a good friend.

There was Mira, too, who had come to the School at the age of sixteen. She was a clever artist without much self-confidence, and we became fast friends since I admired her work. Like Johanna, she had a lot of doubts about her rights to be human, to get angry, or to assert herself. Every now and then she surprised herself and us by putting her foot down and demanding something. When she was pushed to tell someone to shut up, they always did, even Timothy, since it was so startling on its face. There was a sadness about her that she would sometimes forget in our activities, and it was a pleasure watching her laugh. She and I could talk about anything in the way that people who understand one another comfortably do. Even with the serious things, we'd usually end up laughing because we both could see the irony that existed in much of our lives. For much of the class, our concerns were how we related to ourselves, how to have healthy relationships, how to get close to the staff, how not to be overwhelmed by jealousy, and how to balance being taken care of with some sense of independence. Given the School, that last point was not an easy line to balance for those of us who were older, and many of the worst battles were over that issue.

After an armed truce, John and I began to trust each other, which improved things. I would, at least, see reason. Jim would not. After all this time, he was still stubbornly impossible, but that was how it was, so we all had to deal with it. One more point about Jim. He also saw Margaret in session. I had totally forgotten that fact until I went through the historical notes. I must have been jealous and resented it at the time, but I was also secure in my relationship with Margaret, as I had been with Diana. Despite my jealousies and fears, in the end, I believed that I was special to them. Still, it is curious I had forgotten that information—although it would not have made any difference in my later years with Jim. What I held against him was not jealousy over Margaret but how his behavior interfered with my life and how I had to suffer repercussions from his acting out long after he had left the School.

Around this time, John started teaching a formal geometry course to the older kids from throughout the school. He lectured three mornings a week; we had homework and, most novel, exams. The exams were not graded on a curve or really graded at all—to prevent competition—but they were marked to show if our answers were correct. Initially I was very worried about these exams. While I was a good student, I hadn't taken an exam in school since I was eight, eight years before, and I didn't remember those. The tension and the prepping for exams were essential for me to find out how I did under pressure. Eventually taking exams just became part of studying and not insurmountable; although later in high school or college, of course, there would be a number of 3 A.M. caffeined-out moments cramming as if to save my soul. Those early exams with John saved me when I went out to high school, since I hadn't had formal classes as such, except for that one with John in geometry, another in history with Julie, after she stopped being a counselor and became a teacher, and a couple with later teachers. Those classes helped me get used to taking an organized class (and occasional tests), so when I went to high school, I knew I had at least hope of passing. Given all the other things I would have to juggle, such as life with normal kids my age on the outside, I was glad I didn't have to take extra time to learn how to take exams.

John's classroom was a classic formal Greco-styled room, like a large club's sitting room, with light blue walls and white cornicing, moldings, and columns. To make things more informal, we painted each radiator cover a different color, which turned out much better than I had envisioned, since I liked the formality of the room. Johanna worried about the paint and its vapors being toxic and wanted to ensure that whatever food, such as cookies or candy, was kept well away from it. This concern was too juicy to resist and there were quickly rows of Oreos dipped in the various colored paints drying on the newspaper as soon as John's back was turned. Johanna was somewhat horrified but couldn't take what Jim, Jack, or I did seriously. She loosened up, thus preserving what sanity she had, and we learned to admire that she was more resilient than she had seemed.

We had one autistic girl in the class named Patty. Her face was constantly screwed up into a frown; her blond locks, although carefully brushed each morning, ended up a mess in all directions; and she walked with this serious demeanor befitting an aging lumberjack rather than a little girl. Her language skills were seemingly not good, for she echoed back to people whatever they said to her, unless she wanted something. Then her speech miraculously improved. Or, conversely, if she was mad at someone, or jealous that they were getting more attention from John, she could make some surprisingly nasty remarks. She was exceedingly smart, and I always wondered how such intelligence and yet such complete removal from the world could coexist in such a little girl.

I liked Patty immediately. I admired anyone who could be sarcastic and nasty while being amusing at the same time. Her damage was so deep that it was unlikely that she could go on to high school or college and live anything other than a limited existence with someone looking after her. If she could avoid an institution, that would be a huge achievement for her and the rest of us. Life at the School provided her with an opportunity to be herself without being judged, where she was offered the same respect as anyone else. When watching her, I would think sometimes of Dr. B.'s remark that for some kids the years at the School would be the best years of their lives. I just hoped that I wasn't one of them.

One day this pushy yet shy mixed-up kid went off and did something she wasn't supposed to do deliberately and obviously just to provoke John. It worked. He got really mad at her, which she didn't expect. Then Patty delivered one of the great lines of all time: John, not terribly originally, had shouted at her, "Who do you think you are?"

What came back was this meek voice saying quietly "Somebody else." There was a moment of stunned silence while we all digested this brilliant yet sad response.

Timothy had a harder time with Patty. She was the closest to him in age in the class, which ran from seven to seventeen. Timothy could be heard muttering about her being a pest while she walked around repeating to herself "Timothy likes Patty," which would drive him nuts. While they did not battle all the time, it was not, shall we say, unusual.

Given the diverse age range, class was a little like the one-room schoolhouse on the prairie. Teaching so many ages and abilities put a lot of strain on the teacher, but since what was most valued was screwing people's heads on straight, the skills required were equally applicable to all the kids. Clearly different people required different things, but the ability to listen carefully, to see the world from each child's viewpoint, and to attempt to keep oneself from being enmeshed in someone's problems (the dreaded countertransference) made a teacher's life not quite as bad as it might sound. Given what we did to John, however, it certainly was no picnic.

John left toward the end of the summer to go to medical school. I had been in his class a year. Since he lived in the neighborhood, I would run into him from time to time. We have maintained a friendship ever since, which is now almost thirty years.

12

The First Leaving of Dr. B.

The Mohawks settled into being the older boys on our floor. Julie was softening and we had some good times with her, and Mary Margaret had established herself in her own right so that Diana's long shadow no longer covered whatever she did. Leslie was also part of our lives, and the two dorms became more intertwined that any two other groups I can remember, because with Leslie and Mary Margaret such good friends, the borders between our two city-states were almost always open. It made their lives easier, too, I think, because they each had a comrade in arms close by when the wars began or when one of the kids went AWOL.

Leslie is one of the most beautiful women I have ever met: classic features with prematurely gray, now white, hair. We used to tease her all the time about needing Clairol, since her hair had starting graying when she was sixteen. Roger used to go over to her all the time and tell her that we were never going to be able to marry her off if she looked like our grandmother. In reality, however, all the gray hair served to do was accentuate the youth and beauty of her face.

Eventually the Mohawks seemed to rope Leslie's kids into our own version of zaniness. We still had our problems, petty jealousies were rife, frustrations in trying to fill up our various voids were common, and yet we managed to party on. If the party was a bit whacked out and sometimes came to a dead halt because someone was overwhelmed or enraged beyond his ability to cope, at least we had our moments. Now what I remember most are those Mohawk moments.

Also at this time, Bert Cohler arrived. He had been a child at the School in the fifties, way before my time, had left a success, gone to college, and then got his doctorate at Harvard in clinical psychology. He started teaching at the university and visiting with us. At first we didn't know what to make of him. He was neither fish nor fowl. He wouldn't answer any questions: He wasn't going to be a counselor, teacher, or therapist. There wasn't much left, and we figured that it was unlikely he wanted to be the new janitor, even though we had an opening. Rumors started flying. Some were better than others, but we were aware that Dr. B. at sixty-eight was beyond the standard retirement age for the university's professors. We sailed on with a willing suspension of disbelief, since to speculate was quite different from confronting actuality. It was hard to take the idea of Dr. B. leaving seriously. He had formed the School, was such an integral part of our lives, and was judge, jury, and executioner. I imagine that we thought of him a bit like the citizens of any kingdom who had a monarch for the past thirty years, when no one can remember having had anyone else on their postage, currency, or passports.

Finally, when the tension coiled itself as neatly and tightly as a watch spring and we had achieved an equilibrium of sorts, Dr. B. announced it was time for him to retire and that he would be leaving to go teach at Stanford. Our Emperor Franz Joseph was abdicating.* Now it became clear what Bert was doing. If ever there was someone who fitted the saying "Uneasy lies the head upon which sits a crown," it was Bert. We had a couple of months to get used to the idea of Dr. B. going, Bert had a couple of months to take over the reins, and the staff had some time to establish relationships with their new boss. Now, however, staff intrigues started in earnest. Factions, political and otherwise, came to the fore. The staff managed to protect the little ones, but those of us who were older could tell by observing the glances, hesitations, and ultra-cautiously worded statements that there was a lot of things we were not being told.

---

*Franz Joseph was the last Hapsburg Austro-Hungarian emperor. He was born in 1830 and reigned from 1848 to 1916. It was the assassination of his nephew, the archduke Ferdinand, which began World War I.

Bert had his work cut out for him. Dr. B. worked from nine or ten in the morning to eleven every night—and, even on weekends, he worked a lot, too. For the entire time I knew him, if he wasn't putting in seventy hours a week, he was putting in eighty Dr. B.'s duties included the kids, the staff, his classes, his professorial duties, his writings, which included not only his books, but also articles for *The New Yorker*, his monthly column for *Ladies Home Journal*, fundraising duties for the School, dealing with the university, and frequent speaking engagements. It was an onerous schedule and there was no expectation that his successor could continue with a workload so excessive. Some things would have to change. Dr. B. never once said a word about the demands on his time, and, in fact, it never occurred to me to wonder about it when I wanted to talk to him. He was omnipresent and would take whatever time he felt was necessary with us. Of course, part of his skill was in scheduling himself intelligently, and the shorthand in which he spoke may have been due to the limits on his time as well as his wish for us to figure things out on our own. He did not need to spend a lot of time on an issue. Like an emperor with long experience at the helm, he got good at dispensing justice and making pronouncements with a rapidity that seemed beyond the ability of the rest of us mortals.

Those shoes seemed impossible to fill, but Bert had a few things going for him to cushion his transition. He was smart, his doctorate from Harvard gave him credibility not only with us but also with the university, he had been a kid at the School himself so he understood our needs, and he was a decent human being. Those abilities, in the end, would not prove sufficient.

Around this time, just before Dr. B. left, François Truffaut's film *The Wild Child* (*L'enfant sauvage*) came out. Since it was widely believed that the child on whom the film was based (from the book, *The Wild Child of Aveyron*, by Jean-Marc Gaspard Itard) was a nineteenth-century autistic boy and not raised by wolves, as was assumed by his contemporaries, we all were interested in this film. A group of us went to see it at the local art film house with Mary Margaret and Genevieve. Genevieve Jurgensen, who was one of Mary Margaret's good friends, counselored the older girls in the Adolescent Unit. Their table was next to ours in the dining room, so there was a certain amount of back and forth, which grew over time, encouraged by the friendship of Mary Margaret and Genevieve, who, with Leslie, were more relaxed compared to some of their more uptight colleagues. As with Leslie's group, our closeness with Genevieve and her girls derived initially from the friendship of the two counselors.

Through the six degrees of separation theorem, over the years I bumped into several people who knew Truffaut. The first was Mary Margaret's friend Genevieve. She was a dark beautiful Frenchwoman who had come to the school while her husband was getting his architecture degree from the Illinois Institute of Technology. She had trained as a speech therapist in Paris, where her father-in-law was a senior French ambassador. Eunice Kennedy Shriver, wife of the then American ambassador to France, had written her a letter of introduction for an American school for retarded children. After visiting that school, however, Genevieve did not want to work there but fascinated by Dr. B.'s book *The Empty Fortress*, which was a big success in France, she made inquiries about the School. Encouraged by Serge Lebovici, the famed French psychoanalyst who had been coauthor with Joyce McDougall of a well-received book on one of the School's kids who had previously lived in France, Genevieve arrived shortly thereafter.[1]

Genevieve was to become acquainted with Truffaut by coincidence. She had written him a letter; he thought she was someone else, so he called to arrange dinner. At dinner, they had a great time, at the end of which he told her of the mix-up, which naturally made her feel embarrassed, as if she had dined under false pretenses. Truffaut was delighted at his mistake, since Genevieve is smart, chic, and beautiful. Some mistakes turn out to be the best luck of all. Truffaut was deeply interested in Bettelheim and his work and would later revive his acquaintance with Genevieve. During the summer of 1973, Truffaut discovered Jeanne Moreau, a leading French actress, reading the book Genevieve had written about the School after she had returned to France.[2] Truffaut then contacted Genevieve and told her although he wanted to make a film about autistic children and the School, he felt it would be almost inappropriate to have an actor pretend to be so crazy. He did, however, eventually produce a documentary on autism in addition to *The Wild Child*.

Dr. B. continued to hold his three o'clock meetings with us once a week until he left and once talked to us about Truffaut's film, which had captured my imagination, lover of history that I was. I had long ago asked him, after reading Kipling's *The Jungle Book*, whether feral children, whose existence in history predates even Romulus and Remus, the mythical founders of Rome, had ever really existed, but he said he doubted it. He believed they were most likely autistic children who were exposed in the forest and then found by others before they could die. He also told me that Frederick the Great of Prussia had become interested in a similar subject: the natural language of man, something the eighteenth-century philosophers such as Rousseau had debated over and over. Frederick conducted an experiment: He had several children placed in a nursery and forbade the servants to speak a word to them or have any contact with them, except for feeding and changing them. They waited to see what language would evolve among the babies when they got old enough to converse. I asked Dr. B. what happened and he said bluntly, "They all died. Infants cannot survive without intimate human contact." Later he would discuss this further in one of his university classes.

> *Frederick the Great had a keen investigative mind. It was a religious age so he had religious questions. To find out what language God spoke to Adam and Eve, Hebrew or Aramaic or perhaps some other, he ordered children taken immediately after birth by caretakers and brought up in silence so when they grew up, their language would be that of God. All the children died. This experiment was done earlier as reported by Herodotus.*[3]

Our final meeting with Dr. B., when he said good-bye to all of us, took place in a three o'clock meeting, although he came around later to say good-bye to each of us personally. At the meeting, Dr. B. brought Itard's book *The Wild Child of Aveyron* in translation: He had promised to lend it to someone but had forgotten whom. Since it was I who had asked, he gave it to me. I treasured that book as a symbol both of him and of being singled out for my curiosity about other worlds. Eventually, some years later, I returned the book to him.

I was conflicted about seeing him go. I was glad that I wouldn't have to face the Big Bad Wolf and get called on the carpet so often with all of his formidable ferociousness. Yet, also, he had honored me by trusting my judgment as well as my ability to decipher his pronouncements and had provided a stability for the School that was so pervasive, it was impossible for me to imagine life without him. Although I trusted his judgment, even if I disagreed with him, it would be years before I could deeply question some of the assumptions we all took for granted. I had expected him to be there as long as I stayed. It was a devil's bargain: I didn't like all the clauses, but the bad parts were the cost of the contract.

I now see that Dr. B.'s leaving had even more far-reaching consequences than I had realized. Life at the School was different without him, not so much because our daily lives had changed; after all, we still had the same counselors and teachers, we still lived with our dorm mates, and the ethos and purpose of the School had not ostensibly changed, but the quality of thought immediately began to decay. In addition to not seeing him four times a day during rounds, there was no possibility of turning the corner and unexpectedly running into him with all that could entail.

As difficult as Dr. B. could be, his genius was digging out the underlying truth about an issue and seeing it so clearly that he often could get the rest of us to see it, too, such as the example of my word choice with Michael when he smashed my arm into the wall. Much of his guidance took place with the staff, out of our sight, but its effects were felt no less because of that. Without him, the staff could more easily be led astray, since so much of their clarity came from the director—and when the director was unclear, they could not always obtain the needed objectivity to make themselves hone in on the appropriate issues. A large part of the School's structure was not for the kids themselves; it was so that the staff could feel safe working with us. Since many of them deeply cared about their kids, they did not have to live in terror of what would happen to us when they were off; there were set limits and a structure in which they could live and work. It was no mean feat that Diana felt secure enough to put up with all the crap I had dished out and yet still was capable of loving me unconditionally. That came from Dr. B.

The unsettling effects of Dr. B.'s leaving began a year or two before he left, when he was slowly removing himself from the School and beginning, at least in his own mind, leave-taking. I can't tell you how this manifested itself, yet in my bones I am sure that it must have begun to have an effect in creatures as finely tuned to nuance as we were. I was angry at him for twenty-five years after I left. Perhaps part of that anger was directed at him for leaving me, when he had made an implicit promise when I first came that he would see me through.

The fact that I looked on Bert as a friendly face and enjoyed talking to him should have been a warning. I didn't need another friendly staff member; I needed a director who could allow the framework in which we all lived to continue to help us get well. Bert never was able to truly understand the uses and limits of power. Operating the School successfully required a wise and sagacious ruler who understood that while it was necessary to show himself to his subjects, distance was required for the magic of royalty to work. Familiarity breeds contempt, and nowhere is that more apparent than in political life.

As Dr. B. made his rounds for the final time, his shoes still squeaking, the formal Viennese world in which I had grown up began to crumble. The moment he closed the door behind him, it started being replaced by the 1960s' and 1970s' informality to which Bert was accustomed.

13

Bert

While anointed and crowned by Dr. B. as his successor, Bert's few moments of grace did not last long. I, for one, made his life miserable. I enjoyed his friendship and looked to him for support and comfort, all the while knowing full well that this was not his function. We needed a director, not another counselor. Bert's informality worked against him. I had never stopped to think about Dr. B. having problems: One did not question God. Bert, however, was a kid who had made good.

The problems with Bert paralleled, I suspect, parents who try to be friends with their children, which often turns out badly for all involved. In the end, kids do not need or want their parents to be their friends; they need parents to educate, protect, set limits, and love them. The respect learned from and for a parent is unlike any other relationship we have—and those who miss it suffer for it. Bert from the start wanted to be our friend.

A month or two after Dr. B. had left, Bert brought in someone named Ted as assistant director to help him, since it was not realistic to expect him to continue working Dr. B.'s hours. It was a mystery why he chose Ted, an action that puzzled us and infuriated the staff.

Our first warning that there were going to be problems with Bert as director should have been Ted. While Ted seemed to be well-meaning, given the grace and skill of the senior staff to weigh and adjudicate our internal and external lives, why pick someone over them whose only claim to fame was being smart, with no analytical experience? As far as I knew, he hadn't worked with kids with problems before. Ted never had the stature or wisdom to earn the confidence of either the staff or the kids. An assistant director needed to be able to run the School and help the staff, not be merely an administrator. Ted could be an impartial judge of certain situations but was not capable of seeing the nuances that made up much of our lives. He used to describe himself as a thermometer, since he would take the School's "temperature" for Bert when he was absent. We thought this was a bit weird but nothing like his parting remark. When he finally threw in the towel and left, after it became clear that he was never going to win the staff's or the kids' confidence, his parting comment left us all gasping. When asked what he planned on doing after leaving, he responded, "I would like to continue doing the same kind of work that I did here, like working in a museum." I can't begin to tell you the number of comedy routines we made out of that one. The whole episode didn't do Bert's reputation any good or make us feel any more secure.

Also, shortly after Dr. B. left, Bert came to talk to me privately. He called me out of the dorm and we sat on the stairs, informally, to talk. He wanted me to move out of the Mohawks and transfer to the Adolescent Unit. He felt that it would be better for me to be with the older kids, since I was seventeen, rather than being with the younger kids. I resisted and didn't want to go. I liked the Mohawks; I had been there for nine years, and I didn't want to leave Roger, Sean, Timothy, or any of the others. Moreover, despite our distance, Julie had been with me since I was ten and I liked Mary Margaret. I didn't know the counselors over at the Adolescent Unit. Although Daniel was there, it still meant moving to a foreign country.

I refused. But a decision like that is not easily resisted, and Bert, Margaret, Julie, and Mary Margaret wore me down and convinced me that I had to go. If I think back, my refusal was a sign of what progress I had achieved. I had become a member of a group and had made friends; now, when finally offered the opportunity to leave the little ones behind, something I spent the first half of my life at the School trying to do, I didn't want to go.

Looking back, I try to understand why they wanted to move me. I was doing well and was in a good group with good counselors. It was true that I had long had problems with Julie—we battled, not as I had with Diana, which had been based on affection and respect, but on misunderstanding. I craved warmth and intimacy; Julie was distant and cerebral. It was not a combination that led to mutual fulfillment, but we had been together for seven years and Dr. B. had not seen fit to move me. Why now? Bert said that part of the reason was to give me male counselors, since the staff felt I needed more of a man's influence. That may have been true, but Bert had mentioned to us a number of times that one of his major interests was working with adolescents and conducting research on how best to help them. This was the early 1970s; drugs and rebellious youth seemed to be on the national consciousness after the shootings at Kent State and the riots over Vietnam.

On the altar of proposed research, my life was deranged, my worldly belongings packed up to be transported two hundred yards and seemingly light-years away from the Mohawks. What passed for advancement, the Adolescent Unit's separation from the rest of the School, I hated, since it made it much more difficult to wander over to say hello. While I saw Roger, Sean, Toby, and Timothy in class and still spent time with Mary Margaret, Julie, and Leslie, I realized that this was the beginning of the closing chapters on my life at the School. At the time I thought the book was going to be shorter than in fact it turned out to be. Nonetheless, it was clear that at some point that was distinctly imaginable, I was going to say good-bye forever. I understood how Diana must have felt. In spite of needing and wanting to get on with one's own life, leaving cut off a part of oneself that would unavoidably leave a scar. It wasn't leaving the School or its culture that did the damage; it was leaving behind lives so intertwined with one's own.

I entered the Adolescent Unit. In the end, the reasons given were all for naught, since within two years I was back again as one of the older kids within a group of little ones, but this time without Roger or Sean. For the moment, however, Daniel was there, as were Andrew from the old Mohawks and a few others I have not previously mentioned: Todd and Glen. Glen was my new roommate; unlike the dorms, Glen and I had our own room that we shared along with our own bathroom, a degree of privacy and luxury that I could barely imagine. Glen and I had always gotten along. He was very involved with his teacher, and the vicissitudes of that relationship would end up driving us all crazy, but for the moment we got along well. We had a third roommate, Spartacus, an iguana that Glen had gotten when he was a baby only twelve inches long. How Glen wangled permission for a pet, I never knew, but I liked Spartacus. By the time Glen left, after we had been together a year or two, Spartacus was three feet long. An incredible craftsman, Glen could figure out how to construct anything and do it with grace and beauty. He had built a large, elegant cage of wood, wire, and lights for Spartacus that took up the entire top of his dresser. We pretty much gave Spartacus the run of our room, but eventually I put down some ground rules about feeding him. His favorite food was mealworms. After I went to bed one night and found a bunch of them under my covers, where they had crawled to hide from the light, since my bed was next to Glen's dresser, I insisted that we feed them to him one by one.

Glen had lived down the hall from me for years in the old dorm building. We had been friends and friendly competitors. His primary relationship was with his teacher and therapist, Marilyn, who had been a child at the School in the late 1950s before we had come to the School. She had a cultlike group around her, Dr. B. had adored her, and, as far as Glen was concerned, the sun rose and set on her. Eventually she married, had an ungodly number of children—seven, I think—and continued seeing kids in session when she stopped teaching. She was a dedicated professional and far more successful in her career at the School than Bert ever was. However, I was never close to her; in fact, she always made me uncomfortable. I never figured out why. Her class consisted of an awful lot of giddy girls and Glen and a few others. Maybe my irreverence rocked her carefully constructed world too much, or maybe it was that I never felt particularly close to many of the kids she took care of, one of whom was Jennifer, who had been in Sue's class with me and about whom I had been so ambivalent.

It was Daniel's roommate, Todd, who struck me as the cool one. He was good-looking, came from an extraordinarily wealthy family, and was going out to high school with Daniel. They had their own lives now of which I wasn't a part, but how I wished to be like Todd and not myself.

At the time, I wrote a short story about me as I hoped to become, walking on the beach on Martha's Vineyard with a sheepdog, since I wanted to trade Spartacus in for a pet somewhat more relationship-oriented than a lizard. I haven't read that story in over twenty-five years, but what I wrote about was someone else, not me. What I wanted back then and what I thought getting well meant was, as Patty once so elegantly stated, to be someone else. I couldn't envision myself as ever being able to live the life I wanted for myself. At one point, back in the first dorm I ever inhabited at the School, I remember hoping and praying that I would be able to earn $10,000 a year and have my own small studio apartment somewhere. At the time, that was all I could imagine.

Then I wanted to be Todd. He seemed to have it all—wealth, looks, and charisma. He was masculine where I saw myself as confused and not masculine enough. He was not a good student, however, and I was aware at the time how he struggled academically with things that I would have to look at only once to grasp and retain. He left shortly afterward. I would think of him often, hoping he was leading the life I had imagined for myself. One day, a couple of years later, I asked my former teacher, Sue, who by then was working as a therapist, about Todd, since she had been the closest of all to him. She gave me this strange look and said she would talk to me later.

After class, she found me and we sat on a sofa in the unused auditorium. She told me that Todd was dead, having died several months before in an automobile crash. It got worse: He was alone in the car and had hit a tree head-on. No one could answer whether it was an accident or not. I was saddened and incensed that no one had told us. At that point, Bert had left us and Jacqui had come back after leaving for several years to live in California and was director. Dr. B. would have told all of us together. He understood that we needed to know the bad news as well as the good, so we wouldn't have to spend the rest of our lives wondering what they weren't telling us. I never forgave Jacqui for allowing me to think for months that Todd was well and happy, when, in fact, he had been buried. The only mitigating factor in this betrayal was that Jacqui had once been his counselor. The news of his death would not have been any easier on her, either.

There is that poem about Richard Cory by Edwin Arlington Robinson (1869–1935) that appears in many schoolbooks, the one where he is handsome, charming, and privileged and then one day, the man who seemed to have everything goes home and puts a bullet in his head. Whenever I hear that poem, I think of Todd. All the energy that went into keeping that façade shiny and new, in the end, was not enough to sustain him. It was good enough, however, to take me in and for me to look up to him as a hero. Discovering that what I had looked up to was a fantasy was hard. I wasn't yet smart enough to doubt myself and ask why my values were so immature and faulty as to admire style over substance. That realization would wait until long after I left the School. I think for a long time I resented that the staff didn't force me to take a better look at such values or lack thereof, which would have saved me much future heartache. The staff gave me so much grief about relatively unimportant things, I am sorry that they couldn't help me face more important ones. Our mutual horror and sadness about Todd didn't provide an opening for me to deal with my faulty values until years later.

At the time, though, the one person who I insisted be told was Sean. He had been especially close to Todd, and the two of them had shared a special bond. I told Sue that it was unfair for Sean not to know and if Mary Margaret, who was by then his senior counselor, didn't tell him, I would. I got talked to about this threat by Jacqui, but given the School's ethos about freedom of speech, I couldn't be forced not to say anything, so Sean was told. In hindsight, it is curious that I never thought before now how logical it was that Todd and Sean were close to each other. The two most contained individuals, both of whom had to present a perfect façade to the world, had each found a kindred spirit. Perhaps without even knowing it my insistence that Sean know of Todd's death was because I knew he needed to be warned of the all-too-obvious risk of continuing on a similar path.

Our counseloring situation in the Adolescent Unit was unusual. We had three counselors: Mark, who was a clinical psychologist, had three shifts a week with us while continuing his clinical work and seeing patients outside the School; Tom, who always looked to me like James Taylor, also had three shifts; and Mary, who had just arrived at the School, had four. Bert had appointed Mark director of the Adolescent Unit; like his appointment of Ted, he had chosen someone who had little knowledge of the School or its methodology.

Both Mark and Tom were close to thirty or over. Mary was twenty-two; this was her first job after college, and I found her beautiful. Even when I was enraged at her, which later became pretty often as she became more important to me, she usually could melt me with her smile. She had come from Flint, Michigan, a small town, and had trained as a speech therapist. At some point in her youth, she had suffered from a high fever that damaged her kidneys, so she spent a lot of time in the hospital recovering. She had that outlook, maybe stemming from her illness, that she wanted to make a difference and didn't want to waste time about it. When I first met her, she was full of energy and light. And she loved Boz Scaggs' music, which I had never heard before meeting her. In time she became a great counselor, but you have to wonder what was in Bert's mind to allow someone so young and inexperienced to work with a bunch of boys nearly her own age.

In a situation like this, the staff didn't seem to take into account the laws of physics, not to mention biology, regarding the older kids. The staff acted as if the old rules just applied: If they willed it so, they could make it so. Dr. B. tried and failed at that method but was capable of making adjustments because he had the experience and stature to pull it off. Bert had no hope of doing so. You could ignore sexual issues only for so long; then you had some real trouble.

The more I saw of Mary, the more I liked her. From the beginning, we had a different relationship from those I had with my other counselors because I was already seventeen, had been at the School for almost ten years, and was not dependent on her. Once she had gone to get her hair cut and the guy brutalized her, making her feel insecure about how she looked and her sense of style. A small-town Michigan girl in the big city, Chicago, she wanted to be sophisticated and wise to the ways of big-city life. I was taking a nap and she came into my room to wake me up so that I would reassure her. She sat on my bed and we talked. I treasured not being treated as a patient but just as another person. She needed something from me, which was an absurd construct in the world in which we lived. It almost fooled me into thinking that I might have something to offer. Thinking about Diana, despite her taking care of me and all of my craziness, we, too, had also, outside the patient/counselor relationship, simply respected each other as individuals. That was the mark of a great staff member, for they could see us as a person in addition to the therapeutic milieu. Mary did this because she was new and had not yet learned all that Diana had, but I liked the way she treated me no less on account of that.

If I put my arms around her to hug her that afternoon to make her feel better, it was not something unusual, but there were definitely feelings there that hadn't existed years earlier with Diana. It was subtle and something I appreciated, not acted on. The intimacy between us, once established, became important to me. In time Mary would withdraw from me, which caused me a lot of pain and confusion. The problem was not with us, however; it was lack of direction from the top to establish an environment with clear boundaries protecting both staff and kids. Bert was incapable of so doing, try as he might, and his successor, Jacqui, had her own problems in that regard, as well. Clearly the issue was not about sexual thoughts or jealousy; it was about dealing appropriately with the feelings aroused and recognizing that they existed.

My interest in Mary was secondary at that point in my life to my relationship with Mark. I had a crush on him, which would not have been the way I would have described it at the time. Unbeknownst to me, my sexual orientation was a major source of staff discussion. This all came to the fore after I moved to the Adolescent Unit. I was slowly becoming aware of the fact that I might be gay, and, given the Freudian world in which I lived, it seemed a most unwelcome development. It was a subject that I never dealt with at the School, hoping for a long time it would just disappear. In fact, I assumed it would, since I had been taught at the School that when I dealt with my issues, such problems would fade away. I wanted so much to be like everybody else, and here was another diversion putting up one more roadblock. Now, looking back, I can see I was always this way. Then, looking forward, I was terrified. I had never met anyone openly gay that I knew about, and the images I had were all of pathetic people or hairdressers. If I were to be gay, I figured it meant ending up a screaming queen: a Liberace in street clothes. Margaret did comment to me, at one point, that Alexander the Great, a historical hero of mine, was gay and it hadn't stopped him from conquering the world. But he had been dead already for thousands of years. I was still here.

For me, too, the issue of acting feminine had been a long-standing problem that had in part brought me to the School, because it was so obviously disturbing to those around me. As I was to later learn, there is a big difference between orientation (that means gay or straight) and masculinity. I know gay men who are far more masculine than any number of their straight counterparts. While the issues are not totally unconnected, neither are they Siamese twins conjoined at the hip. Back then the confusion of the issue made it harder for me to accept who I was. I did not want to be a feminine male aside from my orientation, which I didn't like, either. Moreover, I felt the staff didn't want to cope with this, so I hoped that if I ignored the issue or pretended it didn't exist, I might, when the School finally "cured" me, find out that I was straight after all. The staff couldn't say "This is how you are, so deal with it." Such a thought, let alone statement, was not in our lexicon, a residue of Freudian absolutism.

All of the issues involving sex and sexuality with the older kids were such loaded artillery that the staff unconsciously avoided them, although if you had asked them, they would have denied it, truly believing that they were open and liberal about all subjects. They behaved in essence like a twisted version of Billy Crystal's complaint to Meg Ryan in *When Harry Met Sally*, "You're the worst kind of high maintenance; someone who's high maintenance who thinks they're low maintenance."

Dr. B. had been accused of making antigay statements. I was never able to find published quotes from him nor could any of the others with whom I spoke. The only written record that I found was in my lecture notes from Dr. B.'s class.

> *Presently, the U.S. is trying to determine whether homosexuality is normal or not. Before, the suffering was limited to a small group of homosexuals; now it is made easier for them with tragic consequences for the rest. If homosexuality goes too far, in the past, such societies have disappeared.*[1]

I do remember his concern about the downfall of society brought about by the more open acceptance of homosexuality. I think he had said something along the lines that by society making it more acceptable, those who in prior times would have dealt with it or repressed it could now act it out. Thus, he believed it was an illness, an aberration. He made clear in his remark that he believed that unchecked homosexuality was inherently evil as well as a causal factor in civilization's downfall. A nonprejudicial view to be sure! It was a subject that we never discussed, nor did I wish to ask him his opinion.

The one time that he had said something to me, it was so cruel, I didn't want to repeat it. There had been a blizzard in Chicago and passage on the streets was impossible so ambulances were using the plowed sidewalks on their way to and from the hospital. The older boys were shoveling sidewalks as part of their civic duty and a few of the Mohawks, like Daniel, who was considered one of the older ones, went with the bigger boys to shovel. I desperately wanted to go, too, but was not allowed. This was in 1967, when I was twelve. At any rate, when, in a fit of sour grapes, I said that I hadn't wanted to shovel anyway, after I had been told I could not go, somehow that got reported to Dr. B.

Julie had been on, so maybe she told him. When he came around at dinner, he came over to me and whispered to me that I was acting like a little girl for not wanting to go shovel snow. I was terribly hurt. It was also wrong, because I had wanted to do my duty (as well as get out of the dorm). Instead, I got a whispered dressing-down and called a girl, too. I was so upset that I refused to tell Julie what Dr. B. had said. Of course, he had said it quietly exactly to make it worse, since he knew that eventually I would have to tell Julie. If I didn't, it would come back to him, since she would ask him and then he would have one more shot at me, this time for keeping secrets. Finally, when I couldn't stand her nagging any longer and it became clear later in the evening that she would ask Dr. B. if I didn't tell her, I finally had to say something. But I refused to talk about it with her. I was betrayed, it was unfair, and I just buried the remark and added it to my pile of little hurts that were too painful to discuss.

I thought I knew what he thought about gays, which was to believe they were sick, a problem, and evil, so I never talked about the issue with him. He did sometimes surprise me, so maybe a discussion about my orientation would have been different from what I imagined. However, by the time I was ready, Dr. B. had died, so our timing was off.

All gay men have a story. Some are worse than others, but everyone in a minority who breaks through to the other side has an interesting past. Although being different is always difficult, it is also strangely liberating, because one gets to make up one's own rules. It just sometimes takes longer. It certainly did so with me, who was an outsider for a multitude of reasons. Dr. B. had great affection for the works of Shakespeare and Dostoevsky and would often say that there was nothing in Freud that they hadn't written first. Suffering made for interesting stories—as Tolstoi had pointed out when he observed that all happy families resemble one another, but each unhappy family is unhappy in its own way. The American dream has always been based on a home, white picket fence, two cars in the driveway so as to better see the amber waves of grain, and children for whom parents sacrifice and start saving college funds for from the moment of their birth. Gays were left out of all that. And in our old age, instead of having grandchildren to dandle on our knees, we would look in the mirror and wonder who was that old man staring back, who once upon a time had forever. Coming out to oneself and to others was more difficult than it sounds. There was always the fear of what would be lost, the doors closed, the jobs forsaken, and having to live on the fringes of a demimonde of which, often, not all of us wanted to be card-carrying members.

It was not a subject with which I dealt at the School. For one thing, it was not something I wanted to look at too carefully. I hoped if I kept it hidden, particularly from myself, it would go away. I kept hoping that as I would get "better" I would be cured from being gay, as if it were some strange disease. I never was. Even though I would pray that God would make me straight for years, all that showed was how far I had to go to accept myself. We were all brainwashed by our Freudian-based theories. All the School's ethos was based on good parenting; if we did not have a good marriage and become good parents, we had not really succeeded in curing ourselves.

From reading the notes, there is a constant theme of concern about my orientation, which the staff all talked about, but not to me. It was simply not possible in that era for the staff to try to help someone make an adjustment as a healthy gay person to lead as good a life as they could. Such a notion was inconceivable. Every time I seemed to be closer to being straight they all breathed a sigh of relief, and when I acted attracted to a male, even if I was unaware of it, these trained observers noticed, noted it, discussed it, and felt that they were failing me. Diana was particularly concerned in the beginning, but I believe that had she stayed with me, she would have been open enough to the possibility to at least force me to look at it and discuss it. The rest of the staff sort of tiptoed around the issue, hoping that if they could help me in other ways, the problem would vanish. It was an unbearable burden that I carried for a long time.

And where was Margaret; why didn't she push me to deal with such an important part of my life? She, of all people, was most concerned in her notes about my orientation—and felt she was failing me whenever she thought I was being more homosexual rather than less. We talked about so much else, how could such a major factor of my life be so unexamined with me, although evidently minutely dissected in staff meeting?

When once one of the staff had said something about me using the word "homosexual," I was terrified. Margaret attempted to calm me by saying she had no interest in labels. What interested her were feelings. That was a fudge, however, since label or not, what were the underlying issues? On any other subject, she would have said, Why does this bother you so much? Or, as we used to say all the time quoting Shakespeare, "Methinks the lady doth protest too much."

When working on this book, it was Diana once again who came to my rescue and supplied the answer. Margaret for years had a relationship with her partner, Florence, who was the other therapist at the School. Although they maintained separate apartments, their relationship was openly known to the staff of an earlier generation, including Dr. B. Clearly we kids didn't have any idea nor did many of the later staff. It was the 1960s and early 1970s, after all, and life then was not as open as now. It was an era that didn't ask and certainly didn't tell. When I heard this from Diana, things fell into place. First, that Margaret and I had missed an opportunity to discuss and work on an issue that was to haunt me for so many years. If anyone could understand how I felt, it would have been she. I also felt bad that when Florence died, I never understood the entire import for Margaret or how brave she was to carry on day by day without us knowing. Much of her life that I thought I had understood—the fact that she never married or had her own children—now made sense.

Now, too, the reasons that we did not talk about this in session became clearer. I felt acutely uncomfortable raising this issue with her. Even long after the School, when she was old, I didn't discuss it with her. I was worried she would think she had failed with me, and I didn't want that. At the same time I felt dishonest, since we had discussed pretty much everything else at one point or another. In the end, this was too close to home for both of us and maybe I sensed that she didn't want to discuss it, for fear of intruding her life's experiences on me. I didn't bring up the subject because something held me back, and she didn't raise it directly because she didn't want to risk imposing her life on her patient. It was so assumed that to be healthy for me meant a straight identification that it was never questioned. On the same theory of why it was Nixon who could go to China,* Margaret must have felt that she had to be completely impartial about a subject so close to herself. I remember how upset she was when I told her I had inherited a streak of her Scotch Presbyterian ethic. This would have been worse.

Perhaps we could not have resolved this before I left, but at least beginning to look at it might have started a process that in the end took far longer than it should have. The flip side is that I am alive. I was still resolving this issue when AIDS was spreading but unknown. My failure to address who I was may have saved my life. Most of my Yale classmates around my age who were gay are dead. By the time I was ready to tackle this issue and face it, we already knew what the disease was and how to avoid it.

All of this came to the fore because, in addition to my attraction to Mary, I was attracted to our other counselor, Mark, which rang alarm bells with the other staff, particularly Margaret. Part of it may have been hero worship: He was tall, strong, and successful, had a kind of confidence and masculinity that I lacked, and was a success in the world. Looking back, it now seems silly that I was attracted to him; like, what was I thinking? This attraction was all new to me then, and I had no help—none—in figuring any of this out in a sensible fashion for a long time. In retrospect, I think homophobia was the reason Jim always gave me such a difficult time, which touched my life in other ways. I couldn't acknowledge it, because like the

---

*A dedicated Republican right-winger and anticommunist, Nixon could make the trip without being accused of being soft on communism, a charge that might have been leveled at a left-wing Democrat politician.

ostrich if I didn't acknowledge that I was gay, how could anyone else? The School, whose stated goal was to make its children find out who they were and become more comfortable with themselves, utterly failed me in regard to my sexual identity. And it was the worst kind of failure, because I had been raised to think that there was no problem with their openness, thus all of this extra weight had to be my failure. It was truly a high-maintenance situation thinking it was low maintenance—and I believed it.

Shortly after I moved to the Adolescent Unit, while this was all going on, we got a new kid, Simon, who at seventeen had been used to teenage life on the outside. If I felt circumscribed at age eight, how in the world did the staff think a seventeen-year-old was going to feel? And sexual maturity, a major difference between the ages of eight and seventeen, just made the situation worse. Bert, as I had said, was fascinated with the issues surrounding adolescents and finding a means of treating them. Simon was admitted to the School to fulfill this interest. I always felt that Bert made a major mistake in loading on Simon's back all of his hopes to solve the adolescent mental health problem in America. I pointed out to him a number of times that it would be hard enough for Simon to do what Simon needed for himself without Bert making him a cause célèbre for an entire generation. Bert did not appreciate my counsel.

Simon came into the dorm, and our lives were disrupted from the moment he walked in until he left a year later. It was a disaster. Simon immediately made Mary the pivotal person in his life. No matter what she did, it was not enough, and he hated sharing her with the rest of us. His attraction to her was obvious, and he frequently played the role of jealous lover. I had done the same thing with Diana, but I had been eight, not seventeen. Whenever they had a disagreement, or if he was upset about something, he would storm out of the dorm, leaving Mary to follow. Whenever he wanted to be with her, he would just walk out of the dorm. As neither Mark nor Tom lived in the School and Mary did, she was on call for Simon essentially twenty-four hours a day. After a very short while, this became wearing on the rest of us, not to mention her. There is no doubt she liked Simon, but she was a young, inexperienced counselor and the rest of us tried to help her. She was also supposedly a counselor for us, as well, but in practice that didn't mean much until Simon left.

I was particularly incensed that Bert didn't give her the support she needed. It was a subject of a lot of fights and was, in the end, what made me turn away from Bert. The whole episode was handled as poorly as anything I have ever seen, and the responsibility falls directly on Bert.

I was not impartial, it is true, because I liked Mary, but I also understood what was going on. The only solution to some of the problems was to insist that Simon had to remain in the dorm, both for his own sake as well as for Mary's, not to mention the rest of us. Despite all of our insistence in the dorm, this was never carried out. Bert couldn't do it. Indeed, he would become angry when things became chaotic, since he felt that any failure with Simon was a sign that perhaps all adolescents could not be helped. Poor Simon really got screwed over.

I had an uneasy relationship with him. We were never friends. I was fascinated by what he could teach me about the outside world, since I knew very little about how teenagers really lived. I am not sure that he was the best person to offer a tutorial, however, but he was all there was.

That year was the strangest one I ever spent at the School. I wasn't going out to high school yet—that was still two years away—but the maelstrom swirling around me just made me more confused than ever. Bert held his three o'clock meetings, but there was now a universal irreverence that never would have occurred with Dr. B. In a moment of weakness, Bert had once confided that hosting three o'clock meetings made him nervous. It was definitely a talk show moment of letting personal confidences replace good judgment. One of the girls made up a verse to the tune of *My Fair Lady*'s "At the Races":

Every boy and girl of the school is here,
Every important member of the staff is here,
What a smashing, positively dashing spectacle the Thursday Meetings are.
Bert comes rushing, his face flushing.
Then he thanks us for making him so anxious.

I had started to get concerned about money at this time. With Dr. B., while we hadn't lacked for anything, life was not over the top.

Now there were clear signs of bread and circuses to distract the masses. I finally blew my stack when Bert announced, rather proudly in a three o'clock meeting, that the School's dentist had come that morning to take a staff meeting and discuss the therapeutic issues surrounding the care of teeth and mouth. This guy wasn't a shrink, he was one of the best dentists in Chicago, and if the staff or Bert couldn't figure out the therapeutic issues regarding dentistry and the mouth, we were in more serious trouble than even I thought. I raised my hand and asked incredulously whether Bert had paid for Dr. Clifford Wilk, who had once repaired Queen Elizabeth II of England's lost filling on an official visit to Chicago, to come to the School and miss a morning of billing his clients. The chance of him coming for free was small. He was a brilliant dentist, but I had stopped using him long ago when my father had complained that my twice-yearly checkups cost more than all of my brothers' checkups put together. When Bert, looking extremely uncomfortable, responded affirmatively, I asked if he planned to have the plumber come and take staff meeting, too, to discuss the therapeutic issues surrounding the bathroom and toilet. I was scathing and tore into Bert in front of the entire School.

It was clear that from the food we were eating (lobster and steak were not as rare as they had been), the purchases of new furniture and TVs, Ted's salary as well as Mark's as director of the Adolescent Unit (both newly created positions), other new staff and consultants, not to mention the money that Daniel and Todd were given to go on dates (including a huge amount of taxi fare, since they couldn't drive while under the School's responsibility), that the School's operating costs had to be escalating.

Katherine of cooking fame, who was Genevieve's co-counselor for the Adolescent Unit's girls on the floor below us, yelled at me for being disrespectful. I wondered where in the Twilight Zone I had landed if I was the only one with such concerns. I could dismiss Katherine, for her attitudes and judgment were fairly conservative and too *orthogenic*, but where were the rest of the staff?

They were fighting quietly among themselves, as I learned later, trying not to involve us in the behind-the-scenes disagreements. A couple of staff spies would send update reports to Dr. B., who constantly undermined Bert. Bert made a horrendous mistake in not putting a stop to Dr. B.'s imprudent intervention immediately, but he was a decent man who stumbled because he made the mistake of thinking that he could run the School acting like an avuncular counselor. Given who he was, he could not have acted any other way. Like all of us, he was limited by his own experience and view of the world, something that Dr. B. had warned all of us about, including Bert, in a three o'clock meeting. Bert was a tremendous success as far as showing how the School could help kids; the fact that he, as a relatively young man, was not suitable to run the School does not take away from his other achievements.

He was generally more patient with me, who attacked him on his performance at every turn, than might have been expected. I think he understood that I wanted the School to succeed and he with it, and hoped to push him to do it. What arrogance! I wanted the School to survive, not just for me, since I was nearing the end of my stay, but also for those to follow so they might have the same or better opportunities that I had. Also, I was truly unsettled by the lack of direction I perceived around me; the situation was so markedly different from our lives with Dr. B.

The passions in the Adolescent Unit were getting overwhelming and Simon had moved beyond running out of the dorm with Mary in tow to running away, period. Search parties would go out, the university police would be called, as would the Chicago City police, none of which, I might add, was doing our reputation in the neighborhood much good. It was one thing to pick up an obviously deranged ten-year-old and quite another to pick up an eighteen-year-old who seemed relatively normal on the outside and then watch him resisting being dragged back to the sometime prison that we called home.

Finally, Simon's running away had its effect on the university and Bert's reputation. Bert informed Simon that if he ran away again, it would be for the last time and he would not able to return. It was far too late to begin laying down the law. If Bert had been clear from the beginning, things might have been far different, since new rules were just part of the overall adjustment. But Simon wasn't about to start listening to Bert after a year. When Simon ran away one more time, that was it. I felt bad about it. It wasn't fair to stick one guy with all the hopes for treating and curing a generation.

Simon was different in many ways from the other kids who had come to the School during my time there. He had his problems, to be sure, but they seemed different to me. For one, he could survive outside the School and not run a significant chance of being institutionalized. That was not true for the rest of us. It was a major difference. If one didn't have to be at the School, why stay and put up with all the crap? Ultimately, I stayed not because I was so happy to be taken care of or because I feared Dr. B. but because I felt it was the only option open to me that would enable me to survive. And I didn't want to just survive; I wanted far more out of life than that.

Margaret kept her head down with all this nonsense and insisted that I do what I had to do for myself and not keep worrying about those things about which I had no control. One of the issues that came up in so many ways was that despite how I felt about Mary, or Mark for that matter before he left, I was basically unhappy and frustrated. It is true that the situation at the School was not ideal, but that wasn't what bothered me. The problem was that no matter how much attention I got (or didn't get), nothing could fill the void inside. I was incapable of simply enjoying an interaction and feeling at peace for more than a moment, which more than anything made me beside myself. The problem, horror of horrors, was me. What made me feel alone came from me, and there wasn't a damn thing Mary or anyone else could do about it. This realization made me miserable, since it was my interpretation of the world and self-loathing that made life so difficult. I tried to figure my way out of that one but could no longer blame everybody else. Solving this problem, I found, would take time.

I felt I had already lost so much time just by being at the School—most of my childhood and virtually all of my adolescence. I was upset to think that I now needed even more time to work this out. I lived in terror that something would happen to Margaret, who was getting older and had had a couple of accidents, such as falling and breaking her ribs. She was my life raft and I needed her to help find land. If she disappeared, whether from illness, death, or even her own free will, I was scared that I would drown. Looking back, it was a pretty selfish view, but I felt I was fighting for my life just to make it to the end of my road at the School. My stomach trouble was slowly fading but was not entirely gone, and I didn't want that bell jar descending over my head again.

I don't remember it, but Margaret's notes make clear that I was angry with her a lot of the time. Part of the issue was the typical transference between patient and therapist. She was central in my life, and at times much of my anger and depression would be directed at her. I was also frustrated that she couldn't protect me from the craziness of the world around me now that Dr. B. was gone. In some ways she fell into some of it, and this was hard for me to realize at the time—I only really did so when looking at the historical notes. Her notes about me and what she told me were two different things. She may have written about me as if I were a patient, but that was never how she treated me.

Nonetheless, I was confused and wanted her to straighten things out. When she didn't, whether it was a realistic wish or not, I became angry. I was also angry at myself for causing so many of my problems, but I couldn't just flick a switch and stop. Poor Margaret had to cope with my anger. Now I am sorry about it, but then, who else was safer for me to be enraged at for all of my failed human interactions and for my emptiness inside? Also, I was frustrated about how she handled my relationship with Mark. I sensed then that there was more to her reaction than met the eye. She never told me, however, exactly what had occurred. It turns out she had been fighting for me, battles that I never knew about.

Mark had told me I would be going out to high school the next fall. I remember none of this, so I must have blocked it out completely. Mark had essentially given up on me and felt I had gone as far as I could go, so the best that could be done was to heave me into the outside world to start preparing for my transition. This, of course, panicked me, since I didn't want to be stuck where I was as the best that could be done. Margaret was also incensed. She felt that my big problem, as always, was getting to my feelings, and going out to high school would focus me on my intellect, something with which we all knew I had no problem. She fought Mark, but of this I never heard a word.[2]

I do remember a sense of confusion and frustration. One of the consulting shrinks, trying to explain what was going on with me, said at the time that the issue was anger and disappointment going back to my infancy and that while part of me was grown, part of me remained infantile. The staff seemed to focus on the infantile, but I was living with the grown-up part and wanted that acknowledged, too.[3]

Typically, the shrink put my problems on my relationship with my mother. And the staff's attitude just made what I really needed to do, such as deal with my depression and anger, worse by my resentment, unknown to me at the time, for being treated constantly as a patient and not as a human being with problems. Dr. B. was gone, the School was an unsettled place, yet all these people knew what was better for me than I did. Of course. The opportunity to look at some of the underlying issues was missed, as well, so I suffered the worst kind of suffering, the one from which I learned nothing.

What also saddens me on reading Margaret's notes is all the time wasted and effort put into trying to solve the insoluble issue of my orientation. Maybe if we tried this, it might work; if not, then we might focus on that. I was gay and that was the end of it. Poor Margaret kept blaming herself for not helping me enough. She also made the mistake of trying to give me enough to fill me up, an impossible task. I needed to gain some sense of worth, this was true, but the issue was why I didn't; it was far too late for it to be given to me by another. I had to figure out how to give it to myself. Margaret thought, however, that if I turned to men, it was somehow her fault, because she didn't give me enough or what she gave me wasn't good enough, perhaps because she was a lesbian. How senseless; it was just a fact of life.

Mark left shortly after this battle. We would soon lose Tom, who stayed on after Bert left for some six months. Both had had enough of the long hours and the lack of direction. Thus Mary ended up in charge of us. I was pretty upset, given all of my conflicted feelings about losing Mark. It was for the best. However, this is a lot easier for me to say with hindsight. Genevieve was also gone by this time, back to Paris. I would not see her for six years.

We got David, an Englishman, to work as Mary's co-counselor. David was right off the boat (British Airways) from London. While I liked him, we never had the relationship that was like those that I had had with the staff in the past. I was too old. David, just a few years older than I, could give good advice; he was never a therapist to me but more a supportive advisor. For the most part, he did not force himself on me, so I could accept him. Mary would remain important to me until I left. However, the primary person in my life was Margaret, not those from my dorm, which was about to change radically once more.

14

Dr. B.'s Return and Life in the Adolescent Unit

Bert decided to call it quits—or was forced to by the university—in the summer of 1972. Bert would leave the School and focus on his teaching. One day we walked into the three o'clock meeting and there was Dr. B. sitting on a chair next to Bert. It was as if we had had a long bad dream and now were waking. I do not remember how I felt about seeing Dr. B. again. I was too surprised, but I suspect that I was both pleased he would restore sanity and order and unhappy to be back under his thumb. After a few weeks Bert was replaced by Jacqui, the new heir apparent. One of the reasons given for Bert's departure was that the hours were so demanding he didn't have enough time to see his children. When I asked how it was going to be for Jacqui, who had a three-year-old son, her response was that she had managed both her group and being assistant director, so she thought she could deal with one little boy. It was masterful Jacqui, able to give an answer that seemingly responded and tied up all the loose ends, but the more one thought about it, the more one realized that she had redirected and not really answered the main issue.

This time having Dr. B. around was different. He was back for one year, and he promised that when it was up, nothing would make him return. He had learned his lesson about meddling, and I imagine Jacqui was wiser and tougher than Bert in this regard. Evidently several people had been offered the directorship, all of whom refused. The hours were long but the primary problem was that Dr. B.'s shoes were too hard to fill, and most people didn't want to set themselves up for failure. Additionally, it was not a position one could take in good conscience to see how things worked out for a limited period of time. The School required someone to commit to at least ten or fifteen years, a complete cycle of kids and staff, and it would be better to stay for two. Not many people wanted to draft themselves into such a life for the next twenty or thirty years. Moreover, living or working with Dr. B. was difficult. It was one thing to have a young professional at the beginning of a career dealing with his comments and lecturing. Yes, the brilliant teaching was there, but so were the put-downs, if not to you, then observed with others. A senior professional at the prime of his or her career did not need to be reduced to being Dr. B.'s assistant for an apprenticeship, no matter how long it lasted. Dr. B. had to take what he could get. This time it was Jacqui.

While Jacqui deferred to Dr. B., he tried not to overstep his bounds. Jacqui had dealt with him for over a decade years earlier and then had obtained her Ph.D., so she was not naïve in coping with him, even as heir to the throne. We immediately began taking in new kids, but the aftereffects of Simon were felt, and this time they were all younger, as crazy as in the old days. In short order we got three little kids, and whatever was the initial point of my leaving the Mohawks was papered over in the onslaught of new little ones. I was now, once again, the elder statesman of the dorm. There was old Andrew, from when I had first arrived at the School, but he was still removed to some extent from our daily life and decided not to interject himself as much in the affairs of the little ones. Mary, who had been the young beauty surrounded by a group of young men, traded in her position for the little old lady who lived in a shoe with too many children to know what to do. She quickly gained a maternal air that was both endearing and frustrating because I knew I would lose out. She had less and less time for me, focusing necessarily on her little ones. She and I had more and more disagreements; I cannot remember about what. I think I wanted more attention than she could give me, while at the same time I had so little self-confidence that each setback was seen as proof that nothing would ever change for the better. I felt that I had been teased; we had once had a kind of intimacy that meant a lot to me, and Mary pulled back, maybe with Jacqui's and some of the other senior staff's assistance, to become much more "professional" with me. The change drove me batty and what I missed most of all was the ability to just plain talk together, where she could be a person, not a shrink.

When Jacqui kept announcing one new kid after the other, I was upset because I had been dragged out of the Mohawks against my will only to be put in the same situation they were trying to get me out of. But that was Bert's doing, and now he was gone and I had to live with the aftereffects.

Michael, who would later smash my elbow into the wall, was first of the new little kids coming to the dorm. Jacqui warned us that he would be a handful, but since most new kids were, the warning didn't sink in as it should have. In hindsight, it didn't matter; nothing would have prepared us for the little hellion who arrived the next day. Most people have a problem with repression—not Michael. His problem was everything just exploded out all over the place. I remember Tom, a few months before he left, that first day, carrying Michael upstairs while Michael found a pencil in his pocket that he used unsuccessfully to try to gouge out Tom's eyes. After seeing that, boy, we knew we were going to have to lock up everything that wasn't nailed down. Later the same day, just when things looked bad enough and Michael was off with Tom or maybe even Jacqui, his teacher came up to the dorm to warn Mary that Michael kept trying to yank the fire alarm. These were all over the place due to Chicago's strict school fire prevention laws. The teacher had barely finished her warning when the alarm went off. We just groaned as we went down the stairs and joined the entire School on the flat Midway across the street, which we were required to do whenever an alarm went off. The rules were really strict. We had a couple of drills a year, but about once a year there was a false alarm—sometimes because someone yanked it, but other times because the system malfunctioned. We would have to wait until the firemen gave us the all clear, and, in the Chicago winter in pajamas, we would freeze our asses off waiting.

We got outside and there was Michael, this little ten-year-old with an unruly mop of black hair, running around yelling proudly "I did it. I pulled it. Yeeppiii!" When the fire trucks arrived, he couldn't wait to run up to the firemen and tell them, too. The firemen, after all these years, knew all about us, but this was a new one, even for them. One started answering Michael back when Michael threatened to cut him up with an ax, of which there were several attached to the side of the truck. I got there first and hustled Michael away because the last thing we needed was the fireman to do something stupid and provoke Michael further. Tom came over to get Michael, but since neither of us knew him, it didn't really matter.

Finally we got him back in the dorm after the fire trucks left. It was an amazing production. Getting him into the dining room for dinner took half an hour. I finally had enough stalling and just picked Michael up and carried him in to his chair. Jacqui followed us in and everyone stared. It was a novel way to make your first entry into the dining room, but after the afternoon's performance, no one was surprised. Over the next few months, I would grow very attached to Michael, who had, despite some obvious character flaws, great charm and could be truly funny. He was also terrified, believed he deserved to be treated as a dog, barking sometimes and trying to eat off the floor, and threw huge tantrums. Even Timothy was impressed.

He liked to wear only red. I remember best the red high-top sneakers, which he wore all the time, even for dress occasions, and he liked red pants, shirts, and socks, too. He said that red was a warning sign, the color of danger, like stoplights, danger signals, taillights, bullfighter's cloaks, and so on. He wanted everyone to be warned wherever he arrived that he was dangerous. I never found him so and, despite how big a pain in the ass he proved to be, neither did very many others, either.

We got a few more young kids, too, but their behavior was considerably more modest than Michael's. At Dr. B.'s three o'clock meeting, which Jacqui almost always attended, Michael would holler at least once or twice, "Dr. B. and Jacqui are gonna fuck tonight!" He also would make a sound, "Unnh-unnh-unnh," his idea of a sex grunt, which he would do every night as soon as someone switched off the lights for bed (or when he wanted to provoke the rest of the dorm). Eventually we older ones, out of his hearing, would adopt the expression, too, since it was so funny and quintessentially Michael.

Between Michael's shouts and grunts, those three o'clock meetings were considerably livelier than they had been previously. I am not sure what was more fun: watching Dr. B. ignore them; seeing the kids trying not to laugh, because although Michael hadn't gotten into trouble, anyone caught laughing was sure to; the expression on Jacqui's face that would have curdled milk because she was not amused but had to ignore the racket if Dr. B. did; or the expressions on the staff's faces, whom I am sure would crack up about this later. We sure did. And Michael got away with it.

As if we didn't have enough going on, about this time we received some very upsetting news about Daniel. He had been suffering from colitis and had been in the hospital, where they performed an emergency colostomy. I didn't understand what had happened. All those years with us and he was fine; now suddenly after leaving, this. It seemed as if leaving well was no guarantee of anything, given what had happened to Todd and now Daniel. I wanted to go visit him, but Jacqui wouldn't let me. Mary had gone to see him in the hospital, and when she came back, I asked to talk to her. Word came back that she was too overwhelmed to talk and that I could talk to her tomorrow. She had never refused to see me before so it must have been pretty brutal.

I felt obligated to go. After I moved to the Adolescent Unit and during all the confusion surrounding the Bert and Simon fiasco, Daniel had kept a comforting eye on me. After all the time we had spent together, I didn't want Daniel suffering alone. But I was scared to death of what I would see. Secretly I was a coward. On the surface, I was angry at Jacqui for forbidding me to go, which I certainly would have done if I had been permitted. But in my heart, I was glad she had said no. I didn't know how to help Daniel with this. For me, with all my anxieties about my body, this was one of my worst fears. For many years afterward, I would thank God whenever I sat on the toilet that I still could. I didn't know how his life would be, but it could not be easy for a young man starting out in life, dating and having to live with a colostomy. In the end, I understand that Daniel married and has done well, so this indignity was something he could overcome.

While we were getting this new gaggle of babies, Mary started dating one of the counselors, Reid. I had never paid much attention to him until I found there was a growing relationship between them. Since Mary had become more professional with me, she never said anything to me indicating a word of how she felt, something that previously would have been unthinkable. I could forgive her for falling in love with Reid (how big of me!), but I couldn't forgive her not bothering to let me know with a look or a smile that something was afoot.

I was incredulous that she could fall for Reid. It wasn't like she was going to marry me or that I even wanted to marry her, but I was jealous nonetheless. At the time, I would point out, as sarcastically as I could, all of Reid's shortcomings. Mary never said a word or indicated that I was right about her deepening relationship with Reid, although it was obvious. The only way I could make her acknowledge that I was right about the romance was by making her angry. Most of the time, for the same reasons she wouldn't or couldn't say anything to me about her relationship, she couldn't give words to her anger about my remarks. If I could take back some of the things I have done in my life, those comments would be among them.

Looking back at the situation, it is a striking example of low self-esteem reacting in anger, jealousy, and pettiness. I had so little confidence in myself and my ability to change my life that every little thing that went against me or hurt my feelings was taken as proof positive that I would remain forever stuck in this rut. A little self-confidence would have given me the strength to think that tomorrow might, perhaps, be better. I had little hope for the future, and the instability within the School at the time made me distrustful of the staff and their decisions.

Over the years, I have seen guys with low self-esteem act infantile; insult or put down their wives, girl- or boyfriends; overcompensate; lie; and constantly misread reality. It seems familiar because I did it to Mary. My behavior just reenforced the cycle, as it usually does, which drove Mary away and made me even more miserable. Worst of all, I found I could not help it.

In a strange way, however, finally having low self-esteem was an achievement for me. Prior to Diana, I had had none.

By the time Mary announced her wedding, there was almost a

wall between us; if we were not arguing, there was a cold silence. Mary had invited us to the wedding, although not the reception, and it was a brave act on her part to bring all of her kids, even the little ones. One of the older boys in the dorm, Clark, who had already started going out to high school, refused to go to the wedding if we were not invited to the reception. He was not going to be a second-class citizen. I agreed with him, but it was one of the only times I kept my mouth shut, since I had said way too much before and, given the chilliness I had caused between Mary and me, what could I possibly contribute to the discussion?

From my earliest days, as I mentioned, shopping had been a trial for me since I had never liked my body. I wanted some new clothes for the wedding. Jacqui herself went through my closet with me. I don't remember why it was such a big deal, but Jacqui didn't want me buying new clothes for Mary's wedding. At one point, she yelled at me that I should read *Member of the Wedding*. I thought she was just hassling me, so I never read the book or, indeed, bothered to find out what her point was. Jacqui, I believed, was trying to push Mary and me apart. Why, I don't know; all I know was that if she had provided some guidance, things would have been a lot easier. I needed to understand what I was doing in a way that made sense to me, and Mary needed to understand that my anger was not her fault. However, that is a lot easier said than done.

My life with Mary went from bad to worse. One day we were going swimming and I didn't feel like going, but we had all the little ones. We crossed the Midway to the pool and something sparked an argument; I got pissed and refused to go swimming, turning back to go home. Mary, for some reason, was equally incensed and grabbed my arm to pull me back, something she had never done before. I instinctively pulled my arm away, but she continued yanking and, as I was trying to break free, she managed to jerk my arm into her face. I was horrified. No matter how angry I was at her, I never would have hit her. I loved her. At the same time, I was also outraged for being put in that situation. She, naturally, blamed me for striking her, but it was entirely accidental on my part. She gave me that hurt, enraged, and long-suffering look that women are so good at throwing at men. It was the first time one of those had been directed at me. There was no joy in finally growing up enough to be on the receiving end of one of those looks.

I just walked away. We needed some distance, or at least I did. I got back to the School, looked for Jacqui, who was out, went down to the kitchen, where there was a phone for the kitchen staff, and called her. I was so upset. I didn't know how to fix this. Something had happened totally out of my control and I knew that Mary would never believe that I hadn't struck her. If the positions had been reversed, I wouldn't have believed her. And, if that was the case, in her eyes what I had done was unforgivable, so I had lost her forever. Fortunately, or so I thought at the time, Jacqui believed me. I was grateful because I could not see any way out of my situation. Jacqui did, however, and within a few months engineered dorm changes.

Mary's wedding finally came that summer a few months before she moved over to the other building with the other kids in the dorm except me. In the aftermath of Clark's objection, we were now also invited to the reception, too. We all attended, the service was simple and dignified, and then we went to the reception. Michael, dressed all in red, instead of his usual remarks about fucking, which we all expected, behaved for a change. The little ones stayed at the reception for a short while to make an appearance and then went back to the dorm. Clark and I remained. I thanked God for the champagne and that no one there was prepared to stop me from having some. I avoided Mary and then suddenly found myself face to face with her. I had the courage of alcohol in my veins, so I went up to congratulate her and shake hands with Reid. Sometime later Mary found me, put her arm around me, and we talked for several minutes. It seemed that the wall between us was coming down. I apologized for being such an ass. If there was anybody in my life whom I loved at the time, it was her, and she knew it. Now that her relationship was out in the open, I could forgive her, for it was not only jealousy that had made me so unhappy: It was the fact she had hidden such a huge part of her life from me. Curiously, whatever reasons had caused her to do so seemed to lessen after her wedding, and we were able to start talking again.

That Mary had come over to me, when she had so many other

guests, and we had been able to talk, meant a lot to me. It may have been silly, but I was eighteen, after all, and Mary's attention made me feel that I was still special to her. As long as I had that, I thought I could manage anything. Instead of dreading this whole event, I enjoyed it as well as the opportunity to meet her family, about whom I had been curious. I don't remember how much champagne I had, but I sure had a headache the next morning. There were a number of my friends from the staff there, too, including Margaret, so the Orthogenic School contingent made its own little circle. I remember being in the hall with Clark and one of the girls' counselors when Clark made some comment that if you couldn't stand on one foot backward on a chair, then you were drunk. "Piece of cake," I said as I stood on the chair with perfect balance. Clark laughed as I got off the chair. He waited for the counselor to leave and good-naturedly said that if you were loose enough to take the test, it meant you were already drunk, just not dead drunk. We laughed and I laid off the champagne for the rest of the evening, which by then was almost over.

I had been a fool with so many things related to Mary but had received little guidance from Jacqui or any of the other staff who might have helped me deal more rationally with all that was stirred up. Margaret felt that her best course of action was to help me deal with my internal issues in session and her job was not to assist me in managing life itself. There was still a lot of politics among the staff that she preferred to avoid.

Following the wedding, while life wasn't easy, it seemed to be improving. However, shortly thereafter, Mary moved over to the boys' floor, taking all the little ones with her, leaving me behind in the Adolescent Unit. In fact, the one older boy she worked with, Clark, moved over to the boys' floor, too, and got one of the counselors' rooms to share with the other older boy who had stayed behind in the dorms on the boys' floor. You can imagine how I felt at Mary's taking with her every kid who had ever meant anything to her but me. I was never consulted, although every inch of my life had been discussed behind my back. I did not want to lose Mary, who next to Margaret was the other primary relationship I had at the School. It is not incidental to this story that while the staff with one breath spent so much time encouraging me to be a man, they only wanted me to do it on their terms. If I asserted myself on my terms, I was, of course, acting out. There they were, worried about my orientation, but when I had a female counselor with whom I was involved, she didn't get the support to help me or to help her withstand my problems. It was another mixed message in a long line of them, and it made unraveling myself and my situation more difficult.*

The day of moving was hell, not just because of how I felt but also because of Michael and the other little ones. Now Mary had a dorm full of six of the youngest and craziest kids we had. It would be an unenviable workload, as she was well aware. At the end of the day, I stopped by to say good night to Michael and the others with whom I had lived and whom I, too, had taken care of to the best of my abilities. I thought they would be relieved to see that I was still interested in them and I wanted to see them as well as Mary. I walked in and Mary, with one of those long-suffering looks, threw me out. It's true she had to be overwhelmed on that day, but Clark was in the dorm, too, and she didn't even bother holding back the sharpness in her voice. She did apologize later, but no apology would erase the sting of her tone. I was convinced that no one could love or have any respect for someone on whom they used that tone of voice. Margaret noted at the time that I felt betrayed by Mary's turning to a man other than me, which also indicated my difficulty seeing reality.[1]

I avoided facing this for a while. Then, too, it was difficult for Mary to forget some of my behavior, including the things I had said about her intended. For a young woman newly in love, those comments would not soon be forgotten. In time, I reestablished my relationship with Mary. Since she no longer had line responsibility for me, we had less to argue about. We passed through the battle zone

---

*In working on this book, I asked Mary about her recollections about the move, because I wondered if she had wanted it, since I was so much trouble. She informed me that while I was difficult, it was not her wish or intention to no longer be my counselor. As Mary was still a relatively junior staff member, she did not feel she could argue with the senior staff who, with Jacqui's acquiescence, felt the relationship, with its constant arguments, was toxic. My arguments with Diana had resolved a lot for me, unpleasant as they sometimes were. Eventually, such arguments were surpassed. What was toxic in the end was that the staff never consulted me or indeed failed to see me as more than a child. If Mary needed a break from me, there were other ways of intervening. Here, I think, is an example of power corrupting and absolute power corrupting absolutely. For the staff, who said they knew what was best for me, this example showed they didn't even really know me. No wonder I was angry.

and she remained a major positive influence in my life until I left. That probably would have happened even if she had remained my counselor; our rapprochement was not due to the senior staff's so-called wisdom in separating us but from me getting over my jealousy and anger and, perhaps, gaining a bit more self-confidence to withstand the imperfections of everyday living.

15

Dictation

Looking back on what is left of the historical notes, I am struck by a number of things. The first, and perhaps the most overwhelming, is to see myself through the eyes of the grown-ups, like Diana, on whom I was so dependent. Most of the notes of my earlier years jibe with my memories and experiences. With the later ones, however, I have some grave problems.

For the early years, I knew my memories are faulty, and I allowed for that. I had so much trouble feeling anything at that point in my life that it is strange to read about myself and to realize, yes, I was that crazy. My initial diagnoses are there, as well, and the prognosis was poor. In any event, the actual details of daily life are recounted, and they are not so different from what I myself remember or saw with some of the other children who came after me when I was eighteen or older, so that I could observe their behavior with more objectivity.

For the last four years, after Dr. B. left, when Bert and then Jacqui were directors, I do not have any actual daily notes. When Jacqui gave me the records in 1992, sixteen years after I had left, she told me that she had removed from the files information that was personal to the staff, since they discussed their own issues that impacted their work with me. Except for four pages, there were no daily notes dictated about direct observations of my actions after July of 1972. (Dr. B. left initially in 1971, and Bert became director; he returned in 1972, when Jacqui took over from Bert; I left in June of 1976.) All that remains for those last four years are various synopses prepared by the staff working with me in preparation for the School's outside consulting psychiatrists, who would meet with me and then have a staff meeting to discuss their interpretations of the reports as well as their direct observations and discussions with me.

The threads of similar issues run through the early and later years at the School, as well as my life after leaving. This makes sense, for I have been the same person dealing with the same issues all of my life. The person who comes across in the later notes, however, is someone I barely recognize, while the person from the early notes I remember. The later notes show just part of me, almost as if the staff couldn't see me as an entire person. From seventeen to twenty-one, all of my behavior and all of my motivations are ascribed to neuroses, which, I suppose, is in itself a vast improvement already. Little is attributed to decisions made of my own free will, whatever that may be, or from choices I made on how I wanted to live my life and spend my time. It's as if the staff was trying to justify keeping me and was working to convince me that I was worse off than I was. Since I still had so many serious issues that would take another twenty-five years to place in perspective, I could have used a more open discussion about where I was, where I needed to go, and how they might have assisted me in getting there. Also, not everything I (or anyone else for that matter) did was due to some deep-seated problem. There were times I just needed room to breathe and live, something that Dr. B. had understood.

> *Don't only think that what goes wrong is important. Performances are important, period. Freud was in pathology, so he naturally looked at what went wrong. There are many things people do that are neither right nor wrong, healthy or sick, but just ARE.*[1]

I was never consulted about the major decisions in my life, and I was already seventeen years old. The School's notes refer to my fears about going into the outside world, which were true; however, the staff did little to alleviate such fears. What I so desperately needed at the time was an objective adult who knew both the School and the outside world and who could assess me and my behavior in terms of actual reality and not the reality of a mental institution, even one as good as the School. The attitude portrayed in these notes is that everything was an escape from myself, and, no matter where I turned, I was surrounded by shadow. It would take me years to find any sun, but I blame the School for part of that, since it did so much to encourage my fears that I would not be able to manage without it. Even Margaret's synopses seem surprising to me for those last years. Whatever is in these pages seems different from what she was telling me at the time and from what I remember.

The attitude in these notes, which were appropriate for a child of ten or twelve, made no sense for one of seventeen and certainly not for a young man of twenty-one who had just finished high school. It is true that it was very hard for someone to get me to see what I didn't want to and all of my intellectual and verbal abilities could be unleashed to defend my position.

Seeing those issues took so much longer than I imagined way back then. The staff could not step back to let me look at myself on my terms, and I was kept so busy fighting for independence that I didn't focus on some crucial issues that I should have.

> *One of the (hopefully) results of psychoanalysis is that in the end, the patient is responsible for his own actions. Sooner or later, if the analyst stays in the background, the patient begins to realize that he is responsible for his actions and realizes the difference between his projections and reality. Freud believed that the analyst should be like the movie screen: white, only reflecting the patient's projections.*[2]

In my case, or in all of our cases at the School, the staff seldom tried to stay in the background. They tried to direct the movie. This may have been fine for a young child, but when I was in my late teens, it denied me my dignity.

In discussing this issue with Diana when I was writing this book, she made two important observations. One was who wants to go back and remember their adolescence exactly as it was? Even if one tries to remember, people block out part of their adolescent memories for good reason. Most people do not have copious notes to which to go back and consult: what a nightmare! This was the reason I hated the movie *Big*. Here you have this twelve- or thirteen-year-old, who skips the worst part of human existence, has a great job and girlfriend, and at the end of the movie he *wants* to go back to live through his adolescence. What was Penny Marshall thinking when she directed this?

The second point was that synopses were prepared for the outside consultants. They were drafted to focus on what concerned the staff most so they could receive guidance or reassurance. Day-to-day living, which contained both ups as well as downs, is missing. The staff didn't need to waste time with an outside consultant to hear about one's successes. It was the uncertainties that were of concern here. As Diana also commented to me via an e-mail:

> *As for the Outside Consultants: we never listened to them, and always told them they were wrong. Sometimes Dr. B. would come in at the end and tell them they were wrong. We liked Dr. Perkins, when you were younger and before he had his stroke, because he would tell us juicy stories about his clients, pertaining to the (somewhat philosophic) nature of love.*
>
> *We wondered why we were so democratic as to ask for an outside independent opinion and then respect it so little compared to our internal thoughts. Although at times it gave us food for thought, it was just another viewpoint, not a guide. So it is not at all surprising that it was the consultants who looked at the glass half empty, and pathologized, because you know what differentiated Dr. B.'s viewpoint from theirs was the respect for the positive, the existential leap in spite of difficulty, rather than letting the problems define the person. Psychoanalysis when it is done badly is very pathologizing and pessimistic and negative.*[3]

Margaret worked with me longer than anyone else, from when I was ten to twenty-one. After leaving, I would see her formally from time to time for another four or five years, whenever I was in Chicago, or talk to her on the phone. My life with her was outside the rest of my daily life at the School. During our sessions, we had our own little world within the slightly larger one of the School, which in turn was a smaller version of the outside world. It was, in a word, very *Horton Hears a Who*-ish.* My memories were of someone who had complete faith in me and of someone who, out of her faith, could give me courage to face the world and myself. Referring to the Freudian symptomania above, Diana, who has not seen any of Margaret's notes, suggested in that same e-mail to me:

> *Similarly, Margaret's reports to them spoke in their language, perhaps. It's a jolly good thing that she sent you off to Lab School with self-respect and a vision of your strengths, instead of that Freudian mumbo-jumbo.*

Margaret tried very hard not to get involved in my daily life at the School so as to keep our time together focused on my internal battles and not the ones that sometimes raged within the building's walls. Given the mechanics of transference and my frequent anger at her, even though I knew that she was not the cause of it, we had our own issues to deal with. In the larger School, she defended me and worked behind the scenes to ensure I had what I needed or what she thought I needed. We had an agreement that what we talked about would remain between us—and that what she dictated about me would never come back to haunt me. It never did, for Dr. B. never said a word about what I discussed in session.

Looking at the notes, however, I found that Margaret had put things in there that betrayed our agreement. Not so much when I was small, but certainly later, when I was eighteen or more, I didn't want my counselors, whom I didn't look on as my therapists or parental figures in the slightest, and certainly not the rest of the staff being privy to my innermost thoughts. They were all there in these synopses prepared for the outside consultants, and then these issues would be discussed by the entire staff. What I had thought was between us was shared behind my back with others. Had I known it, I am not sure what I would have done, since I was dependent on her as the main adult (and sometimes the only one) in my life whom I trusted. There would have been a major row, and I would have tried to ensure that she stop taking notes or telling others what we talked

*In that famous children's book by Dr. Seuss, an elephant discovers a tiny world—and a tiny creature in that world finds one even smaller.

about. I guess I am glad that I waited so long after her death to read the notes, because I was so angry and disappointed when I first looked at them. However, if I read them while she was alive and before she had her strokes, maybe she would have explained her rationale. She must have had her reasons. Since she seemed to do everything else in my best interest, I assume she did this for that reason, as well. She was dishonest with me, as she well knew, because I would have raised the roof. This was the one thing that might have made me walk out the door of the School.

Looking at her notes, I was struck by something else. There is appreciation of me but little joy. I think my anger was hard on her—more than I ever knew. She thought that my turning from women to men was her fault in some way, since if she could have given me enough, I would have been "normal." I think, in the end, it was that sentiment that drove me crazy and created more difficulties between us. Although I have always been sensitive enough to pick up nuances, this was one that remained hidden for as long as she lived. It saddens me.[4]

I also think that I blamed her for not protecting me enough from the mixed messages and the misunderstandings of the rest of the staff. I wanted someone to consult with me about my life and to permit some growth externally as well as internally. She had a hard time with this, because she, too, was a creature of her time and place, so once again I was left alone to figure out how to fight my way out of a series of tough situations.

16

TEDDY

My remembered time line has become less clear, but one date I am sure of is that four years before I left, when John was still my teacher and Dr. B. had returned, the School got the youngest child it had ever taken in. Teddy was four, Eurasian, and very small for his age. He came into Leslie's group. At the time, I was already in the Adolescent Unit. He was so much like a baby that I remember asking Jacqui before I got to know him if he really needed to be at the School: He was so little. She told me in time I would see. And I did. If there was one person who helped me make sense of the world and gave me courage, it was this little boy. When I first saw him, I never thought that he would have such a profound effect on my life. He was the size of a two-year-old, with delicate features and blue-black hair.

During one recess in John's class, we had Teddy's class visit so that his teacher could go to a staff meeting. This happened all the time, and the teachers would take turns so that every week they could attend the daily staff meeting while we had a combined recess. Only the big Wednesday one was held at night, so everyone could go. John had a lot to do with so many kids, including Timothy and Patty, who were doing their normal battle dance, so I spent most of the hour looking after Teddy, since he was so little and new to the School. For someone so tiny, he exhausted me in just the one hour. Teddy liked to spin around in circles until he was so dizzy he would fall down. We tried to prevent this, but distractions worked only for a minute and holding him to stop him was a lot of work, since it had to be done gently, firmly, and constantly. He kept trying to run away, so I kept running after him and made it a game, by pretending to catch him while stopping him from spinning. Later I would learn that the running and catching game was something he never tired of. He would play it for hours as long as someone was willing to catch him. Finally, toward the end of the hour, I was thrilled to discover he liked sunflower seeds, so he would sit patiently waiting for me to crack them open and give him the kernel to eat. We had ten minutes of relative peace. I was sitting in a beanbag chair and he snuggled next to me while I cracked open the seeds. At the time I didn't think about it, since I just assumed he was so little he liked to cuddle. It hadn't occurred to me that he had chosen me to snuggle with and me to feed him.

A couple of weeks went by and one Sunday afternoon a whole bunch of us were in the TV room watching the World Series. Teddy walked up to me, smiled, and said, "Teeb gonna catch Teddy." I was stunned. Not only had this child remembered that I had played a game with him a couple of weeks before, he also remembered my name, which he always pronounced in baby talk, and had come forward to ask for something that he wanted. For an autistic child, particularly one so young, this was quite remarkable. I felt honored. So that afternoon I played with him, chasing him, keeping him from spinning, feeding him more sunflower seeds, and finally settling back on one of the sofas with him in my lap. Such physical contact between kids was not allowed, but I was dealing with a baby here and I had run out of options. He had worn me out.

Whenever we saw each other, he would seek me out and made it clear that I was special to him. Since he was becoming special to me, it worked for both of us. I slowly became responsible for him, if not legally, then morally. Now there was someone besides myself to worry about. Over the next four years, I tried to spend at least an hour a day with Teddy as often as I could, doing whatever he wanted. When I went out to Lab School for high school, it became harder, but I still tried to visit with him almost every day. It was an unusual relationship within the bounds of the normal of the School. And I, after all this time, hesitate to say that "normal" was a word that could be applied to our lives there. Now it was I who was neither fish nor fowl. I wasn't a child with Teddy but one of the crucial adults in his life, yet I was not a member of the staff. Leslie, in particular, who was the major person in Teddy's life, appreciated what I did with him, as, to some extent, did her co-counselor, Bob, and Teddy's teacher, Melissa. My staff were ambivalent about it. They felt that I needed to focus on myself and my missing needs and not worry about a younger child (whom they thought I viewed as another younger brother and was hiding my anger and my jealousy). I was no longer ten. What I needed was to feel good about myself and to feel that I mattered so that I could gain enough strength to fulfill my own needs. They felt if I just sat back and let them take care of me, then all would be well. We were on different planets.

There were a number of disagreements with my counselors over the time I spent with Teddy, but once I had made that commitment, I never went back on it. In the end, despite some arguments, no one was prepared to force me to do so. I knew I had to pick my battles carefully—and this was one about which I never wavered. Teddy had chosen me, after all, and I never forgot it.

Looking back, it was one of those fortuitous happenings that sometimes occur in life and bail one out of difficult circumstances. The golden days of the Mohawks were over, I was still struggling to find myself, my battle with Mary was a deep emotional morass for me, and Jacqui cornered me seemingly at every turn. Things got easier in some ways once I went out to high school, but that just mitigated the tensions I felt being at the School; it did not alleviate the stress from my own internal life. In fact, it just brought new stresses to bear, but they were external ones and ones at which in time I proved I could succeed. I do not know why Teddy selected me or what he saw in me that could meet his needs. All I knew was that I cared for him, felt responsible for him, and, whatever else happened, he depended on me. I needed to hold myself together not to let him down.

Teddy gave one clue about why he chose me. He was fascinated by my blue eyes, which he would point to every now and again, telling me "Teeb has boo eyes." I never learned from him what my blue eyes meant, although he was fascinated always by the color blue—blue bath oil beads, blueberry muffins, "booberry," as well as my eyes. In his own iconography, they meant something and were a factor in his choosing me to take care of him.

It was the first time in my life that I felt the weight of responsibility for another person's soul, and it was a sobering realization. At the same time, it was an anchor for me that I would return to whenever I needed to reestablish my priorities. I felt like a parent. Given all that I knew, I wanted to be a good one.[1]

Life continued for me and Teddy was now part of it. He looked forward to seeing me and sometimes would come over to sit in my lap during three o'clock meetings. When he did it during Dr. B.'s meeting, I expected Dr. B. to tell me to give him back to his counselor, but he never did. Thus, I knew that he approved, for he never missed anything and he certainly would have said something to me about such an important issue as my caring for one of the other kids so intimately. And there was a lot of intimate care. Teddy was terrified of going down the drain. He talked about it repeatedly. "Not gonna go down the drain. Not gonna go down the drain," he would echo for hours. The only way he would take a bath was if Leslie gave him one. After the first one, she learned to put on a bathing suit, since she was as soaked by his splashing and panic as he was.

I thought his fear of going down the drain was only in his mind and tied to some deep psychological issue. One day during another recess, he needed to go the bathroom and there was no one but me to take him. I carried him down to the bathroom and found that he needed to defecate. There was not a potty seat for him in this bathroom, so he had to use the regular toilet. This was a tiny, tiny child. I put the seat down for him and he climbed on, braced himself, and set about doing what nature required. He was so small and the toilet so big that he had to hold on for dear life. I could see now why he was scared about going down the drain. Falling into the toilet was something that was a good possibility *in his reality*. All that talk about going down the drain, which I had arrogantly assumed was mere craziness, made a lot more sense now. I could see what Dr. B. had meant about looking at the symptom from the child's point of view. I felt humbled at my failure to understand and thereafter tried to be less quick to make assumptions.

When he finished, it slowly dawned on me on who was going to have to wipe his bottom. I looked around, but I was the only one there. So I did it. Prior to this, I had been fanatical about washing my hands and not wanting to touch urine or feces. Even when I had first come to the School, I would refuse to take a bath after Paul or

Francis unless Diana sterilized the tub, since they often peed in it. If I touched a doorknob in the bathroom, I'd wash my hands. Now I had to make a decision: If I immediately ran over to wash my hands, I would give Teddy the message that I thought what came out of his body was bad. Since I did not want to do that, I just redressed him and carried him back to recess. I didn't wash my hands, although I had been careful to keep them clean. I lived. (I washed them later when Teddy wasn't around.) I guess from that point on, I could no longer be called obsessive compulsive, although I had never been truly so, merely fussy. Teddy never knew what a moment this was for me. Not washing my hands, whoa! I felt like I was changing my child's diapers—I wasn't crazy about it, but it needed to be done and I did it for him.

Some of the other kids resented my relationship with Teddy, but we lived through that. One night Teddy came over to our table in the dining room, since it was next to his, and climbed up in my lap. I was pleased to see him and didn't see why he shouldn't visit. Jim, however, began acting up, making snide remarks and being insulting, not just to me, which I cared less about, but also to Teddy, which made me angry. He was four and Jim was nineteen. David was on duty and, as per usual, wasn't prepared to confront Jim and didn't say a word. I thought it was better for all concerned to take Teddy back to his table, which I did, but I deeply resented doing it. I felt that David was useless if he wasn't going to defend a four-year-old from Jim's malevolence, let alone me, for whom he was allegedly responsible. In the end, I didn't expect much for me. I was waiting to get out. I just wanted to be able to protect my own—and having a testosterone endurance battle with Jim would not have served Teddy. I did want one of the staff to call Jim on his behavior just once when it was directed at me. Until the day he left, it never happened.

Teddy's counselor, Leslie, did heroic work with him. Slowly I tried to push Teddy to talk more and act up less. His spinning slowly stopped, he started to learn how to write his name, and I would sit for hours with him drawing butterflies and trying to get him to read and write his name, on which his teacher worked with him. At swimming, at those times I did go, between Michael and Teddy, I had my hands full. Once during the winter, I had dressed Teddy while I was still in my bathing suit and had laced up his miniature hiking boots against the Chicago cold. He was mad about something and stomped with all his might on my bare foot. Without thinking, I shoved him off my foot. I had never done that before and he didn't like it. He didn't cry; he just looked surprised. But he never tried to stomp on my foot again, either.

Cole was in Teddy's dorm, and the two of them didn't get along well. Cole was jealous of all the attention Teddy got from Leslie, and Teddy was well aware of how Cole felt about him. I was over in their dorm one day, after Teddy had been at the School a year or so, and Teddy walked out of the bathroom clutching a now-empty box of blue ("boo") Vaseline Intensive Care bath oil beads that he had just dumped on his head. I suspected that Cole had put him up to dumping the box in his hair. The blue bath oil beads and the fear of going down the drain were connected in some way; I just wasn't sure how. What concerned me more, however, was that the soap concentration would burn Teddy's scalp. Leslie's co-counselor, Bob, was on. He took one look but decided to wait for Leslie to give Teddy a bath the next day, given how difficult it was likely to be. I decided to try, and Bob, although he figured I had a hound's chance in hell of succeeding, did not object. I ran the bath and told Teddy we needed to wash his hair, deciding that I would do it no matter what it took. Surprisingly, it took very little. Teddy let me. He understood that "Boo gonna hurt Teddy." He held the towel against his eyes as I rinsed his hair, and, when it was all over, I asked him if he wanted to stay in the bath and play with some toys. I'll never forget the look he gave me, which clearly said, "Are you nuts? I let you wash my hair, but that's it, you moron!" What he said out loud was "Not go down the drain!" as he vaulted out of the tub into my lap. I was honored, given all of his fears, that he let me give him a bath. No one other than Leslie had ever done so before. I was only moderately soaked.

The time I spent with Teddy suddenly made the world saner. What I wanted was for him to have a good life, to be able to go to school, if only high school, and find some means when he grew up and was no longer a cute four-year-old able to climb on and off people's laps of having people still want to help him and be his friend. I often remembered Paul, the autistic boy in my dorm from my first days in the School. The idea of Teddy past puberty, in some institution, being restrained so that he wouldn't jerk off in public was one that put the fear of God in me. Whatever fears that I had for myself, and they had been legion, now seemed petty and self-serving. There was some balance being learned. Yes, I had been in danger of having a difficult, unpleasant life, but I could talk, I had full use of my intellectual facilities, I could fight for what I perceived as mine, I could relate in the "real" world from time to time, and I had had such abilities all of my life, even when I was four.

Teddy at four was much more limited. I had it lucky because I was with him when he was little and cute—and I would not have to deal with him as an adolescent or an adult, when he would be stronger, more belligerent (testosterone is a powerful drug, even for autistics), and not able to accept or be given physical care in the same way that I could so easily do it when he was little.

The School fostered a Madonna worship, a form of iconography that the good mother was a be-all and end-all. Despite Dr. B.'s titling one of his books *Love Is Not Enough*, the overarching image of a good mother (read counselor) could do much to reach out and save a fumbling and unhappy child. There was no doubt that the heroic attempts of many excellent staff did much to alleviate the suffering and distance of their kids. Diana's incredible patience and work with me provided a life rope so that I could eventually form an intimate relationship with her and, once I trusted her, begin the process of civilizing myself. The idea that "love was not enough" was true, but too simple. A more exact definition might have been the all-knowing mother therapist who fights through whatever to save her child. It was educated love applied in a professional, disciplined therapeutic setting, but in the end the professional meant far less than the attachment that formed naturally from the heart between one staff member and one child. Some children could not engender this kind of affection and for them the school was a colder, less successful experience. Whatever it was in their makeup—such as Georgina's (the "valedictorian" who thought "shoulder" was a three-letter word)—that kept them from attracting those who would be there beyond reason or above duty, it had a profound effect on their lives. Diana was certainly therapeutic in her approach to me and put my needs before her own, but that was not the underlying basis for her success with me. What made it work was that she loved me and it was vital to her that I have a good life. She was prepared beyond reason to ensure that she could catch me before I fell to the bottom of my personal abyss. Whatever gifts I had or didn't have, I was able to spark her interest and affection.

Teddy was able to do that with me. I tried with all of my skills to do what I believed was best for him, to bring him into our world, whatever that was, and to help him use his mind with as much freedom of which he was capable. I was not a free agent to do just what I wished or what was merely fun for us both. I was a creature who had been bred, so to speak, from the age of eight in this specialized milieu and understood the balance needed to try and catch someone as they were falling. Bottom line, however, was that I was involved with Teddy beyond reason because I loved him, and love, by definition, is not reasonable.

The question that has played in my mind for years is how Teddy knew that I had such capability inside of me. Looking back, he sought me initially and trusted me to take care of him from the first moment. I think that was his gift for survival—to find those who could care for him. I did whatever I could to help him, but in the end, it was not enough. Maybe that was what "love is not enough" meant. Despite love and professional discipline, the others, particularly Leslie, who was responsible for him as Diana had been with me, and I were not able to do enough. When I finally left the School, I was terrified but also so happy to get the hell out and away from my counselors and Jacqui. I didn't even care so much about not seeing them as in being able to live my own life without having to fight every inch of the way to make decisions about my own life and to be taken as capable of making them. Leaving Teddy behind was one of the most difficult things I have ever done. I had nightmares about leaving him for years; even now he appears in my dreams more often than you might think, given how long ago all of this was.

I visited him when I went back to the School. He was always pleased to see me but there was a distance, a hurt, because he did not understand why I did not come to see him every day. In his world, how could I explain it so that it made sense, other than I was selfish and had chosen my life over helping him? In the end, after spending some six or seven years at the School, I understand that he went back to his family to be placed in an institution for retarded and autistic individuals. Those were good years for him, and I pray he has continued to have as good a life as possible. Whatever damage that had happened to him was too deep to fully repair. His history was kept confidential, although, as I recollect, he had been a twin with a sister who had been the favored child. He had progressed apparently normally and started talking; then one day prior to age two he retreated into autism, not an unusual story for an autistic child.

I do not know whether his parents did anything to him that would account for such damage or whether there was some biochemical imbalance that didn't permit him to process life the way the rest of us do. Or some combination. Autism describes a set of behaviors; there is no simple test that can tell us what the disease is, as there is with strep or cancer. I have long believed that the etiology of such responses may be several different diseases that result in seemingly similar disconnections from the world. Thus, the word "autism" may cover several diseases.

Dr. B. believed that autism was caused by a child facing an extreme situation. He defined "extreme situation" to mean a cataclysmic life experience, such as being in a concentration camp. Brainwashing was another means of placing an individual in an extreme situation to gain a calculated response, such as retrieving information in times of war. There were certainly parents who behaved in such a fashion as to place their children in such an extreme situation. *The Empty Fortress* describes the backgrounds of the children in Dr. B.'s case studies—all of them had been in extremis. Since I knew some of those kids, I understood what he was talking about.

Later Dr. B. was attacked for blaming parents for causing autism, when there were so many examples of decent parents with autistic children who could not, by any reasonable explanation, be said to have placed their child in an extreme situation. But Dr. B. had a knack for provoking and enraging others. This was his theory on autism, and those autistic children he chose to enter the School were those who had been psychologically damaged, intentionally or otherwise. He did not choose his kids lightly and his selection may have skewed his interpretations.

As I said, autism describes a set of symptoms that may reflect a variety of underlying diseases. In that case, there is room for differing opinions. From what I could observe, often there may have been an underlying biochemical problem. However, not always. To give Dr. B. his due, I knew kids who certainly had been placed in extreme situations. Like all infants, these children when tiny had no self-defenses whatsoever; however, they were completely dependent on extremely disturbed parents. It never struck me as implausible that some of the situations about which I had heard could have resulted in such a profound disorientation from life.

My life has had, perhaps, more highs and lows than most. Throughout all of them, I have carried the weight of my failure to do more for Teddy than I did. Part of me tells myself that I am not God and cannot work miracles on another, much less on myself, but I would give anything to walk into a fancy Manhattan restaurant one day and have some young man, now in his thirties, come over and reintroduce himself to me. In many ways, I was able to get far more out of our relationship and use it to further my life than Teddy could in any practical way. Nonetheless, I was there to support and nourish him on many levels for four years, and I know that it meant a lot to him, too. In my heart, he will always be my firstborn.

17

Ready for His Close-up

The end of Dr. B.'s final year, which I believe was 1973, was marked by the arrival of a French film crew who were shooting a documentary about the School and Dr. B. Previously Dr. B. had guarded our privacy and had never permitted outside film crews to shoot us. A series of films had been shot about particular children that Dr. B. used for educational purposes in his classes and to compile a research record on certain case histories. Probably the most famous of these was the footage taken of Marcia, whose case history is detailed in *The Empty Fortress*.

Most of that footage was shot by one photographer hired by Dr. B. who came to know the School's children well. I do not remember his name, for he was only at the School a few times just after I arrived. Adamant about refusing the television news crews who wanted to do specials, Dr. B. did not want our faces shown on TV. He did permit a *New York Times* cameraman to shoot some stills to accompany a cover story on the School for an article in the *New York Times Magazine* of January 11, 1970. However, he had final choice on the photos selected, and no child was identifiable from the photos that ran with the article.

This French documentary was another matter. We had been promised that the series, eventually shown on French television to great acclaim, would never be aired in North America. It was the end of his tenure at the School, and, while Dr. B. had managed to return after Bert's demise, it was clear that Jacqui wanted to run her own show. This film was to be his swan song and provide a final record of his life's work. Maybe, somewhere, he already knew that such a monument to sheer willpower would not long outlast him so he wanted future generations to know that once upon a time there was a school that believed that emotionally disturbed children's symptoms were their highest form of expression and coping, given their view of the world. A place that didn't believe in drugs or restraints or locks on the doors. In retrospect, it was a wise decision, since the School as it once was is no more, and sadly those kids who could benefit from its uniqueness, despite its many faults, can no longer do so.

Tellingly, given what happened later, Jacqui was against the filming but felt she couldn't prevent it. She held her peace and let Dr. B. have his final moment of glory. As she frequently did, she would later have the last word long after he was gone.

At the time, I wasn't capable of thinking of the film crew as documenting Dr. B.'s lifework, nor of Dr. B.'s wish to leave some record of himself for posterity. All I saw was that our lives were turned upside down for a month as the crews filmed dorms, classes, meals, meetings, and conducted a number of interviews with us. It was anathema to me to be featured on film; I didn't know what I would be able to achieve in my life, but I remember my old fantasies of running for president and didn't want local news shows running clips of that footage with me in it during a campaign. I carefully stayed out of the line of the camera and worried about the potential effect of others being able to identify any of us in the future. Teddy made a good subject since he was little and cute. I was enraged that he was being filmed without being able to understand what it meant.

In the end, it was fine. I was overconcerned. But you have to remember that this was still an era where any mental problem was a huge disability. It was not an idle worry; in those days people kept seeing a shrink secret. People could and did lose their jobs. Thomas Eagleton was forced off the presidential ticket as a candidate for vice president when it came out that he had had psychiatric treatment. America was a much more conservative place. I did not know then if the future would hold greater acceptance or less. I had no interest in having any more risk in my life than I felt I already had.

The crew, all of whom were French, made some friends among both staff and kids. We lived cheek by jowl, and they would join us for snacks or would sit chatting with us in the side yard when they weren't filming. It was the first time outsiders had lived with us who were not professionals in the field or trainees under Dr. B.'s authority. One of the cameramen, Bernard Martinot, who later directed a well-known television documentary in France called *Le Bébé Est un Personne*, was a particular favorite, as was Daniel Karlin, the director. I liked them both and would speak with them often. The denouement of this filming took place, of course, in one of Dr. B.'s three o'clock meetings, where he had a final parting shot.

I have no recollection of that meeting, but on my first trip to Paris I reconnected with Genevieve, who gave me Daniel Karlin's phone number. I wanted, finally, to see the series, which he kindly arranged. I went to the French television studios, in those pre-video days, and a projectionist showed me all of it. It was dubbed in French and my French was not that good, but I was able to understand a good deal.

What I remember most was that last three o'clock meeting with the film crew. I had thought I had kept myself out of the entire picture, but there I was in my trademark red sweater, sitting on the floor with everyone else. I hadn't wanted to be there but felt coerced into going. I didn't want to be the only kid not there and single myself out for some snide remark from Dr. B.

I was surprised some five years later to see myself raising my hand and asking Dr. B. about coercion. "What about those of us who don't want to be in here but feel compelled by you to do so?" I asked in response to his asking if any of us had anything we wanted to talk about. His answer was a classic and one I had heard many times before: that no one could make you feel anything. What we felt and how we responded to outside pressure was up to us.

> *What is important to us is not what happens but what we make of it. That is, when we try to do something about a chance occurrence and fail is when someone begins to feel defeated. . . . It is the parents' reaction to the child which is important to the parents, not what*

the infant does. What really shapes us is our reaction, and our reaction to our reaction.[1]

He was right, of course, but sometimes in unfair power situations, such as a child with a parent, a patient with a therapist, or even a concentration camp inmate with a Nazi, there were limits as to one's ability not to be coerced. Seeing this so many years later, I realized that he was disingenuous here. On one level, yes, it is true we are responsible for ourselves and our choices, provided we are free to exercise them. As he certainly was aware, concentration camps could coerce and make people not only feel things they did not want to feel but commit acts that they would never have committed otherwise. Former inmates often spent the rest of their lives trying to wipe out the horror of not only of what was done to them but also of what they themselves did.

In the School we were not all free agents. Some of us were fighters, as I was, and we could rail against unfairness and despair in a way that some of our less fortunate citizens could not. To say that they were free agents who couldn't be coerced was misleading.

It was equally telling that I was the only person who challenged Dr. B. on camera, who questioned the man who was passing beyond human stature into mythological proportions. Of course, the fact that I could ask him shows that I had more freedom than I thought at the time. In some ways now, I feel badly that I rained on his parade to the small extent that I did. On the other hand, I was pleased that I stood up and questioned him on so sensitive an issue: how free were we really to be in or out of this film? It might have been better if all of his flaws had been shown, since when they finally did come out, Dr. B. was already dead and could not defend himself or even give an explanation.

The series was a huge success in France, where Dr. B. was already a big star.* Even to this day, more of the French, German, and Ital-

---

*Evidently, the night the series was shown, there was a strike by French state-run television staff so that the series was broadcast as a "programme unique" on all three existing French television channels, thus reaching a far greater audience than it would have otherwise. Nina Sutton, *The Other Side of Madness* (London: Gerald Duckworth & Co., 1995).

ian intelligentsia seem aware of his work than Americans. The show also made Daniel Karlin's career. Afterward, he wrote a book[2] about his experiences with Dr. B. After seeing the shows, I went to Daniel's apartment for dinner, where he, his wife, and I talked for hours.

Genevieve also became well known in France for her work at the School. A year after returning to Paris, she wrote a book on her experiences with a wonderful foreword by Dr. B. I read it and liked it very much, but the work could not be published in the United States for the same reasons that the documentary could not be shown.

18

NEITHER FISH NOR FOWL

I was eighteen in those waning days of summer as we got used to having Dr. B. back and Jacqui as our new reigning empress. A former counselor, Kathy, also returned to Chicago with her husband, Marc, a clinical psychologist. He wanted to learn how the School operated in a more direct way than he could from his discussions with his wife, so he came to work as a teacher, while Kathy returned to work as a therapist. Kathy had been a great friend of Diana's—she had been the counselor of the girls' dorm below the old Mohawks, when so many years before we traded places so that the girls could stomp and jump over our heads and we could hear what it was like.

Marc began by visiting the various groups and getting to know the School. Dr. B. announced that there would be class changes to make classes and teaching more manageable, and he wanted each child to choose the teacher he or she preferred. Such a request had never happened before in memory, so there was a lot of consideration—including where one's friends were going. I had a problem: By this time, my former counselor Julie had become a teacher, my old teacher John was leaving; what should I do? I had not been close to Julie for a long time, but she had looked after me for seven years. All of the issues that I had suffered over choosing between Diana and Margaret to sit at my birthday table came to the fore. I didn't know if it was a good idea for me to be back with Julie again or if she wanted to have me. If she wanted me—and asked to have me in her class—I was willing to go. If not, it didn't matter. But if I chose her and she didn't really want me, then I had just shot myself in the foot. I didn't want to have to start fighting again with someone with whom I had managed to escape our battles and regained a sense of comfort in our dealings. If I chose someone else, then I ruled out having her choose me and possibly insulted her. I couldn't decide. When Dr. B. came around, I told him I did not have a preference. His reaction was to yell at me, "It is only you and Jane (who was our youngest girl at six) who are incapable of making a choice. It's difficult to know who is less mature!" He turned and stalked out of the dorm. I was hurt beyond measure that he didn't give me the benefit of the doubt or ask why I was having such trouble making up my mind. I wanted his advice and instead I was reduced to tears as soon as I could lock myself in the privacy of my bathroom. Mary, who had witnessed this scene, was very supportive. It indicates a lot, I think, that Dr. B. could still reduce me to tears when I was eighteen with such a comment. Those sudden seemingly offhand remarks were the worst, because I never could see them coming.

I was placed in Marc's class. He was a gentle man, and I remember his quiet laugh most of all. That year with him was a good one. Marc must have taught classes, but I do not remember any of them. I remember his working with me on my writing, since I wanted to learn how to write fiction and improve my school papers. I also remember his patience. The year passed. Maybe life in the Adolescent Unit was so difficult that it was nice to have a few hours of calm, with a grown-up who actually could provide some stability, where I could focus on my needs for a change.

After Mary moved to the other building, taking all the younger kids with her, the Adolescent Unit became an empty place to me. Paulette joined David as our second counselor. She was cordially disliked by all of the older boys. She was pushy, inconsiderate, incapable of truly acting in a kid's best interest; instead, all of her actions were directed to fulfilling her need to perceive herself as helping others. Within a year we started getting young kids with whom she often set up situations to provoke them so she could ride to the rescue. I always felt she was completely unsuitable to be a counselor and her hiring was a major mistake of Jacqui's.

I was still resolving my issues with Mary for a long time. One night I knew I would not be able to sleep unless I finally talked with her about some of the things I had done. I asked David to get her for me, since I knew she was up front at one meeting or another. I waited up for her, since I knew if she got my request, she would certainly come. But she never did. I found out later that it was decided that she shouldn't come talk to me because I needed to separate from her and form bonds with my new counselors. I was in the process of separating from her, which was why I needed to settle some things that had happened and resolve what I had done. I knew that I had a lot to answer for.

I had thought at the time that David had made this decision alone, but if he did, there was a lot of pressure for him to do so—the same pressures that moved Mary to the other dorm without me. I was enraged that David hadn't the balls to ask, let alone tell me, what he had decided beforehand, thus giving me some say in my own life. Instead, I was left to wait all night without any explanation. Thereafter, I made it clear that he better not attempt to treat me as a child again.[1]

As for Paulette, I wouldn't even give her the courtesy of listening to her advice. Since Glen and Jim, two of the older kids with me in the dorm, just walked out of the room whenever she entered, I felt that I was doing well by being civil, which was more than she deserved, since she mistook any act of civility as an invitation to try to play a role in directing my life. There was no point in discussing it with her; I just learned to ask her to leave and give me some privacy.

Sometimes at night or late afternoon, Margaret and I would talk about things downstairs in the living room. If Paulette were to walk through, she would automatically sit down and attempt to join the discussion. This was my therapist, for Christ's sake, who had been with me a decade. I was polite, but Paulette always forced me to ask her to leave after a couple of minutes, so that Margaret and I could continue our discussion. No other staff member would have dared to be so intrusive as to sit down, not even Dr. B. As long as I remained at the School, Paulette never gave me that courtesy.

Later, as things improved between Mary and me, we also got together to talk in the living room. While not part of my daily life, Mary was certainly part of my world—I would often spend time in her dorm so we could talk as well as give her the freedom to leave for a break. It was my gift to her, and, in addition, I liked the kids. Paulette also attempted to join our discussion when I was alone with Mary, which, given how little free time I had with her, was precious to me. As with Margaret, I always had to ask Paulette to leave.

More new kids came into my dorm and they were a lot of work. I wasn't prepared to accept being told what to do by either David, whom I actually liked, or Paulette, whom I didn't. Life in the dorm was difficult. Jim was now there and as difficult as ever. He pushed the envelope in permissible behavior to limits that even I thought were improper. Jim was by now at U-High as was Jennifer, the princess with the limousine. They were close to each other—what the extent of their relationship was, I never knew or wanted to know. In many ways, I thought they deserved each other: two perfectly ordinary people convinced of their superiority.

Jim had been Jacqui's youngest kid when she was a counselor and she had taken him into the School. There was still an almost maternal bond there, and it blinded her to some of his misdeeds. When Jim and I had any disagreement, he was often particularly ugly and David or Paulette was useless. I quickly learned that saying anything to Jacqui was equally useless if I were really annoyed by something, since she would either blame me or think I was exaggerating. Because my counselors couldn't control Jim and he knew it, and Jacqui wasn't prepared to do anything, he took full advantage of making my life miserable. My counselors were worse than useless to me later, when we got some little ones, since I would have to straighten out some of the riots when David or Paulette got in over their head. Unlike the dorm building, there were no other staff next door in the Adolescent Unit. I suppose I could have walked out, but I felt I owed it to the little ones. After all, someone had done so for me once.

For a time after Jacqui had returned to the School, she had been warm and friendly to me. When she told me I couldn't do something or restricted me in some fashion or other, she would take the time to explain it. I felt consulted about my own life even if I had little say. After Dr. B. left, that warmness slowly disappeared. I think Jacqui, to her credit, was realizing that she needed to be a director and not a counselor. She wanted to avoid making the same mistake that Bert had made. But she went a bit too far the other way, and, in time, our relationship became adversarial. I just avoided her more and more. Margaret continued to be my life raft—she was the only staff member working with me who had any sane or therapeutic effect on my life, except my relationships with some of the smaller children.

One evening the entire School was called together for an emergency meeting. Heretofore, such meetings were only for dire events: someone's sudden leaving, which was never good, or someone's dying. Since I knew Jacqui hadn't bothered to tell us about Todd, I figured it really must be bad. We all gathered together to hear of the tragedy, which turned out to be that Jim and Jennifer had been picked up by the campus police for drinking a beer at a high school basketball game. I think that they were both nineteen or twenty, so they may have actually been of age, even though they were high school students, but I couldn't find it particularly shocking that two high school students had been caught with a beer. This was hardly a teen pregnancy. Given that Jacqui had ignored every other sign of their behavior, why take it out on us by calling us together late at night, scaring me and disturbing the young ones, who did not understand fully what this was all about? I did all too clearly and was enraged beyond belief.

After the meeting, I told Jacqui what I thought in a blind rage and then added that Dr. B. would have called us together only for a true emergency, not something so petty. She was furious.

Later, in the spring, Dr. B. returned to the university to teach a few classes, continuing the research and writing into what would turn out to be one of his better-selling books, *The Uses of Enchantment*. He was teaching "Understanding Human Behavior" (Psychology 251), an in-depth overview on behavior, which also touched on fairy tales and their underlying psychological messages. I had been with Marc a bit less than a year when I started going out to audit Dr. B.'s class.[2]

It was probably one of the best courses I have ever taken. But oh, was I scared. It was my first venture back into real academia since I was eight, and I was beset with doubts. I didn't want to make a fool of myself in front of him and his other students. After so many years at the School, I had little confidence in my abilities. Yet I felt so happy to be able to go out to school where I could see what it was like. In addition, there were a couple of members of the class who had formerly worked at the School whom I liked, and it was nice to meet up with them, on the other side of the grave, so to speak (given our attitude that once someone left, they were no more).

The class illustrated Dr. B.'s ability to synthesize information from disparate intellectual realms and put it together in a way that not only made sense but also made his students (and staff, kids, and readers of his published material) ask "why didn't I think of that?" Despite occasional episodes of ill humor, not to mention sarcasm, his classes illustrated why so many put up with so much for so long. This was no ordinary mind.

Birds have a purpose in "Hansel and Gretel." They led children to the gingerbread house, ate the crumbs left to show the way home, and led the children home on the back of white duck. When Hansel and Gretel left, there was no water, yet they had to go over water to get back home.

To understand both stories and people, you have to read them forward and backward so that at the end you understand them. For a person and his behavior in the present, you try to go backward to understand why.

The white birds prevent them from going home and lead to the gingerbread house and then lead them home in the end. The birds force the children to progress; going home is regressing, so birds want the children to grow.

Why a stepmother? A mother first provides all satisfaction, but at weaning, food stops (cow in "Jack and the Beanstalk" dries up). This turns the all-giving mother into a frustrating one, because the child had every reason to expect a good mother to continue to be all-giving. Toilet training, too, makes demands, which also make the mother evil. In "Cinderella," the good mother still provides from the grave: The memory of the good mother can sustain a child through life if cultivated.

First Hansel uses white pebbles to mark the way home, but that leads them back home where they were before. Regression doesn't solve anything. Afterward, Hansel cannot think of anything other than food to solve problems (oral fixation). The children grow up along the forest and must have known that animals eat crumbs. Story shows oral fixation and regression do not make a good solution. View of the stepmother has to change for the children. The witch is at first nice and warns the children not to eat her house: symbolically, eating the mother's body. Then, after eating the house by throwing caution to the winds, the witch retaliates, an eye for an eye. The children eat the witch's body, so she is going to eat the children's bodies. After this, another oral regression, kids are able to act rationally and kill the witch [We were told earlier in the lecture: *"Killing means that someone is not up to the task and that a rebirth is necessary."*], *freeing themselves from oral fixations and regressions. Then they are able to take advantage of the witch's jewels, so she has something to offer them.*

Crossing the water, River Styx, babies living in ponds before birth, baptism, and water rites; all change someone to a new life. Water is a boundary to new life; now that Hansel and Gretel have solved their oral problems, they are ready for a new life.

There is a difference between Oedipus' rejection and Hansel and Gretel being led out into the forest. Rejection is one thing, abandonment is another. Every child must be abandoned eventually, so they can finally grow up and become independent. The dark forest represents the unconscious: of traveling and finding oneself.[3]

The class turned out to be a wonderful experience. I was proud that I could finally see Dr. B. outside of the School in his element. It was a mark of how far I had come since I was a child. Also, even though I audited the class, I did all the work, including the papers, which I really struggled over, because I wanted to do well and make a good impression on Dr. B. There were a number of people in the class I liked and going was the high point of my week, because it let me stick my toe into the water of going-out-to-school in a way that gave me some reassurance when time came for me to go to the Lab School. There were a lot of Dr. B.'s three o'clock meetings in his class. I found that he treated his class as he did all of us in the three o'clock meeting: It was a comforting revelation that he never bothered to talk down to us.

The sisters in "Cinderella" are at various stages of development. Cinderella is at the highest stage. At the beginning of the story, she separates good lentils from bad. She gets help from the birds. She knows the difference from right and wrong, good and bad. From her ability to know this, all her good fortune accrues. She KNOWS. (We are the dead generation. No one in his classes ever remarked on this—and he has given this assignment for four or five years.)

Her sisters were blinded because all they could see was material things, while Cinderella could see the spiritual and what was important to a person's soul. Children generally know stories by heart. They know justice because they feel unjustly treated. If one skips a part, a child will question what happened: "You're wrong!"[4]

Unfortunately, my counselor, Paulette, was taking the class. She thought it would be a good bonding experience for us to go together. She would come and try to get me to walk over to class, try to sit next to me, and then want to walk home with me. If I was talking to someone, she was known to make an embarrassing scene about how I needed to come back—and, bitch that she was, she knew that at age eighteen, the last thing I wanted was to call attention to myself in that class. I really would have been looked upon as a guinea pig. And the class filled one of the larger lecture halls, containing over a hundred people.

As an example of Paulette's modus operandi: Two years later, I was to make a trip to be interviewed at Harvard and Yale for their admissions departments, the first time in memory that any kid from the School had achieved such an opportunity. Even Bert had gone to Harvard only after completing his undergraduate degree at the University of Chicago. Jacqui and I had a fight about Paulette taking me in the cab—I wanted to go by myself. I was being given $200 in cash for the trip, since I didn't have one of my parents' credit cards with me. Paulette refused to give me the money before we left—she waited until we were at the airport where she could count it out in front of everyone in the departure lounge, thus publicly demonstrating her authority and power (as well as exposing me to pickpockets). I was then two months shy of my twenty-first birthday.

19

U-High

Jim, my old nemesis in Luitgard's class so long ago who had continued to dog me in the dorm years later, left in the spring of 1974 to attend a small midwestern college. In many ways I wasn't sorry to see him go, but at the final moment I had a pang. I felt left behind. By now there were only a couple of kids who been at the School when I had come in 1963 and I was the only Mohawk left of the original group. Except for Margaret, Jacqui, the boys' floor maid, Theresa, and some of the cooks, no staff remembered me as I was when I came. It seemed as if time was passing me by.

The previous year I had started to go out into the neighborhood more on my own, since I was tired of being cooped up in a dorm of younger kids. I would bump into John, my old teacher, from time to time, but that bothered the staff, since it was felt I needed to establish relationships with staff who were at the School. They had a point, but I didn't think life always had to be so black and white or that I had to give up a friendship with someone who was a positive influence. In the end, my outside jaunts were curtailed. My choice was to leave the School or stick around more. One day, after a fight with my counselor David over this issue, I just walked off in disgust to go sit in a quiet corner to read. David couldn't find me, which was fine by me, and thought I had run away. I was sitting around the corner from him when he asked Glen (this was just before Glen left) to help him look for me. I just sat there enjoying this, since I was five feet away from him. Eventually he got Jacqui, who wasn't worried in the slightest and whose immediate response was "He didn't run away; where would he go?" She was right. She knew me well. I couldn't go home. I could manage there for six weeks or so, but I couldn't go back into my old environment for the next two and half years until I finished high school and was ready to leave for college. Later, when I went back up to the dorm, David yelled at me for scaring him and making him run all over looking for me. I felt bad, but not that bad, and must have mouthed off that I was sitting five feet from him most of the time, so I had been right under his nose as I was supposed to be. Jacqui hadn't been annoyed for my taking off to read, but she was pretty irritated that I didn't come forward when I knew (and could hear) that David was looking for me. The fact that I referred to him as a blind moron also didn't win me any points. I had made the jailer squirm, but it was not one of my better moments.

Also at that time, I had another rite of passage that reminded me of my earlier existence. I returned to the Becks for more testing. They still lived in Hyde Park and were still worldwide experts in giving and interpreting tests, including the Rorschach. I hadn't seen them since I was just short of my eighth birthday. I had always remembered my father taking me to see them, and I had retained some vague memories of the test itself. It was an event that presaged my being so unceremoniously ripped from my suburban world to a prewar Vienna existence. I was very nervous about taking the Rorschach test—and what it would show. The idea that someone could poke around in my mind and gain insight out of my control terrified me.

Margaret told me that the second test showed that I had undergone a complete personality reintegration, not as if there were two different people who had taken the exam but one who had made a major personality change. She seemed pleased, for such an event is rare. To me, however, I was still me and I hadn't yet been able to become someone else. Damn! While writing this book, I looked over the Becks' notes and found that while I had made major improvements, the diagnosis was clear that I still had a long way to go. Things were not as much a cause for celebration as Margaret had led me to believe.[1]

The report details that the unbearable conflicts and pain are still being resolved through my fantasy living. My intellect is still impacted by my anxieties and by the enormous energy that I am still expending on my fantasies.[2]

I guess, however, given everything, being neurotic was a lot better than the previous alternatives. There was also a lot of focus on this test about my feelings about my mother, my frustration, anger, disappointment that I feel as a "never healed wound." This may be correct, but also at this point, I was battling with Jacqui and often feeling castrated, restrained, frustrated, and incapable of taking a more active role in my own life. The Becks quote me verbatim in one reaction (description) of an inkblot. It could be my mother, as I suggested at the time, or it could be my views of Jacqui at the time.

> *"Two angels in flight or lifting up this female figure in the center—to rescue her or take her to heaven . . . I am tempted to say she is being rescued from her children—they are so angry at her they want to be rid of her—she felt put upon, caged in . . . my mother I guess . . . but instead of hands she has claws or pincers—so dangerous, or evil—but why then to heaven?—if she is in heaven, we won't have to put up with her."*[3]

I would not have been able to think of Jacqui back then; it was unthinkable for me to articulate that she, as director of the School, could be wrong, evil, or castrating. In our lexicon, putting all of that on my mother was much more acceptable and probably safer, too. If anyone at that point was a mother with pincers, Jacqui fit the bill.

The mixed messages, the control, the constant barrage of intimidation had a deleterious effect. The worst were the mixed messages: Everyone urged me to assert my masculinity and be myself, which was okay as long as I was given permission. My ability to be my own self, however, when it was exercised independently and on my own behalf, threw the staff into a tizzy and earned me Jacqui's opprobrium. It seemed like she had an impossible time with independent men, not just with me but also with male staff. The constant underlying message of castration brought me back to some of my oldest fears.

I was not then what I had been when I first came to the School. I was much stronger, with a much better sense of self, and my main defense mechanism, which was to fight, was already well developed and, here, appropriate. What got me into trouble and cost me many years of unnecessary misery was that I continued fighting after I left the School, since it was what I knew and it had served to protect me so well previously. I lost the opportunity to deal with this issue while I was at the School, since fighting was a sensible defense mechanism in the circumstances against a group that tried to pigeon-hole me, not necessarily maliciously, into a space of their making. I had no interest in being a good patient; I wanted to be a decent, independent human being, and I never let the staffs' machinations take my eye off the ball of achieving life on *my* terms.

The insidiousness of all of this was unfortunate and truly had a *Hush . . . Hush Sweet Charlotte* or *What Ever Happened to Baby Jane?* quality to it. Here were these people saying that they had my best interests at heart and the fact that I couldn't see it, as they would inform me, was an example of the work that I still needed to do on myself. They were convinced of the propriety of their efforts. The situation defines conundrum. I was so confused and desperately needed someone who could independently advise me in awareness of all the facts of what was truly happening, but there was no one capable of doing so, until I myself finally figured it out when I could create enough distance, a mere twenty-five years later.

In effect, Jacqui's control and seeming hostility to true growth on my part or the development of any true masculine independence made the School unbearable for me. I also knew that I could not return home to live with my parents, because I wasn't yet strong enough to go back to the environment that had driven me to the School in the first place. Once again life had seemingly positioned me into another corner where my options were impossible.

Years later, I studied chimpanzee behavior in an anthropology of law course. I proved in my paper, by applying the same tenets used to determine legal systems among primitive peoples, that chimps had a vestigial legal system. (My professor said it was one of the strangest but most interesting papers he had ever received and gave me an A+.) In writing this paper, I discovered one of my favorite research stories. A group of researchers were trying to calculate chimpanzee intelligence and set up a test to measure creative thought. They piled bananas behind a window in a high partitioned wall—and the chimp had a choice of figuring out how to use a crane to lift the bananas over the wall or use a bunch of building blocks to build a staircase so he could climb over it. As I remember it, the test was to be timed and each detail had been carefully worked out in advance.

The door was opened, the researchers clicked their stopwatches, and the chimp entered the room. He looked around and saw the bananas in the next room through the window in the partition as well as the crane and building blocks. He took a chair, tossed it through the glass window, shattering it, and climbed through to eat the bananas. Time elapsed: some ten seconds.

Looking back, I felt like the chimp, for I tossed a chair through the plate-glass window of my existence. I did what I could not do when I was a child and found another way amid the impossible choices presented to me. I worked to keep my sense of self whole by fighting back as much as I dared and spent my energy on a new goal, which was to get myself out of the School and into Yale. It was my Holy Grail and, when I began my quest, my chance of success seemed just about as likely as that of the Knights of the Round Table.

There was something else that I did to bolster my self-esteem: I spent time with the smaller kids. In the same way that the staff had used their work with us to promote their self-growth and to uncover their hidden motivations and problems so that they could reintegrate themselves to gain true strength and understanding, I used the smaller kids to help me assert my sense of self and my deep concern about their welfare. In this way I could assuage my guilt for what I had done or wished to do in the past to my brothers as well as for the survivor guilt I felt about those at the School who were less fortunate than I.

Diana made the observation to me many years later, apologizing for not thinking of it at the time, that my need to be a "better mother" was not just a symptom of feminine identification but also an example of my decency. I was trying to protect my brothers from suffering what I had. It was distorted and bizarre and not terribly well grounded in reality, like so much else that I had done when I first arrived at the School, but it was an exercise of a decent soul with a sense of honor. So I divided up my time in that last period of my life at the School to pursuing my goals, independence, and the smaller kids, thus making it through.

Every summer there were fireworks by Rockefeller Chapel around Midsummer's Eve. The carillon would play Handel and the entire neighborhood would come and sit on blankets, often picnicking under the Chicago summer sky. Those nights were magical for me, since I loved being part of the community at large. I still remember the smell of the summer night tinged with the smoke of the fireworks. I went that summer with the other groups, not my own, since most of my dorm mates were too small. Some of the Lab School kids with whom I would study that fall were there, sitting near us, and we talked. I did not know at that point that I would be going out to high school that fall, although I knew it was a possibility. A few days later, when I went across the Midway to U-High to play tennis against the backboard, some of the same kids were on the courts. We recognized each other and began hitting the ball.

I have always been a terrible tennis player—I didn't practice enough when I was young, but, in addition, I have trouble in three dimensions, such as when parking in one of those up-and-down garages that I mentioned earlier. We had a good time and agreed to play again the next day. I would later become friendly with all of the players at U-High.

David, of course, was concerned when I got back and said I had made a date to play with them tomorrow. This was not part of the orthogenic handbook, meeting strangers and then going to play tennis. Also, his reaction was fallout from the Jim and Jennifer beer fiasco, which would dog me for the next two years until I left. He said I couldn't go. I just laughed at him. I finally meet some normal people who live in my neighborhood with whom I can play tennis and you really think I am not going to go. Right! To cover himself, he called Jacqui. It was a Saturday, I think, and Jacqui came around that evening to talk to me, obviously returning from an evening out, dressed in a long gown and a necklace of red coral brachia that I always liked.

We had a long discussion and she convinced me that I couldn't go careening around the neighborhood and make tennis dates with strangers. She did agree that I could keep the meeting I had arranged, but I could not make any more. Looking back, I ask myself how much of a revolutionary I could have been if I acquiesced to this, but what choice did I have, unless I wanted to leave? I hadn't even started high school, I wasn't sure how I would manage living in the outside world, and I had very little self-confidence. I had grown up in the School and it was, by then, the only life I knew. I couldn't just throw it all away for a tennis game. At the same time, the issue wasn't tennis; it was living a real life and having some measure of independence. I needed to do something. I was now nineteen years old. When I went to play tennis the next day, I tried to be cool. For my teammate, it was just hitting a ball. For me, it was a lot more complicated.

When I thought things couldn't get worse and didn't know what to do, Jacqui told me that I would be going to U-High that September as a junior. Just like that, without consultation, my fate was decided. All of my doubts came to the fore. I wasn't sure I wanted to go, since I was sure I would fail. I was terrified, but not so terrified that I hadn't wanted to enter as a senior, because I was already nineteen and had lost so much time already. Jim had entered as a senior and left one year later when he graduated. Jacqui wasn't going to repeat the same mistakes that led to the beer drinking episode. She insisted that I go for two years after we had battled out some of my fears about going at all. She knew that by insisting that I go as a junior, it would give me an additional year at the Orthogenic School. If I didn't like staying an extra year I didn't have to go out to high school at all. I was not in much of a position to argue. And I was terrified.

Later I would not see the point, since outside of Margaret and Mary (and Jacqui herself, if truth be told) there wasn't a lot for me being at the Orthogenic School that final year. But Jacqui did not want me back into my parents' home for a full year. Even after all of this time, it would have proven difficult for me.

Now that I was faced with really being in the outside world with a group of kids who had been there all of their lives, all of my self-doubts began wriggling. Nothing had prepared me for life on the outside. Despite Martha's Vineyard, Augusts at home, trips in the neighborhood, all I had ever heard was how many problems I had and that I if I wasn't at the School, I would come to a bad end. In truth, I was aware of how many problems I had, just not what to do about them. I was not by any means a happy-go-lucky individual, I had no idea of how to relax, I still didn't like myself very much, if at all, and I had no idea of how I could possibly earn a living. Worst of all, I might find out that maybe I wasn't as smart as I thought. Moreover, I sensed that I still could not interact appropriately with others. I had improved greatly but was still so overcompensating for my perceived inadequacies that I was not easy for others to cope with. Nonetheless, I was proud when I told Roger and Sean, my good friends from my Mohawk days, that I was going out to school. In our world, that was big.

Despite all my complaining that she was the wicked witch, I was grateful to Jacqui for pushing me out. My low self-confidence prevented me from taking the steps on my own; I desperately wanted out but had no idea of what would happen to me. While my memories seem harsh in much that transpired between Jacqui and me, I do not forget that there were many times I turned to her for advice or comfort. As an adolescent/young adult, I needed to rebel against authority—and at that point in my life, she was the authority. The battles seemed to take on a life of their own, and remembered carnage seems a stronger memory than softer conversations and interactions. Despite my anger for what I thought went wrong, much was also right.

My parents were proud and pleased and probably really relieved. I had been away from them by now eleven years, and although they never said anything to me, they had to be concerned about my fate, too. I couldn't stay at the School forever, but Dr. B. had scared them so much that they were unwilling to do anything that might rock the boat, including ask questions. I went over to U-High to meet the guidance counselor, who would help me find appropriate classes. She was extraordinarily kind and patient, having had some idea of what it must be like for me. I was to take French, English, biology, math, gym, and something else that I don't remember. Math was a problem; I needed to be in a certain class so I could complete all the appropriate pre-calculus classes prior to college. In the back of my mind I was thinking about going to medical school to become a child analyst. It was, at this point, my family business. Jacqui was concerned that the pressure on me would be too much to take the more difficult class, because I didn't have as much trigonometry as the rest of the students, so I would have to make it up. It was the first big fight and it ended with a threat that I might not be allowed to go at all.

After all of this, I went home for my summer visit. I had learned to drive the previous summer at home. My brother David, an excellent driver, was horrified that his older brother still didn't have his license when he already did. For a suburban kid, that was a fate worse than death. After I got my learner's permit he would sit beside me while I practiced for the driving test. Given our rivalries, it was also a pretty bad fate learning with David. He inherited a lot of my father and could be cutting and sarcastic, not unlike me. After one drive with him, I was so angry that I got out of the car and walked home just so that I wouldn't have to look at him. It was a three-mile hike. After that, my parents signed me up at a driving school.

Driving was a more sensitive issue for me than for most. When I was five, I had been with David across the street playing and he wanted to go home. We went to the corner and I told him it was safe to cross the street, but when he was halfway across, some nineteen-year-old was speeding around the corner and hit him. Luckily, it did no permanent damage, but I had nightmares about it for twenty years. Even after I received my driver's license, I used to have horrible dreams that I was driving and my brakes would fail or that I was too small to reach them. Eventually, probably as I dealt with my anger and guilt, those nightmares receded.

Since I was generally exempted from customs (where the staff searched returning kids' luggage), when I returned to the School that fall, I smuggled in a stick of deodorant, which was verboten, since Dr. B. had forbidden it on the grounds that permission to use it meant the staff thought I smelled. The logic here now made no sense, although it may have earlier. In any case, I didn't want to start off high school with my classmates wanting to move upwind.

My first day at U-High I went to all of my assigned classes plus one. I also went to the more difficult math class, determined that my premed studies were not to be screwed up by Jacqui. For the first month, I took both math classes. I survived. I was up front with the other kids that I was from across the Midway from the Orthogenic School. By then a number of kids before me had recently come from the School, including Jim and Jennifer, so having kids from there was not so unusual, if you call having the local mental institution send patients to sit in class next to you usual. I suspected from some of the conversations that came to a dead halt when I came around the corner or the ones that I overheard bits of, there were some strange ideas about us. On the other hand, a lot of my classmates were the children of University of Chicago professors, and those at the university cultivated a reverse snobbism. Professors were called Mr. or Miss, not Dr. as in so many other places. The culture was, hey, we aren't mere MDs, we are scholars and researchers, so don't confuse us with the tradesmen. Northwestern University, Chicago's major rival in the area, was cordially looked down upon as rah-rah preppies who were smart enough to go to football games and some even to play, but not to invent the atom bomb or win Nobel Prizes.

From that vantage point, coming from the School was not necessarily a drawback. As long as I didn't do anything really stupid; like a chimpanzee riding a bike, it wasn't so much what I did, but who was doing it.

I was supposed to go back to Marc's class on my free periods and for lunch. I weaseled out of that immediately. I would eat with my classmates and spent a lot of time in the library, which had a record collection, headphones, and turntables so we could study to music. Since I had never owned any records (kids were not permitted to at the School), I loved to go grab a couple of records, put on my headphones, and study. Carly Simon, who had a house on the Vineyard, was always a big favorite, and, as luck would have it, she was rather popular at Yale, too, with friends in my college, so I got to lay in something that would later serve as happy memories.

I started to lose my connection with Marc. After I started at U-High, Marc would come to see me Wednesday evenings before the large staff meeting so we would chat, and then he would stay to have bedtime snacks in the dorm with us. His presence bothered some of the newer and younger kids, who made it difficult for us. I felt they would calm down in time as they learned to be comfortable with Marc and realized that they could not successfully push all of us around. Marc decided, however, that visiting with me in the dorm was creating too much disruption and stopped coming. I never forgave him for that. I felt that I was getting very little from the School and, indeed, had asked for very little outside of Margaret. I spent much of my time, when I wasn't actually in classes or studying, with those children, looking after them and keeping peace, given that we had two relatively new counselors. There was a constant battle about my leaving the dorm to go downstairs to study, since by this time Jacqui had knocked the walls out and I no longer had my own room. I found it difficult to concentrate amid the racket of five little boys running around, to most of whom I was just another grown-up.

That Marc was not prepared to spend that time with me not only demonstrated my place in the firmament but also the contradictions with which I lived. I was old enough to assist new staff (not that they wanted it, but Dr. B. had approved when he was there) with gravely ill youngsters. I was also old enough (and considered strong enough) to be deprived of seeing my teacher Marc in the evening so as to not interfere with those same youngsters because it was considered better for them (although not necessarily for me). At the same time, I was not considered capable of deciding how much I needed to study or the best conditions under which to do it. Once again I spent more energy fighting or ignoring directives than was necessary. Maybe Marc was right about not visiting and I was incapable of seeing it out of my own self-interest. He wouldn't see me outside of the dorm, either, since he said he didn't want to take me out of dorm at bedtime for the young ones. I figured if I was so unimportant, I didn't care enough to challenge it; you can't make people like you, so I drifted out of his class and spent hardly any time there.

I did like to go back to his class from time to time because there were a couple of kids whom I liked. Among them was Stuart, age 11, who was in Mary's group. He paced back and forth all over the School. It was an effort to confine him to the classroom, so someone was constantly going with him, since none of us were sure what he might do without supervision. Once in a minute when he was alone, he wandered into the bathroom, found a bottle of shampoo, and drank it. The whole thing. After a rather unpleasant trip to the emergency room, he came back to the School. This action reinforced for us the fact that we couldn't anticipate what he might do next. I might add, after this, we had to lock up all the shampoo.

Stuart had a lot of trouble eating and would throw up as soon as he felt someone was pushing him to eat or to do something that scared him. He threw up so often that we would just keep a bowl next to his place setting at the table. Once, when I was about to eat a really good chocolate candy wrapped in foil, he asked in his own idiomatic way to see it. I handed it to him without thinking, and he crammed the whole thing in his mouth, foil and all. Mary was right there, fortunately, and got him to spit it out. She was not happy with me, although I hadn't expected Stuart to shove the candy in.

He clearly lived in his own world, except for rare moments, and would pace talking to himself in a discussion we could not always understand. Every now and then, he would pop out onto common ground and startle us, almost as if testing us, saying "Surprised you guys, didn't I?" One afternoon he began counting in French for no seeming reason. Another, he started reading a passage from a book over and over. I didn't know he could read—and French, he must have learned that long ago. We were given to understand that once he had been a good student, but one day he had suffered a nervous breakdown from which he never recovered.

He also had a sensitivity that I loved. I had come back to Marc's class during the day when I had some free time—probably early on when I still bothered to adhere to some of Jacqui's pronouncements. I was upset by something from U-High—adolescent angst over social issues, I am sure—and I sat in a beanbag chair quietly trying to read, but not concentrating. Stuart came over, sat down on the beanbag with me, put his arm around me, and said, "There there," in his own special way, and then walked away to pace around the room. My only action that day was to try distractedly to read yet he picked it up. He was so extraordinarily sensitive that I can't imagine the data that constantly streamed through that head of his.

His being in Mary's dorm meant that my interactions with her brought him into my world and vice versa. When I visited her dorm, sometimes even when she was off and I looked in to say hello (or Mary's co-counselor would ask me to spell him awhile so he could go to the bathroom), or when there was one problem or another that involved a kid running out of the dorm, it was not unusual for me to look after the kids. It was in one of those periods that I had my epiphany with Michael, when he was jumping from bed to bed, and thereafter my time with those kids was relatively calm, since they felt safe with me.

In the end, Stuart didn't stay very long at the School. He got too big and too difficult to control. Being restrained, which became more and more difficult as he got bigger, set him off. His long conversations with himself suggested hallucinations, and, in the end, he required a place that could handle his violence and give him the medications necessary to control his visions. For me, I always remembered him as a frail boy who came over to say "There there."

Basically, I did not spend a lot of time in my dorm. When Paulette was on, I stayed out as much as possible. I would go over and see the Mohawks, or Mary or Teddy. With David, it was easier, so it wasn't usually the high drama when I went in or out. I would study a lot downstairs in the living room of the Adolescent Unit. U-

High was very demanding. What passed for high school courses there could have been college courses elsewhere. I had three or four hours of homework a night minimum, and I worked hard. I understood that coming from the School was nothing to be ashamed of, but it wasn't something to be proud of, either. A really good college would wipe the slate clean, if I managed to get myself in. If I ended up at Yale, I figured, although I had a rocky start, I had caught up. I wanted the School to have a smaller place in my future among the major events of my life.

Almost from the beginning, there were fights about how much time I was spending out of the dorm studying. I tried to ignore them and just did what I needed to do. Jacqui was the hardest one to fight with, because she had the authority and could stop me from going to U-High. In fact, I am not sure she could have done so, but she led me to believe she could and it was the one thing I lived in terror of. I couldn't risk being thrown out of the Orthogenic School having any impact on U-High. I had to get that diploma to go to a good college. If I wanted to go to a community college, I wouldn't have worried. To get into Yale, I knew that if there was any funny stuff on my transcript or my recommendations were not glowing, or if there was anything at all questionable about my application in any way, coming from a mental institution, I would not be granted admission. Jacqui had me and she played it whenever she needed to.

David was basically a good guy and didn't want to rock the boat with Jacqui or with me. He cut me a lot of slack, for which I was grateful. Money for one. All of our allowance was supposed to be locked up, but he knew I kept mine out so I had money to buy a Coke or lunch, if I didn't want to come back to the School to eat. I also got money from my parents, which was strictly against the rules, and kept it locked in my locker at U-High. The old rules didn't apply anymore. Or, more exactly, I didn't apply them. It was time to move on. As I learned in a high school Shakespeare course, "Presume not that I am the thing I was." The line is uttered by Prince Hal to Falstaff, his old drinking and whoring buddy, when Falstaff comes to see his friend after the old king dies, leaving the prince as the new King Henry V. It sums up so elegantly the change in life from youth to responsibility, from rowdy prince to monarch.

Paulette always tried to get all of my money to lock up, but I never told her and just sidestepped the issue. She made my life difficult, but with all the little kids upstairs, once I walked out, there wasn't much she could do, since without me there, she couldn't leave them alone. I felt bad for the little ones, because they deserved better than her. When I was there I could shield them from the worst of her excesses, which was to provoke them when they were calm and then scream at them when they were provoked. Conversely, when someone was really upset and needed help, she had a hard time recognizing it.

Eventually Jacqui found out that I was taking the two math classes. By this time, the teacher of the easier class thought I should move into the more difficult one. Although Jacqui was angry that I had flouted her, she felt obliged to take the advice of my teachers, so I moved into the more difficult class with Mrs. Matchett, who, while chain smoking the entire time, tutored me in trigonometry twice a week for a month. She did it without pay; I would just come to the math department office and we would sit for twenty minutes going over what I needed to know, so by the time we reached that point in class, I was prepared. It must have made me look nerdy or a teacher's pet, but I never thought about it at the time, since I felt I had so much to make up. I couldn't let other people's opinions of me stand in my way, and I had little ego where my future was concerned.

Despite all the restrictions on my life, I had never had such freedom, except for the few days I spent on the Vineyard, which was more vacation than everyday living. If my friends at U-High knew what I put up with, they wouldn't have believed it, but it was the price I had to pay and I knew it.

I also had gym, which was obligatory, and we were graded on it. I was acutely uncomfortable changing and showering with the other guys. I finally had decided that I might have hormones after all but in which direction I still wasn't sure. I just sure as hell didn't want to find out in the locker room.

The U of C operates on the quarter system, so instead of two semesters, we had three quarters plus the summer quarter for those who wanted it. In fact, what it meant was that we had twelve classes each academic year instead of ten, so it was a heavy load. I had my first finals and was a basket case until I got my results. Excluding gym, for which I had gotten a B or B+, I had gotten all A's except for English, where I got a B+. It was the only academic B that I received in high school. The English teacher came up to me in the hall and said, smiling, thinking it would make me feel better, "You were right between an A– and a B+ and I couldn't decide, so I gave you the B+." I thanked her and walked off in a daze. If I was right between, why not give me the better grade? Why torture me by telling me? With that B, I already felt Yale starting to slip from my grasp.

My parents were thrilled. This was the top high school in Chicago, and they, at least, knew that if I could hang in there, I would get into a college somewhere. For them, now the sacrifices looked worth it. Even at the School, the staff were impressed. For the most part, my grades shut them up about how much time I was spending studying, since it looked like it was paying off. It was not, however, clear sailing for me, and there were so many unpleasant battles that I am happy that I can't remember them all.

From the moment I walked in, the other kids at Lab School seemed to me to have a lot more going for them. My insecurities had no effect, of course, on my perception. I was one of those kids from "over there," which may have been Mars as far as they were concerned. It certainly felt that way to me. If there was one thing that Dr. B. pounded into our heads it was about competition—that the only yardstick we needed was our own. We needed to measure from where we had come from. Comparing oneself to others at the School was futile; it only made you feel bad and, if Dr. B. found out, often got you into trouble.

In the final analysis (one of Dr. B.'s favorite stock phrases), even he didn't believe totally in his theory: Sandy Lewis, the counselor from my childhood who had found my flip-flops, had already gone to Wall Street and was making a fortune—later he would send his private jet to pick up Dr. B., and Dr. B. would often cite him as an example of the School's great successes. When one of the kids in one grandiloquent three o'clock meeting asked why he seldom cited George, a formerly extremely disturbed child who was working as a janitor, as a great success, it was a fair question, given the self-measuring yardstick talk. Dr. B. turned him into sushi in seconds.

In our own little world, the self-measuring yardstick did indeed matter and could work, but nobody cared outside. All they saw was what you brought with you when you walked into the room, and no one was interested in your case history, unless they were a shrink or even more whacked out than any of us. At Lab School, here were all these kids who had such interesting backgrounds and experience:

actors, musicians, writers, travelers, the children of politicians, millionaires, brilliant scientists—and then there was me. There was also Lenore who came from the Orthogenic School with me and had joined Lab School as a junior, too. We had different classes, but she was a comrade in arms in the battle of the inmates from across the Midway, so I was able to take great comfort in our friendship. Lenore was a lot quieter than I was and never managed to get herself into the constant battles that I did. She, at least, knew what my life was really like—both sides of it. It was as schizophrenic a life as any I could imagine. Now, looking back, I can see that there were probably many others who felt their home life was bizarre and in direct contrast to their public high school lives. I tried to keep the two aspects separate, which was difficult if I was at Lab School and one of the dorms came by. Everyone would wave, for it was a big deal for them, too, that one of us had made it out into the real world. They just didn't see all the doubts I had on the inside.

Once Leslie's group was going shopping and Teddy came over to climb in my lap. I literally can't explain all the thoughts that were in my head and heart at that very moment. I was at nineteen sitting with a bunch of high school classmates three years younger, all of whom were more advanced in some ways than I, yet here I was with a child in whom I had so much vested and to whom I was so important. For one second, I didn't care what anyone else thought. Then, for another, I was pleased that maybe outsiders could see that in my world, I had stature and responsibility. I guess, looking back, I was proud. And here was my Teddy wanting me to draw him butterflies, totally oblivious to the moment and its import to me.

It is telling, I think, that I have not kept up with any of the people with whom I went to high school, except for one who now lives in Paris. None of them have cared to keep up with me, either. It was such a difficult experience for me that I like leaving it where it belongs: in the past. At the time, it was so exciting and new that I was thrilled, but like the shark that needs to keep swimming forward all the time or it will drown, I couldn't stop; I had to keep moving.

If you had asked me at the time whether I had any friends, I would have answered of course and recited a long list of names. But I still didn't know then how to really be friends and share the back-and-forth that constitutes normal human relations. In high school, there were so many things that connected us: classes, concerns about parents, college, as well as other activities, that there was always a mutuality of interest I could use to cover up the fact that I couldn't truly relax and didn't know enough to discern what I wanted or needed. Just making it out of the Orthogenic School into U-High, I thought, was such an achievement that I didn't have to worry so much about social issues. In truth, the issues weren't social at all but internal, where I still was so confused about so much of life.

Here I was at nineteen and I had never had a date. That part of my life didn't bother me, and that should have been a warning sign. Sex was still a Pandora's box. While there were those around me who were more aware of my leanings than I was, given from whence I came, there was enough doubt to fudge the issue. There were one or two guys who were friends to whom, in retrospect, I was attracted but didn't recognize it at the time. In the end, it was my obliviousness that was scarier to others than my orientation. In the mid-1970s, the world was a different place. But the world has never been so different that someone who had such trouble knowing himself about such a basic issue was not going to have a problem. Additionally, I didn't know how to have the give-and-take of real friendship—I had been raised to believe that sharing intimacies about one's psychological makeup constituted the base of friendship. Often, when people confided things in me, I made the mistake of assuming that they were becoming friends, because why else would they have mentioned something personal to me. I didn't realize that, to many, confidences were more easily told to comparative strangers, who were told precisely so that the tellers could avoid facing the issue once it was off their chests.

I also made a lot of cracks that I thought were funny, but many were mean or insulting, as I overcompensated and tried to be what I thought at the time was sophisticated. I just turned everyone off. Moreover, many of the shared experiences in high school I couldn't share. For one, my life was too difficult to codify or explain. Also, the conflicts within me were still almost Herculean in proportion, and I was struggling to find my voice if for no other reason than I should know it myself.

In a fundamental way, I was alone. I just didn't let myself know it. In fairness to Jacqui, she could see this and tried to do something about it. At the time, however, what came across was only more restrictions. She never sat me down and got me to see what was missing. I do not blame her for that: As I quoted long ago in these pages: To those who understand, no explanation is necessary; to those who don't, no explanation is possible. Nothing, and I mean nothing, got through to me for a long time so that I could have some glimmer of what I was missing right in my own head. It wasn't sex, or intelligence, or ability to relate with others; in a fundamental way, I did not know how to relate to myself. I still approached the world as a gladiator girding for battle.

All I knew was how to argue, to postulate, to attack, and to rebound with a verbal quip. Often I was funny; more times, sad. I was suspicious of others, expecting to be put down and unwilling to give an opening to be attacked. I had spent so much time guarding myself from the sudden swift put-down or the smack in public that such protection was so deeply ingrained I didn't understand that there was any other way to live. And before I could understand that there were other ways of living, I had to see how I was living, which I couldn't do.

The reason Dr. B. got to me so much was that his modus operandi was already how I saw the world, so my approach focused on protecting myself, leaving as small an aperture as possible for another to land a weapon upon my person. Such defenses do not make friendships, lovers, or even business partnerships easy or even, at times, possible.

Although all the time in the back of my mind there was a nagging suspicion, I never consciously thought there was anything wrong. How could there be, since I had been in the School for so long and here I was, outside, alive, and seemingly well? The process of denial or, to be more accurate, blindness continued after high school. It almost destroyed my life, for I felt that I had earned the right to be part of the human race and couldn't understand why I never seemed to fit in. I blamed the School, or prejudice when I was on Wall Street, since it was never noted for its liberalism, or whomever. Then one day I began to see it was what I did that made things so difficult for me. Since I was already forty when that day arrived, I wasted a lot more time than I had when I entered high school and was already concerned about how much time I had lost. My outside success would cover up a lot. But not, in the end, enough.

Be that as it may, I was earning the respect of my classmates: I knew what I was talking about, contributed to class, took some of the most difficult courses, and looked upon the opportunity given me as a real gift.

One evening I was leaving the dining room after dinner and stopped off to ask Jacqui one question or another relating to school. We ended up talking about college, and I said that I wanted to go to Harvard or Yale. This was not something we had discussed before, despite this being my brass ring on the merry-go-round for a long time. Jacqui fixed me with a glare and yelled at me in front of whoever was left in the dining room about having delusions of grandeur. I might have understood a more gentle attempt to lower my expectations, but this broadside enraged me. In hindsight, it was the best thing she could have done. It gave me the strength to prove her wrong.

The end of the second quarter came around and this time I pulled straight A's, proving that the first quarter wasn't a fluke. Even my brothers were impressed. A copy of my transcript had been mailed home, and my brother David, who hated school and cut as often as he could, commented that he had never seen so many A's in one place before. I just smiled and kept plugging away. The double life I was leading made less and less sense to me. At home, back on the good ol' Orthogenic School ranch, life settled down into a modified truce. Margaret, whom I saw two or three times a week, was a great help in reassuring me and getting me to make sense of the world. Mary and I also got together several times a month in addition to the time I spent in her dorm. Beyond that, more and more, I wanted out of the School. I felt pangs about leaving Teddy, Michael, and some of the others, but in the end, they had their lives and I had mine. Much as I wanted to affect their outcomes, I could not. I was tired of the battles over how much time I spent in the dorm and how much time I spent on homework. I told Jacqui I wanted to leave. I was terrified, of course, but it seemed the best alternative. I could finish U-High either from home or living a few days a week at Ruth's house, my mother's old friend whom I had seen since childhood around the neighborhood. Since I would have access to a car thanks to my uncle, it was time to go.

Jacqui flat out refused. She said that I had gotten into Lab School from the Orthogenic School on her say-so; if I wasn't at the School, there was no assurance that Lab School would grant me admission, particularly if she did not give me a recommendation. They would not take the risk of my mental stability. Looking back, I was one of the better students in my class, my parents could afford to pay tuition, and I had already completed almost a year, so it was not as if I was an unknown quantity. If I had really wanted to push the issue, I probably could have made it work. There was one other problem: Margaret. She said that if I left the School without Jacqui's blessing, she would refuse to see me in session. Hers was a threat I heeded. Margaret has been dead for seven years, but if you were to ask me now whether I ought to thank her or be angry at her for her stance, I would not know what to say. As I have explained, I still had a lot of work to do on myself, but I did not need to remain at the School to do it. It would take me another twenty-odd years, so one year more or less wouldn't have made a big difference. I don't know even now what Jacqui told her to say. Technically, Jacqui was her boss, but if Margaret felt I was ready to go, she could have made the case and Jacqui would have listened. In the end, it was Margaret who blackmailed me.

I did not discuss my wish to leave with my parents to see whether we could work out a better arrangement. From the beginning, I had never involved them in my internal life at the School; it was part of our unwritten deal. I knew they made sacrifices to keep me at the School, so it seemed poor sportsmanship to say how much I hated being there. And once I brought my parents into it, I might lose control over the situation. I wasn't prepared to risk my parents agreeing to pull me out and have Jacqui work against me at U-High by refusing to give me a recommendation. I could suffer through one more year with the knowledge that my time in purgatory was coming to an end.

Dr. B. was back again for the spring quarter at the university, which comforted me in some ways, knowing that he was around. He was teaching a graduate course and let me audit it. We would talk from time to time. He always seemed pleased to see me and have a word with me. As with many things at the time, I was ambivalent.[4]

Sometimes after his class I would accompany him across the Midway back to the School, where he still kept an office, and some of the staff would drop in to talk to him, although Jacqui ensured that he had no operating role. One discussion that long has stuck in my mind took place when I ran into him and we walked back to the School together. He asked how things were going and I told him not too well. I felt the odd man out at U-High—not that I was ostracized, but I wasn't part of the inner circle, either. I tried hard, but my social skills were not as polished as those of the others and I felt awkward and gangly much of the time. My lack of vision and the difficulty I had seeing others' points of view added to the problem. All I told him was that things were tough. He asked me how were my grades, knowing full well what they were. I answered, "Straight A's."

"Too bad," he said. I looked at him. "Too bad?" I echoed. This was a new tack, even for him. "Yes," he responded, "because if you had bad grades, at least you would know what was bothering you." We had reached the School by this point and said our see-you-laters. I went off trying to figure out what he was telling me. I finally decided he was trying to point out that maybe I should look at some of my achievements and try to put them into perspective. However, as I could have pointed out to him, that wasn't much help, since I already knew I was good at academics. Life itself seemed to trouble me. At the time, however, the comment served its purpose, and I tried to gain some more perspective

I wanted his advice about colleges, so one day after his class I asked him. He asked which ones I was thinking about. I told him. He glared at me and demanded severely, "Why can you never be satisfied with being like everyone else? Why do you always have to be special?" At least, unlike Jacqui, his point was not that I couldn't do it but that I shouldn't feel like I needed to. Like his postcard of the solid gold cradle with the heavily embroidered coverlet as being most uncomfortable for the poor infant, I think he was addressing himself to my need to make myself the center of attention to cover up for how little I thought of myself.

When I got back to the School, I found my old dorm mate, Roger. He asked how the discussion went. I asked, "Wanna see the bullet holes?" and we laughed. He understood. The weird life we led was his, too.

Of course, once I actually entered Yale, someone told me that he had overheard Dr. B. discussing the School's successes, one of whom was attending Yale. At that I permitted myself a small smile.

I finished out my junior year and had my last summer at the School. U-High ended mid-June, and I had a month to go before going home for my six weeks. It was an uneventful period, as I remember. But I hated sitting around in Marc's class, back to the same old drill. I felt like a canary with its wings clipped.

That summer, I also went back to the Becks for the third and final time of testing. This time they gave me an intelligence test. In actual fact, while I have spoken about the Becks, I only met Mrs. Beck, who actually administered the tests. Then both she and her husband (or maybe just her husband) interpreted the results. I was very uncomfortable about going to take an intelligence test. Given all my concerns, why Jacqui didn't ask me about this or talk to me about it in advance, I do not know. Paulette just arrived at Marc's classroom door one morning and informed me that she was taking me back to the Becks. Again, something was just decided on my behalf, and I had no warning to discuss it or ask questions. I refused to go. This put Paulette in a panic, since we would be standing up some of the foremost testers in the world. That wasn't my problem, however, since I hadn't been given the courtesy of anyone asking me what I thought. While I had understood the reasons for a Rorschach test, I wasn't sure what the point was in an IQ test. I was smart enough, whatever the number was. Determining it exactly would make no difference in my world. However, it might have been necessary for the School's records. If so, they should have asked me, not just made the decision just figuring I would go. And the last person to tell me should have been Paulette. In the end, after some pressure from Marc, I went.[5]

My intelligence rated high and I had continued to improve although the Becks found my emotional issues still interfered with my intellect and overall life. Although I may quibble with certain interpretations, it is amazing to me, looking back at all of the Becks' work, how much they were able to divine from just a few hours' testing about who I was, what troubled me, and what the future might hold. They were generally correct in their judgments, even if in reading some of their analyses now, I find that I disagree on a specific. Overall, I can't argue with any of their conclusions.

One interesting result from the test is that the Becks postulated that I might require a "stress-free" environment to compete successfully academically with others my age. I sure as hell did not live in one at this point of my life and, in fact, found that Yale had no more stress than those last few years at the School. It was interesting to note that both the Becks and staff automatically assumed that I lived in a stress-free environment and that it was only my internal problems that made things difficult for me. Not so. My problems existed and created obvious difficulties. So did living in a place that denied me any autonomy, had trouble allowing me grow up, and where the staff consistently misjudged its own actions and rationale while telling me this was all in my head.

I was to work for my uncle that summer when I went home and wanted to start when U-High was over but was not allowed to. The hassle was that I couldn't drive (and certainly couldn't have a car) while I was at the School—the idea made Jacqui's eyebrows practically jump off her head. She wanted me to spend what free summer time I had at the School, using what it had to offer, since I was no longer focused on Lab School. I was less interested since what I wanted to learn was how to manage in the outside world.

When I did go home, finally, I was a rising star. My grades were good enough and I had made it through my first year of regular high school with flying colors. My outward success covered over the fact that I still had to grow and develop both my personality and self-confidence. I worked for my uncle although I took a few days off to go to Martha's Vineyard.

On the Vineyard, also staying with my Uncle Sy was the son of one of his Washington neighbors, Jeff Kampelman. Jeff was about to enter his junior year at Yale and invited me to stay with him if I went out to do a round of interviews. I was grateful for the invitation, although I doubted I would be able to take advantage of it. I did, however, ply him with questions.

Now that I had my driver's license, that summer at home I spent my time working primarily for my uncle, who owned an automobile agency. When I talked to him about working for him, he said he would pay me either $3.00 or $3.50 an hour. When the time came to pay me, he paid me the lower figure. I was very upset, but my father was amused and was not-so-secretly pleased. He said, "I know you are angry, but let that be a lesson to you. You didn't come to any agreement before you started. Why shouldn't he give the lower figure? He is a businessman and you left it up to him." Every day that summer, I knew I was earning fifty cents an hour less than I could have. Although I realized that it was done to teach me a lesson and I was fortunate that the loss of the money had no real effect on my standard of living, I was still infuriated.

It was a difficult summer on the job. I was "da nephew," and everyone in the place looked at me like I was a spy. It was a typical story of a student working with blue-collar workers who enjoy a little fun at his expense. The mechanics were from a different world. I just tried to hold up my head and survive. One of the more forceful members of the staff was the old black foreman, who seemed ancient and, as the grandson of slaves, was from a different generation. He took a liking to me, after he saw how hard I worked, and his acceptance made the summer easier. By the end of the month, the mechanics had taken me under their wing so I was no longer the enemy. The old foreman was from the Deep South, and I always wondered what stories he had that I never had the nerve to ask him.

I quickly learned how powerless I was in this environment, where brains counted for little. It was one thing to realize there were many things that happened in the world about which I could do nothing and quite another to see one before me. A young Vietnamese immigrant worked for my uncle sweeping the floors. He and his wife had been some of the lucky ones to escape the Viet Cong. They had arrived in America virtually penniless and started over from scratch, not a particularly unusual story. Eventually I learned this man was paid less than the others who cleaned up. I have to assume because he was Vietnamese and his English not good enough to argue for equal pay. I was incensed that he was paid less for doing the same work and he needed the money, since he sent money overseas to relatives.

We would talk from time to time as best we could, given his English, since I clearly didn't have a clue about speaking Vietnamese, and I grew to like and respect him. He worked hard, never complained, and was grateful that he had a job. His pay was similar to mine, but he had to live on it. And I worried about my fifty cents! I pushed all summer to get him paid the same wages as the others. Because I was "da nephew," I knew that everyone thought I reported everything back to my uncle, so I had to be careful and work through the general manager. He didn't care. My uncle, as I have said, was tough. Finally I took it to my uncle, who refused to overrule his general manager.

At the end of the summer, on my last day, the former Vietnamese, now trying to become an American, came over to me and said in very broken English, "Thank you for being my friend." That phrase echoed in my mind for a long time, because I felt honored but also ashamed that I had failed to do anything for him, except like him. I hoped he had friends who could help him more than I could but was worried what the others he had encountered in his new American life must have been like if he considered me, who had done nothing for him, a friend.

Also on my last day, the old black foreman sought me out to say good-bye and pay me what I think was a compliment. He said, "You are all right with me. Even if you suck a mule's dick on the corner of State and Lake (a major downtown Chicago intersection), you will still be all right with me." I never knew if he was telling me that he knew I was gay and it was okay or that no matter how strange I seemed, he would still respect me. In any case, I figured by his remark that our worlds were even further apart than I had imagined.

20

Getting Ready for College

I returned that fall from my summer visit home where, as a senior, I geared up for the SAT and the college application process. I got the *Barron's* study guide and did practice tests for hours. When I went to take the SAT, I was so nervous I didn't even mind that Paulette insisted on taking me. I was even thankful she had brought with her extra number 2 lead pencils. This was it—the moment of truth. If I was going for a gold medal in my personal Olympics, this was the qualifying round. There were a lot of competitors out there.

The first time I took the test, my results were respectable but not as good as I hoped. I retook it, getting a better score. My initial results were good enough, however, so I knew I was in the running.

Back at Lab School, we had the usual fall art exhibition. I had always liked taking photos and wasn't bad, particularly with children and nature. I didn't know a lot about studio lighting, but with natural light I became reasonably proficient. That summer on the Vineyard, I shot a series on Vineyard life and entered several in the exhibit. One was of a naked little girl walking a dog on the beach. Another was of an old lady sitting in her rocker on her porch. I had been walking around near Alley's Store photographing and had passed her house one day. Her face fascinated me: so alive and so old New England with those eyes looking out from deep wrinkles and crevasses, thin with her blue veins showing through. I asked if I could take her picture and she let me take several. Then, in true Yankee fashion, she brought me a glass of lemonade.

I had one more in the exhibit of a spider's web covered with dew, glinting in the sun. Not particularly original, but it was not a bad shot and the colors behind the web, of muted tans and greens of the grasses drying out in the summer sun, were what made the picture as much as the flashes of light on the web itself. I won the Principal's Award—although it did occur to me to wonder if I won because I was good or because the principal lacked artistic judgment. Still, I wrote up my "achievement" in my college applications.

Like the rest of my class, I got the applications and worked over and over on my entry essay. I understood that I had to market myself just right. As Diana once put it to me later, when we were discussing the process, "No college wants kids showing up and committing suicide on their doorstep." I decided to write about how Dr. B. used his experiences in the concentration camps to create the Orthogenic School, thus turning an experience of evil in his own life into something useful not only to him but also to us. This indeed meant a lot to me. But it would be less than truthful to say that I was unaware that I was trying to demonstrate to the admissions committees that despite my having spent the beginning of my life at a place like the School, I was determined to build on my life and, from the ashes of my past, resurrect myself into a beautiful new phoenix. It was denotation versus connotation. I just hoped that they would like my essay and understand my point.

I had to type and retype the essays and application responses on each application. Thank God for White-out. With my straight A's except the one B-plus from English and my SAT scores I knew I had a fighting chance, provided I had brilliant recommendations and wrote a good essay. In the end, I decided on applying to Yale, Harvard, Wesleyan in Connecticut, and the University of Chicago. I figured that if worse came to worst, I would go to Chicago, where I could always try to transfer out if I wanted to get away. It was not a bad safety factor and I was virtually assured of getting in—both through the School and U-High. The university looked after its own. I wanted to get away, however, and begin life in a new world.

Chicago was far too close to home and to the bell jar from which I needed to escape.

I had my teachers' recommendations in order (Bert Cohler, out of the goodness of his heart, wrote me an incredible one), mailed off the applications, having gotten checks from my parents, and crossed my fingers as well as any other part of my body that I thought might help. This was it, my ticket for a different future from my past. I was trying to change worlds.

I went to talk to Bert who, despite my past behavior, was friendly with me. Having been to Harvard himself, he understood what I was up against. He arranged for me to be interviewed in Chicago by a Harvard alumnus who interviewed candidates on behalf of Harvard admissions. So I went. This guy took one look at me and my application, handed me a glass of wine, and said, "Look, officially I am supposed to tell you it doesn't matter whether I interview you or you go to be interviewed at Admissions. In your case, however, you are only twenty sides of paper in a folder somewhere. Given your background, if you really want to get in, you'd better go and let them know you have two arms, two legs, and one head like the rest of us." Funny thing, after talking to this guy and my father, Jacqui let me go. Harvard had a program that arranged visiting applicants to room with students. Yale did not, but that was not a problem, since Jeff Kampelman had told me that I could stay with him. Jacqui didn't like the idea of my arranging to stay with someone myself. She wanted me to go through the admissions office, but since Yale had no official program, I got to call Jeff. Even if there had been a program, I would have engineered it so that I could stay with him. I wanted to be with someone whom I knew.

One more thing. I was flying back to Chicago from LaGuardia and wanted to see Sy and his wife, Liz, who were now living in New York so Liz could attend NYU Medical School. Jacqui said no; I was going to see colleges, not visit relatives. Although it made no sense to go all that way and not see them, it wasn't worth arguing over.

I got myself ready, packed an overnight bag, and went to O'Hare. I was finally going to Harvard and Yale. True, it was only for interviews, but I knew that by being granted interviews, I had already won half the battle.

I was mindful of my father's story. He was from a small town in Upper Michigan and ended up going to high school in Neenah,

Wisconsin. A great athlete, he played both varsity basketball and tennis. It was 1945, and after high school he went into the army like everyone else. He applied to college from his army barracks, writing the dean of admissions at Harvard for an application. The dean replied there was no point in sending one: He would never get in. My father had a few strikes against him in addition to being from a small town in Wisconsin. He was from a public high school and, moreover, was a Jew, and this was the 1940s. The dean left a loophole. He wrote that if my father still wanted to apply, he should write an essay and send it back. If they judged it of suitable caliber, they would send him an application. Three weeks after sending in his essay, my father received his application in the mail. My father told me, "When I got that application, I knew I was in."

I felt similarly. They had agreed to see me—they already knew my grades, scores, recommendations, and that I had grown up as one of Bettelheim's kids. If I could just prove myself as a relatively sane human, I had a good chance. As we roared down the runway on my American Airlines flight to Boston, I was too excited to calculate my odds.

First stop was Harvard. I went to the admissions building and had a cup of coffee as I waited. It was a disappointing meeting. I remember at the time thinking that they didn't seem interested in me. There was confusion about my interview, and it seemed perfunctory. The person who saw me was polite in that way that busy people have when they think they are doing you a big favor but don't want you to notice, which was not what I expected. This was a big deal and I was a legacy, after all, since my father was class of 1950. After the interview, I had some time before going over to meet my hosts in the dorm. I think they put me up in Winthrop House, where my father had lived. I wandered around and ended up at the old gym, which had photos of all the varsity teams going back to the Stone Age. I found my dad's team. He was younger then than I was—and didn't look at all like I expected. Despite aging over the past forty-five years, to me he has always looked the same. So does my mother. Maybe that is because with the people you love, you really only just look at their souls. It was certainly true of Teddy. He was half Chinese and had blue-black hair, but I never really thought about it. He was just him.

My hosts were fun. What I remember most was sitting up late that night in the suite's bunk beds, talking about nothing into the early hours. In the morning I had to race to the train and take Amtrak down to New Haven. My Harvard experience had not been overwhelming.

From the train station in New Haven, I shared a taxi with a Yale divinity school student, who told me that admissions and the divinity school were in the same direction. They were, but the divinity school was farther away, which was our first stop. He handed me half the fare and I then went to the Office of Undergraduate Admissions. Even I, with my faulty sense of direction, could tell that the div student had just ripped me off for two bucks. Not an auspicious omen from a man of the cloth.

Barbara Bernardi, whom I would come to know well over the next few years, was the dean of admissions' secretary. Tall, thin, filled with patience, she always made me feel welcome and comfortable as soon as I saw her. She had seen so many of us hopefuls arrive over the years and knew just how to defuse the anxiety. I was taken in to meet Worth David. We talked for about thirty minutes back and forth. I guess he was reassured that I was unlikely to start drooling if admitted. To make sure that he hadn't missed anything, he had arranged for me to meet with the head of student mental health. My eyes must have shot up in alarm. "Dean David," I protested as quietly as I could, "I wish someone had informed me of this earlier. I understand that you need to know that I won't crack up on you. But by the same token, this puts me in a very tough position. Most applicants do not see your mental health department. Your psychiatrist can ask me anything he likes and I will be forced to answer, since if I don't, it will appear I have something to hide. But some things may be private that I do not wish to discuss with a stranger, particularly one who must enter them into a formal record for my admission file."

Dean David paused for a second and said that I didn't have to see the shrink if I didn't want to. He added that they had arranged the interview in case I had any questions to ask about campus life or the mental health department that I might feel more comfortable asking a doctor. Clearly, this was not a service extended to your run-of-the-mill candidate from Andover. Not having a choice, I said that I would be happy to see the psychiatrist because I had nothing to hide.

I have always believed that it was this dialogue that swung Dean David off the fence on my admission. I had objected courteously and politely, stated my case, which brought him round to seeing my concerns, and yet I went anyway, because I knew I had to do so. I don't think then I realized how much pressure was on Dean David to make a right decision, but my willingness to get vetted by the psychiatrist was a big point in my favor. At least they knew I had nothing to hide.

At the time and in retrospect, it was as good an interview as could be hoped. Dean David is an admirable man who tried to see underneath the surface of this young applicant in front of him, both to protect me and to protect Yale. He went out of his way to anticipate for me what I needed to know. Later I would visit him at least once a semester just to say hello and let him know both how grateful I was and that he hadn't made a mistake. After Yale, until he retired, I would go see him whenever I happened to be in New Haven.

He got me to see the shrink, so he was covered in case they did let me in. It was a good sign that they took my candidacy seriously enough to arrange my meeting with a psychiatrist. Otherwise, why bother? While at the time I was concerned about not getting in and/or being asked personal questions that I absolutely had to answer even if it was none of their business, the real pressure would be on the psychiatrist. If something untoward happened, someone was going to point a finger at him. If he didn't clear me, my parents and I might have questions. If he did and there were any problems later, he would be the one they would point to: "Well, he said it was okay."

I went to see the psychiatrist and haven't the slightest idea of what we discussed. Dean David, I am sure, must have communicated my concerns, since the questions were reasonable and completely within bounds. He did indeed advise me about the pressures and said they were manageable and that the aptly named DUH (Department of Undergraduate Health) had counselors available for students if I should feel the need to talk to someone. We finished the conversation and I went over to Jeff's room, trying not to tear out of student mental health like a bat out of hell. In contrast to Harvard, I felt good about this interview and the one with Dean David. Yale really cared about whether I went or not and went out of its way to determine if I would be able to fit in successfully.

Jeff lived in Morse, one of the two newer colleges built at Yale. The room was heated through the floors, so it was nice to get up in the winter and walk barefoot to the bathroom without freezing your feet. I ate in the dining hall, met some of Jeff's friends, and we ended up later in the evening at a local dive, which I would later come to know much better, drinking beer and eating popcorn.

Feeling so good about my day and my chances, I wanted to share it with somebody, so I called my Uncle Sy and arranged to meet him for lunch the next day before my flight. Getting him to make time for lunch wasn't usually easy, since he was a busy investigative reporter at *The New York Times*, but this was a special occasion. The crazy nephew was coming back from college interviews at Harvard and Yale. That was worth lunch and a good bottle of Frescati, easy.

I had never been to New York before and didn't know uptown from downtown or the West Side from the East. I had heard stories about Manhattan all of my life but had no idea of how it was laid out or how to get from a to b. I arrived at Penn Station, found my way out without getting mugged, and jumped into a taxi to Sy's house. He took me to a small Italian restaurant around the corner that I loved and would return to every chance I got for sentimental reasons until it closed. It was my first time eating out in the big city. Sy promised to get me to LaGuardia in time—I don't think he realized what concerns I had about missing that plane. I had no intention of telling Jacqui I had stopped off in Manhattan despite her command. Sy put me in a cab and off I went to finish up both the Orthogenic School and U-High.

My counselor David met my plane, which was a good thing for I had gone through most of the $200. I knew better than to say that I had gone to see Sy in Manhattan, but Jacqui somehow knew anyway. It was as if she had set it up that way. Although I hadn't planned on going in advance, it was obvious. She knew I was going and I knew I was going. If it was so obvious, why say no, except to show she could? She refused to speak to me at all rather pointedly. After a couple of weeks of this, which was both an unintended pleasure and a curse, I finally asked her why she still wasn't talking to me. She replied, "Since you obviously don't care what I say, why bother talking to you?" Once she had made that point, she started speaking to me again. At the risk of being sexist, it was such a female thing to do.

Two days after I returned, I got a "possible" from Harvard. In those days, sometime in February admissions staffs mailed applicants "likely," "possible," and "unlikely" cards. Very few people got "likelies," since getting one was tantamount to being admitted. You really had to screw things up after that not to get in, such as not graduating or getting arrested, but otherwise you were in the clear. The vast majority were "possibles," which only meant that you had appropriately selected your choices and hadn't been a fool about weighing your chances. There were very few "unlikelies," either, since most people had a shot, unless they just wanted to say they were applying to Harvard. Guidance counselors tried to prevent this. In other words, this formation represented a perfect bell curve. This also meant that Harvard had no intention of admitting me, for they had mailed out my "possible" card *before* they interviewed me. If seeing a kid from the Orthogenic School in the flesh meant no difference in the application, it could only mean one thing: They were going to say no anyway but wanted to show my father, an alumnus, and Bert Cohler, who was a Harvard Ph.D. and a fellow professor, they had made the good old college try.

My "possible" from Yale did not come for several weeks. I was hoping for a "likely." It was a long two months from the beginning of February to mid-April when the acceptance letters would go out. I had finals for winter quarter coming up at the end of March as well as my twenty-first birthday. My parents gave me an electric typewriter, which lasted me years, and I was thrilled with it. For my birthday activity, David took me to see a play I wanted to see, *The Belle of Amherst*, with Julie Harris. It was just the two of us; the others in my dorm were too little. A few days later Margaret took me downtown for a lobster and champagne dinner. I was now legal, not that it made much difference in my daily life, but I felt it inside. Legally I had the right to state what I wanted and how I wanted to live.

At U-High, the seniors still had a lot of work to do, but there was a lot of anticipation and anxiety. I again pulled straight A's, and it was known among my friends that I had gone to interviews at Harvard and Yale, which meant that I was a serious candidate. For most, it was just part of the competition of going to a private high school.

There were a couple, however, from whom I sensed some resentment, in part connected with the Orthogenic School. It was like, why is he interviewing there and taking a slot from me when he doesn't deserve it? Let the normal people get in; let's leave the crazies out. It was unsettling, to say the least.

Letter day arrived. I had already heard from the University of Chicago, where I had gotten in. At Lab School, some of the kids had gone home to check the mail several times, as did I. I went over and found that the mail hadn't been delivered. Next, I found out it had been delivered, but there was nothing for me. I went down to the kitchen and the maids made me lunch because they liked me and I didn't know where else to go. I went back to U-High and a number of people had gotten their acceptance letters, a couple from Yale. There were some sad faces, too, for those who had been rejected from their first choice. I returned across the Midway for the third time and asked in the office again if I had any mail. No, I did not. In desperation, I finally went up to the dorm for a few minutes of peace, since the other kids were still in class, before going back to U-High. There, on my bed, were some letters. David later said he put them there right away, thinking that's where I would go look first and where they would be safest. I drew a deep breath and figured that I would be able to live with the consequences of what was about to happen. Oh, but please, God, if you ever loved me, let it be now! I walked slowly to my bed and looked down. There were three envelopes: two little and one big. Two rejections and one yes. The big envelope had Yale University, Office of Undergraduate Admissions on it. YES! I was in! It had been worth it. I had, with this one small package, wiped the slate clean. I had been given the chance to change worlds. I knew what this meant! Now I had to open the envelopes. Harvard, no. Wesleyan, no. Yale—"The Admissions Committee is pleased to offer you a place in the Class of 1980." I sat down quietly, savoring the moment with tears in my eyes. Maybe I would be a success after all. It hit me how long it had taken for me to get to this juncture in my life and how many sacrifices Diana, Margaret, my parents, who had kept me in this school for thirteen years despite the horrendous expense, all the kids I had lived with, some of whom I had loved, and I had all made.

I also wanted to shout to some of my classmates across the Midway, Look at me, because I didn't feel like a second-class citizen any longer. If I had been smarter then, I would have known what Dr. B., Diana, Margaret, and Jacqui had been trying to get me to see all along. Yale was a great achievement but it didn't replace learning how to accept myself. I needed to respect myself because of what was inside of me, not where I went to college or what I did.

I went up front looking for Margaret. I wanted to share this with her first. She had been with me eleven years. She was in staff meeting so I got one of the office staff to get her out. I told her with a huge hug. She was pleased, too, since she was worried I was going to be bitterly disappointed. I called my parents to let them know. "Dad, I have some good news and some bad news. The good news is I got into Yale. The bad news is I am going."

Not missing a beat, my father replied, "Your mother and I are very proud of you, but you do realize, if you go, I will cut you off without a cent!" Spoken like a Harvard man. Then my mother got on the phone, very happy. "Oh, don't listen to him. You go where you want." It was a big moment for them, too. It had been a very long haul. I told my father I hadn't made it in to Harvard, but he already knew. As a courtesy, they had informed him a few days before. He had figured as a legacy, my best shot was Harvard, and, if I didn't get in there, I wouldn't get into Yale, either. Later I found out that my father wrote a letter to Harvard complaining that if I was good enough to get into Yale and Chicago, why not Harvard? He commented to them that in this new age of admissions (where Ivy admissions committees were trying to diversify classes and legacies were no longer, as they had once been, at the top of the list), he hoped being a legacy would not count against a student. That got their attention. Eventually, word came back that if I wanted to transfer to Harvard, there would be no problem about admitting me. I told my father they could go stuff it. Besides, I really wanted Yale, it had always been my first choice; they had wanted me, and that meant something. Quite a lot, actually.

U-High, when I returned, was in full buzz mode. None of the seniors was pretending to do anything else but discuss who got in where and who didn't. Mindful that I had won my gold medal, I did not want to rub it in to those who had been less lucky. Eventually, one of my friends asked me and I told them. Since the senior class was some ninety-six people, it took about five minutes for that piece of news to get around: "Orthogenic School Kid Makes Yale" read the verbal headline. Actually, in my class there were several Yale acceptances, several Harvard, two or three Princeton, and a collection of others. Our class had done well. Now I had to let this all sink in and graduate. And return to the School, where I would sleep that night in a dorm in the Adolescent Unit with six kids, four of whom were under twelve. A big reality dissonance.

My daily routines, such as they were, carried me along until graduation. Through everything, I carried the knowledge that I had beaten the odds.

In all the changes and joy in success, I had always had doubts about leaving Margaret, just when I would need her most as I transited from a kid at the School to someone living on my own back in the outside world. I was sorry that I hadn't left the previous year, because then I might have felt more ready to leave for New Haven in the fall. Daniel with his colostomy and Todd's death after they had left had scared me about what might happen. I was worried I might crack up on the outside or how I might cope. How healthy was I really now? What would happen if I were to get really upset about something? What was my sexual orientation? How would I fit into dorm life? Would my stomach trouble suddenly return to paralyze me?

I had heard horror stories all of my life from Dr. B. about what happened to kids after they left; some had relapses or never managed really to make it on their own. What he told us to scare us was not what he told the outside world. I had seen a number of them, none of whom I envied. Why was I going to be so different? Moreover, I would be totally on my own in New Haven.

I called Dean David to ask what would happen if I postponed for a year so that I could continue to see my therapist and take classes at the University of Chicago. Could I get credit at Yale for what I studied? Dean David said to go ahead and enroll in Chicago and we would try to work something out. I trusted him, so I did.

Two weeks later I received a formal letter from him on Yale stationery telling me that I had been granted permission to transfer into the Yale Class of 1980 with full credit for my year at the University of Chicago, provided that the trustees of the university approved a transfer program that year. I called him to ask what that meant and he explained that it was a formality; each year the trustees voted to approve a program allowing some students to transfer into Yale. He said he felt fairly certain there would be one next year. He wished me luck and said he looked forward to seeing me in New Haven the following year.[1]

21

Final Days

I was going first to Chicago. I had pangs about giving up my freshman year at Yale. It was a big sacrifice. The rest of my Yale class would have already undergone their bonding and being unsure of themselves together by the time I would arrive. Once more I would have to try to fit in with a crowd who had already gotten to know each other and already had a history. But for me, it was the only way I could go. Otherwise, the anxiety would have been too overwhelming. I was more scared than I could admit back then. I had to dampen my anxieties. Dr. B. had articulated this well in his classes.

Repeated clinging to a response typifies a neurosis. But it serves a purpose: to reduce anxieties. There is a difference between the purpose intended and the purpose served. The tragedy of neurotic behavior is not that it does not serve a purpose, but that it serves so ineffectively that it aggravates the situation and makes it worse. Anxiety prevents using the normal means most likely to succeed. With a relaxed mother, when we are relaxed we can think of many solutions, but when anxiety is high, it prevents us from finding an effective solution to reduce anxiety. The tragedy is the higher the anxiety the less the person is capable of solving it. One needs more ability to find a solution when anxious, but that is when one has less ability to cope. Neurosis comes out of anxiety. The greater the anxiety, the greater the neurosis. Analysis has the purpose of reducing the anxiety to manageable proportions. The basis of all mental disturbance except physiological causes is anxiety. The severity of the disturbance is the result of the severity of the anxiety.[1]

I felt freer to spend more time at the School, now that I knew I was finally getting out. I spent a lot of time with Teddy and Michael, slowly saying my good-byes, trying to impart whatever I could to help them for when I wasn't there. I knew they were in the best hands possible, Leslie's and Mary's, and there was nothing really I could do once I said good-bye. I was going to miss being part of their lives more than they would ever know. Roger and Sean had been my best friends for years now, and the idea of leaving them behind pained me. At Lab School, too, there was a sense of leave-taking among the senior class. We had already had our rites of passage and all that remained for us was to get our diplomas, say our good-byes, and move on to college.

Every year in May, Lab School celebrated the Rites of Spring, a fair to raise money for various school groups, such as the French club and the track team. There were rides, the machine where you throw a ball and, if you hit the bull's-eye, you dunk the guy sitting over the pool, fortune-tellers, booths for all kinds of foods and candy, and, in the grand finale, the high school would put on a play, whether Thornton Wilder or Shakespeare. I had gone to this fair since I was little, and seeing those plays had always been a high point of spring for most of my life. As this final one approached, it was bittersweet to be on the other side of something I had looked forward to for much of my life as an "outside" moment from the School; this time I was on the other side as a participant helping to raise money. One of the girls from the Orthogenic School, who was at Lab School with me, had a starring role in the play.

U-High graduation rolled around. My life was pretty much a blur. My parents came; so did Diana and Margaret. To be in caps and gowns in a graduation ceremony in Rockefeller Chapel seemed surreal, since the chapel was a scene from much in my life, where I had been going from age eight both for vespers and to play in the building's halls and on the lawns surrounding it. After the ceremony I didn't get to spend much time with Diana, who brought me a fountain pen that I still keep as a memento on my desk. The staff chose for me a sterling silver letter opener, which still sits in my living room although I have hardly ever used it. There was no subtlety there, since I had insisted that I open my college replies myself, instead of having David or Paulette do it, as they did everything else. It had been a long fight over the past couple of years. The gift was symbolic of all the ambivalence in my life—on one hand, it was a thoughtful gift commemorating my achievements; on the other, it was a reminder of how much I had been denied.

My parents took me to a celebratory dinner and then drove me back to the School where they would come and pick me up the following week for the last time.

I slowly started packing. Jacqui was clearly different with me and had been for a while, dating back to my Yale acceptance. I was no longer in her sphere of influence. To her credit, she was gracious about letting me go. I had had so many conflicts with her over the years, but that didn't obscure the many good things she did on my behalf. I remain fond of her after all this time for all the good deeds she did and for the help she rendered during the last few years of Margaret's life, when Jacqui managed her financial affairs, as Margaret was no longer capable of doing so.

I minded that she and the rest of the staff had so much trouble figuring out how to deal with me as a young adult. I also disliked the slow disintegration of the School. In the end, Jacqui had her own resentments against Dr. B. She ran the School until her retirement. During that time, when I came back to visit once in a while, I always pressed her and the assistant director who served under her to keep the research going and publish. They did not. Jacqui wrote one small book[2] during her tenure, but it was not a work that received the kind of commentary and notice that Dr. B.'s did. She was not cut from the same cloth. Whatever her vision was, it was derivative at best, and the School did not continue advancing knowledge. For whatever her reasons, her impact on the School, which clearly had to change after Dr. B. if it were to survive, was to destroy much of the vestiges of Dr. B., except the loveliness of the buildings themselves, which remain until this day. In time, the School would separate from the university, have its endowment given to a board of directors, and go its own way. The university was pleased to see it go—a foolish decision—because it was worried about the ongoing expenses of operating the School and the fact that the university's mission was as a research institution, not a treatment one. The university had also phased out its clinical psychology program for the same reason. For many years, under Dr. B., the School had been the source of a series of acclaimed books, and Dr. B., with his writings and speeches, including a role in Woody Allen's movie *Zelig*, was one of its most famous professors. The university had reaped the benefits for a long time, and now, in letting the School go, it seemed to exhibit the worst of the business world ethics, the what-have-you-done-for-me-lately syndrome.

The School separated, I understand, without a mission statement or a written charter stating how it was to be run, what the endowment was to be used for, and any underlying principles for future operations. I am told that instead of being a place dedicated to understanding childhood problems and respecting a children's symptoms as being their highest form of expression given how they saw the world, the School is now focusing more on behavior modification. There has been no research that I have seen coming out of it, and it is often a high-priced holding tank funded in part by the State of Illinois for problem children that it doesn't know what else to do with. Due to its high operating expenses, the School needs to take these children to pay overhead. In the old days, there was a waiting list to get in from enlightened parents and social agencies that wanted the best for their children. So much opportunity has been wasted. Also, the world has changed. We now live in an era that seeks quick solutions, a pill here, a limited number of sessions there. "Managed care" doesn't believe in funding long-term psychiatric care.

I have long wondered why Dr. B., a master of reading others and seeing, if not straight to the heart of a matter, at least to the questions that would eventually uncover the underlying psychic motivation, failed to read the hearts of his chosen successors. How could he have left his legacy in their hands, not to mention my life?

Alas, the story is as old as the Bible and it is the tale of fathers and sons, whether they are actual progeny or children of the mind. For Dr. B., Bert was one of his kids who had made good. As for Jacqui, she had learned from Dr. B.'s knee, as it were, coming to the School as a young girl from Radcliffe to start life as a counselor and eventually working her way up to being assistant director prior to her departure to get married.

In one of Dr. B.'s classes, he made an offhand comment that I noted which perhaps presaged some of these events. Of course, this observation may have been only coincidental.

> *While Freud was the inventor of analysis, he also was a beginner and made beginner's errors. Freud paid a high price for this by having his early disciples turn against him. They didn't like being taken for a ride by having themselves be analyzed by Freud who was trying to make good analysts out of them. Jung didn't want to be groomed for succession, so he retaliated by turning against Freud.*[3]

There is one possibility that maybe, somewhere, so deeply hidden that he himself had no clue, Dr. B. wanted the School to fail without him. A failure would prove to the world that such a grand enterprise could succeed only with him at the helm—there was no one else who could have done what he did. His greatness would be without question, since only he could have achieved it. I do not believe this. Could such a thought have flitted through the silent recesses of his mind? Probably; he was human and had been subjected to numerous insults from the psychiatric establishment, but in the end, he valued light over darkness. The School was his monument against the Nazis and all that they had done to destroy his life and the world he had known in Vienna so long ago. His suicide, finally, on March 13, 1990, the anniversary of the Nazis' entering into Vienna, seems as powerful a statement as any that he spent his life battling history and his enemy. I do not believe that he wished to destroy the School, even to make himself seem greater. He was never shallow.

For a long time I believed that his suicide in his mid-eighties, after suffering his wife's death and a stroke, was an affirmation that he wished to live life only on his own terms. He was playing his hand from the cards that he had been dealt. When he could no longer play on his own terms, he decided to exert what remaining control he had over his life and end it. However, looking at the date of his death, the state of his life at the time, and the situation of the School, I now wonder whether his death was a final cry of desperation, for despite all he had done, his life's work was fading as was his memory and one man could do only so much. In the final analysis, his work was not enough to change the world in the way he envisioned. It was, however, enough for me.

Why, I have asked myself a thousand times, didn't he develop a group of successors, or at least one, suitable, sage, and capable? Yet, as I have also seen on Wall Street, this is not a problem limited to Dr. B. The succession problems of strong, talented chief executive officers who fail, even when forced by their boards of directors, to have an appropriate successor are well known. Often those CEOs manage to sabotage their own arranged succession. Emperors of any sort do not go quietly into the night. Maybe it is primal, this knowledge that there is only a true successor when the chant begins, "The king is dead, long live the king." A child, spiritual or otherwise, seems to offer some protection from that death, at least more than a stranger would, although history is replete with examples of sons and heirs putting the lie to that theorem. Perhaps it all comes down to the Woody Allen line: We don't want to achieve immortality through our work; we want to achieve it by not dying. Maybe Dr. B. hoped he could live on through his chosen successors, but it was a vain hope, which reverberated in my life and the lives of all of us at the School forever after.

As for my own impending parting, while I was sad about leaving the School, I would be in the neighborhood for another year yet and knew I would see people from time to time. I would return to the School twice a week to see Margaret. The new kids who came after me could look at me and wonder, as I had once done, whether they would grow up to be like this strange guy wandering over for sessions.

Looking back, I hope I conveyed the sense of adventure we all had together. For all the bad times, in a strange way my years at the School were some of the sanest of my life. One of the worst things one could do in our world was to lie. We were a community with a common purpose, dedicated to truth and to helping each other to overcome the personal obstacles that made us miserable and interfered with us having any form of normal life. Our world was greater than the sum of its parts. The troublemakers or criminals in our little world were understood and not often judged. Amid all the difficulties and backbreaking work, there was real joy and satisfaction in doing something that mattered for oneself and for others. We had a sense of adventure and of belonging to a great work in progress. On my own, I would still move forward (like the shark, perhaps), but I wasn't so egotistical to think that such personal forward momentum constituted great enterprise.

As I settled down at the School during my time there and slowly stopped looking at the world only from the vantage point of my emotional issues, the joys grew, since I could understand the structure and purpose of the School's world. The problem came as I began to grow and became more independent. The further from being an actual child I became, the harder it was for the School to give me what I needed. I really didn't need the School that last year or two; I just didn't know it at the time and had no way to make an educated decision. I had to trust what I was being told, despite how hard I fought against it, because that was all I had.[4]

The final day arrived. My worldly goods were packed up in many more boxes than when I had first arrived. I was stepping out into a different world from the one I had left—the assassinations of the 1960s and the Vietnam War had ended the vestiges of the 1950s' sensibility, and the pill and women's liberation were changing mores and culture around the world. I had entered the world smack in the middle of the baby boom, and here I was leaving the School to reenter my place with all the other fish swimming around the vast ocean for a bit longer, before most of us would head back upstream to the world where we were spawned, to have families and begin the cycle once more. For me, I could never go back up the river from where I had come because I had changed beyond recognition from what my family knew in ways they didn't see. The School was like the village in the film *Brigadoon*, coming once every hundred years, so if you left, you could never return. I would be forced to find not only my own way upstream but also my own stream. I had been granted choice, not deliberately but by fate, and for all its freedom, it was to be a lonelier life than I had expected. I have long had the sense of being a time traveler, touching down in so many distant lands, having so many backgrounds that have gone into who I am, none of which is truly my own. Like the lone postman making his rounds, I have been the only common link between the people from these different worlds—none of whom had any knowledge about the others except from me.

With its Freudian-based principles, the School believed that health and sanity required a happy family life and being a success at one's life's work. For many of the girls I grew up with, their highest achievement was to be a good mother to their children, thus breaking the cycle that brought them to the Orthogenic School. Dr. B. always said it took three generations for one of us to arrive at the School, the first to create problems in their children, who then married and passed on the problems of the first generation plus a few more of their own, which gave us all each other. Part of my struggle after I left was that I had a hard time facing the fact that I was never going to swim upstream to spawn like everyone else. Most gay men don't. I was so thoroughly inculcated in the ethos of the School that it took me a long time to realize that I was not a failure because of that.

The last day I dressed in a sports coat and tie after I had finished packing. David was helping and went to the last drawer where I had hidden my deodorant. It fell out when he pulled out the crumpled pajamas I had worn the night before. I had figured no one was going to look there (and they never did). David had taken the PJs to put them in my suitcase, the same gray one with the nail polish stain I had brought with me thirteen years before. There was a clatter and out fell the stick of deodorant. He just smiled and asked how long I'd kept that hidden. When I told him years, he gave me this attempt at a wounded look, then we both began to laugh at what a bizarre life it sometimes was. Despite the battles, I had great affection for him. He went on to be a good counselor for the kids and later, back in England, continued his work with children and education.

I walked into the big classroom that had once been mine, with its multicolored radiators still brightening the formality of the Greek columns and friezes that we had painted with John while dipping Oreos into the paint. The entire School was seated in a big semicircle and there, near the door, was the seat of honor where I would sit. Mindful of my extravagant tastes—my father's nickname for me, the dauphin, had been well earned—the staff had ordered a tableful of canapés from Gaper's Caterers, then one of the best in Chicago. Jacqui stood in front of the assemblage and said a few words of introduction, telling everyone that I had been accepted at Yale and had deferred a year to see Margaret, which showed, she said, how far I had come since I knew what I needed and could balance my wish to move into the world at large with my more immediate personal needs.

It was time to make my valedictory. After all the times that I had imagined what I would say and how I would say it, I got up and faced everyone just before my life was to be sundered from theirs forever, the people who would understand me better perhaps than anyone else has ever done, the ones who were now going through what I had before, some who would go on to glory and some who would need custodial care for the rest of their lives; my voice cracked.

All I could say as I looked around at these faces was "Thank you for making this my home." My voice choked up, I who hadn't cried in public since I was twelve, Dr. B. having inadvertently taught me well to hold it in until I could find someplace private. I stood and faced them all for a few seconds more, drinking in the sight of these faces in a look that I thought I would remember forever. Alas, it has faded, too, as with so much else in the march of time. I went to sit down and Jacqui handed me the gift selected for me as one of the customs of the leaving ceremony. It was a heavy and huge lavishly wrapped and beribboned book of Renaissance art. Then the kids who had shared my life for however long they had been at the School, since by now I had been there almost longest of all, came to bid me farewell. Except for Jacqui and Margaret, and one or two kids, there was no one there to remember that skinny kid with the bright blue eyes and the big mouth. Whatever I had been had vanished into what I had become. By the standards of our little world, I had more than done well: I had earned respect, and it seemed as if I had conquered as much as Alexander in the context of our lives. I don't think that any of us envisioned at that time how much longer it would take me to truly come into my own, and if I do not truly always like who I see in the mirror, at least I no longer dislike him. The balance that eluded me all of my life was finally achieved after my midlife crisis in my forties. Since, however, my midlife crisis probably began when I was twelve, perhaps it is a lesser achievement.

Leslie was one of the first, leading Teddy by the hand. We hugged and then I picked up Teddy and held him tight for the last time before I crossed over into his past. He understood and said, "Goodbye, Teeb." He smiled at me and then wandered away. There have been very few days since then that I have not thought of him at one time or another.

Like a reverse Noah, leaving behind his ark that had long provided refuge from the rains and floods outside, one by one they came to say good-bye. I was too overwhelmed to remember much. Mary Margaret, Julie, the Mohawks, Roger, Sean, Timothy, and the others, Leslie's kids, the little ones from my group, Michael, and Mary's other kids all came to wish me well. The other staff came, too, and then it was time. Jacqui held open the door as I turned to wave, and the voices that had over the years shouted for so many others now shouted for me and called out a chorus of good-bye. As the door swung shut behind me, at that moment the Orthogenic School became a moment of history for me, as it had for so many others before me. I walked up front to meet my parents, all of us somewhat nervous because now it would just be us together as a family once more after so long an interruption. We walked out of the bright yellow door at 1365 East 60th Street. David helped my father and me load up the station wagon.

Then we drove off, back to the outside world.

NOTES

Prologue

1. Jacqui informed me before she sent me the records that she had gone through them, removing those discussions pertaining to the staffs' personal issues. Indeed, every page sent has been initialed by her in the corner—it must have taken her days to go through the records, since the complete dossier sent comes to over a thousand pages. However, after thirteen years of reporting, that is just a portion of the record that existed when I left the School. It was explained to me that once Dr. B. left, dictation virtually ceased, although staff still made written reports about important issues or in preparation for the outside consultants who would conduct staff meetings on each child about twice a year. Thus, very little recording of actual events during either of Dr. B.'s successors was available. Why Jacqui felt it necessary to go through the records so carefully and why she spent the time to do so is an open question. I had requested that any records not sent be destroyed, thus only Jacqui knows what was in them. However, while the early records from Dr. B.'s era are on target and report life as I remember it, allowing for the distortions with which I saw the world at that time, all the later reports do not seem to recount my world nearly as closely. While the staff's opinions are based on my actual actions and activities, therapy is an interpretive art. Reason and motivation have to be inferred from actual events. It is the interpretations and motives that I question. Moreover, these years after Dr. B.'s death were a period of great public controversy about Dr. B. and the School. It is my belief that Jacqui wished to protect the institution.

In addition to the actual reports taken by the staff, there were a series of monthly notes written for each child by their counselors, teacher, and therapist that were sent over Dr. B.'s signature to parents and called by all of us, not too surprisingly, "monthlies." Thus, each month, the only contact my parents would have with me was a two-page letter describing the major events of my life. These monthlies are not nearly as useful to me as historical documents as the actual staff dictation, since I saw them as carefully crafted instruments of propaganda, used to reassure parents that their kids were progressing and to give them some knowledge of their children's lives as well as to encourage parents to keep their children enrolled at the School. At the same time, our confidences were protected to best of the staff's ability, so that parents were not given information that they could use or misuse in any way. In fact, my parents never once, in the entire time I was at the School, mentioned anything they had learned from a monthly to me.

Finally, in my files I found a notebook with my notes from two of Dr. B.'s University of Chicago classes given in the spring quarters of 1974 and 1975, respectively. His lectures reflect his mind and observations and are not all that different from what he discussed with the children of the School in his once-a-week meeting with us (the three o'clock meeting).

1. Setting the Stage

1. Bruno Bettelheim, "The Problem of the Beautiful in Nature and Modern Aesthetics" ("Das Problem des Naturschönen und die moderne Aesthetik"), 1938.
2. Bruno Bettelheim, "Individual and Mass Behavior in Extreme Situations," *Journal of Abnormal and Social Psychology*, October 1943.

2. Some Additional Backstory

1. "He wanted to know why castration makes an ox a better work animal. I asked him what he thought and he said that maybe the animal is no longer afraid because the worst has already happened."

—Transcribed dictation, Julie Neumann Dunn, June 10, 1967

2. "The boy gives evidence of assets, emotional and intellectual: but scattered, unintegrated. Dynamically, the evidence points to insecurity centered in his thoughts about the mother; with anxiety severe enough to indicate an early trauma, from the pain in which he fled into his fantasy world; and there became fixated. The pathogenic processes have already progressed ominously; but the residual assets warrant the effort at reversing the present malignant course.

"The severity of this arrest is most obvious in his fantasy activity, a primitive inner world into which he must have very early retreated and which now dominates his character structure. In quality it is essentially all infantile, archaic; at times dream material; in moments an Alice in Wonderland world. Quantity is very high for his age; evidence of the important recourse it is for him; and also the disproportionately high amount of mental activity which he diverts into this sphere. The much energy which he invests in these associations testifies to the strong feelings with which he lives this inner world; and whether he always distinguishes these moments from reality is questionable. Judged as quantity alone this imagination could, in a healthy child, be an asset. In this boy, the themes, like the structure, are largely regressive, symptomatic: i.e., aggressions; paranoid; insecurity. . . .

"The picture as a whole thus shows spots of growth, signs of ability, scattered within a personality matrix that has early become set in an ungrown state.

"The essence of this boy's present structure is a lack of purpose and self-direction, signs that these are of a defective ego state. Seen in the light of the deep and much introversion, this process has progressed to pathologic degree; is essentially schizophrenia; and yet in a transitional stage. In view of the grip on reality which he does achieve, even though this breaks down, and more especially in view of his outgoing emotional trait, a treatment program looking toward reversing the present serious outlook is strongly indicated. It is bound to be [a] long-drawn-out program, with the results from these test findings, uncertain. The boy has assets, the salvaging of which is challenge that he presents."

—Samuel J. Beck, Ph.D., and Anne G. Beck, M.A., Test Results, February 23, 1963

3. *The Initial Cast*

1. "Initially Steve packed his things away with great neatness and exactness and I offered to help and he said I could if I wanted to under his direction. Everything had to have a very particular drawer and he did not bring all of his things but just about what you would take to camp for three weeks, summer clothes, a summer jacket, three great big fat books, hardly any toys, a fancy camera, a tiny checker set that you get from a vending machine. . . . He kept trying to dash out. Two or three times he tried to dash to the fire doors, which had been a game between he and Ugo when he visited and he continued to do this. He said he forgot something in the car. What did he forget? Well, he always forgets something. Then he admitted he wanted to say good-bye to his parents again and we told him that no, that wasn't a good idea and to stay. A little bit later he said something about jumping out the window.

"He presents a very self-assured, needing-nothing exterior and he is not looking for approval in contrast to Daniel [who was to be my chief rival in the dorm] who very much wanted to succeed here. Steve does not care. Along with his self-destructiveness and his suicidal statements about jumping out the window, there is a very terrible desperation about this little kid. He is quite a braggart, and everything that we introduce to him or give to him he has had fourteen of them or he had a million or his neighbor had some."

—Transcribed Dictation, Diana Grossman Kahn, July 8, 1963

2. "After the short party we had at three o'clock Steve asked, while lying on his bed on his stomach with his back to the dormitory and face to the wall, 'Close the curtains' because the sun was on his bed and he was rubbing up against the bedspread and holding his penis and he told me to come over and said he felt sick. I went over and sat down next to him and said, 'Well, what can we do to help you feel better?' He said, 'Aspirin' and I said no, that this was probably the hardest time of his life. That was presumptuous of me but I meant that it was hard and of course this is strange to him, this new place. . . .

—Transcribed Dictation, Diana Grossman Kahn, July 8, 1963

3. "At one point Francis came over and I exchanged one short sentence with him and Steve jumped off the bed and gave me the minutest pinch on the arm. . . . I apologized for taking my attention away from him but told him that he is to touch neither the counselors nor the kids that he has to keep his hands off."

—Transcribed Dictation, Diana Grossman Kahn, July 8, 1963

4. "As we were walking back to dinner, he kind of cuddled against my side and

took my arm. He put his arm on my stomach and said, 'You look like you are pregnant.' This was great news to me so I said, 'No, I am not.' Then he asked if I was married and I said no and, as we walked into the dining room, he said, 'My mom is pregnant like this' and indicated a huge protrusion in the stomach. 'It looks like she is going to have twenty babies,' he said. 'Oh,' I said as he dramatically wandered back into his seat."

—Transcribed Dictation, Diana Grossman Kahn, July 8 1963

5. Lecture Notes from "Understanding Human Behavior," Psychology 251, Bruno Bettelheim, University of Chicago, transcribed by Stephen Eliot, April 15, 1974.

6. "At the end of the game he said something about him not being a cheater and he declared [it] with a certain pride but also a certain embarrassment and ambivalence. But I am sure it is clear to him that at some levels he cheats like mad and he is very inventive in his cheating but he is a complete cheater."

—Transcribed Dictation, Diana Grossman Kahn, July 8, 1963

7. "[He] started to tell another story and it was strange each time I fetched him up, most kids would smolder in silent resentment after being squelched so thoroughly and repeatedly but he immediately started another story. But this story, to my relief, was about a girl who was trying to cross the street on a tricycle but the signal didn't work, so she just rode up over the rainbow across the street. He said proudly that he made it up."

—Transcribed Dictation, Diana Grossman Kahn, July 9, 1963

8. "In the morning I discovered that he was playing dead or putting one over all the while, but he seemed to be deeply asleep and I never caught him opening his eyes and I let him sleep until eight and then I opened the curtains and tried to wake him by talking and I still was fooled and thought that he was still asleep and then I touched him gently and he would not wake up and then I finally got the idea that nobody could be sleeping that soundly. . . . Francis was in the middle of dressing and I went over to dress Francis and this finally roused Steve. I had gotten out his clothes under his direction and he had suddenly stood bolt upright in bed and said he would have all his clothes on before I put on Francis's shoes and socks which was all I had left to do. And he raced and put it on very quickly as he had left his underwear on the night before under his pajamas so he got everything on very quickly until he came to his shoes and socks when he stopped suddenly. I asked why and he said that he had suddenly discovered that he had silk socks and he couldn't put them on in a hurry. That was not true, they were brand-new cotton socks, and then he wanted to wear his thongs."

—Transcribed Dictation, Diana Grossman Kahn, July 9, 1963

9. "I told him that . . . he was a smart boy and this is something that I have told him from time to time. About once a day, there is some provocation for me to say that he is a smart boy and he is always visibly relieved and impressed and, at the same time, he thinks he is smarter than everybody. He thinks he is not smart from this reaction. I told him that I knew that he was a smart boy and he said was he smarter than Francis? I said that Francis, too, was a smart boy but he had difficulty but he certainly behaved a whole lot better than Francis in lots of ways in that he didn't do many of the things, many of Francis's symptoms. He was able to do some things that Francis couldn't do. Later on in the day, when Francis was being yelled at by Daniel, Steve took the opportunity to get back at Daniel and to please me by saying to Daniel about Francis, 'You shouldn't yell at him. He has problems like the rest of us. He's here because he's got problems, not because he likes it.' That is an

indication of Steve's attitude. We had a staff meeting about him and there has been remarkable and marked change since last night and since, I think, today. He has suddenly decided to stop grieving and carrying on and telling us how much he doesn't like it here constantly. This statement about Francis has to do with his own rationalization at this point, which is he will stay but he won't admit or give in to something that he likes it. He is here because he has problems and there was a kind of atmosphere in this statement like 'We are sick, we are sick, we are mentally sick,' like a song, 'Poor me, I'm mentally ill, therefore I have to have what I want.'"

—Transcribed Dictation, Diana Grossman Kahn, July 12, 1963

10. "Steve was saying to me while I was sitting on his bed 'Throw me out the window, I'm going to jump out the window.' We have already had conversations about the window, that is less and less so but in the beginning, he was going to jump out of the window and I hold on to him at such times and say that I won't let him and the windows are locked. Also, in the Side Yard, he will say, 'I'm going to commit suicide. I'm going to hurt myself and you can't stop me.' I just hold him firmly and tell him that I certainly will stop him. That seems to [do it], not the talking, but the holding on to him. I think it's because I'm bigger and it seems as if I could stop him is reassurance. When he told me to throw him out of the window, I took him on my lap and held him and it seemed to be exactly what he wanted so much so. It seemed to me that his telling me to throw him out of the window was simply an invitation to do the opposite; that he couldn't bring himself to initiate but that he wanted me to. He sat on my lap for a while and then he asked if he could ask Paul to play with him and he went and played with Paul."

—Transcribed Dictation, Diana Grossman Kahn, July 14, 1963

4. *Luitgard's Class*

1. Bruno Bettelheim, Monthly Parent Letter, June 5, 1964.
2. Bruno Bettelheim, Monthly Parent Letter, November 30, 1964.

5. *Settling In to the Mohawks*

1. "Immediately after Steve has been reprimanded or [told] to stop doing something or to be quiet or not run or not push ahead of everybody, he doesn't wait half a second and immediately asks some question like 'Where do turtles live in the winter?', something which I cannot connect to the previous conversation. But the function of the question seems to be either to distract my attention from my anger, whatever way I have been admonishing him or bawling him out, or else to reestablish contact and to make sure I am still his friend even though I am bawling him out.

"Also, I think it is an attempt on his part not to think, not to let his mind dwell upon his misdemeanor. . . . Because I think that if he lets himself feel that he has done something bad, he becomes flooded with feelings of being no good and this is an attempt not to let it sink in. I guess it is also an indication that I shouldn't get angry at him and I should just stop him from doing things and not make him feel guilty. He cheats but, at the same time, he cannot be permitted to hurt himself, to run, to touch or destroy other kids toys. The things that I call him on, he can't do, usually not my personal humor, but I think that there is something in between that

I can take a firm stand against delinquency but at the same time not come down on him too strongly—so that the feeling of badness is too much for him to tolerate."

—Transcribed Dictation, Diana Grossman Kahn, August 29, 1963

2. "At snacks, Steve complained that nobody played with him and he was sitting in my lap. . . . It was clearly a case that they were all playing together and I have seen it so many times I could tell exactly what had happened. That Steve has the rocket ships take off without the other kids in it. That is that he gets carried away with his own fantasies and also there were monsters and dinosaurs and Steve suggested that we kill off (that is, they kill off) the grown dinosaurs and leave the baby dinosaurs in a nice way. But, at any rate, the other kids didn't like it so that there is no compromise; he wants everybody to do what he tells them. He wants to run the game. So I said well that was very unfair of them not to listen to you, with some irony, because Steve is very upset about the kids not playing with him; however he does not wish to change his behavior one iota. What he wants is for everybody else to change and to enjoy what he puts out and that just ain't possible, because no kid would enjoy playing with him under the circumstances, at least in a fantasy game, that he puts out. He gets carried away and is completely heedless of anybody else. Steve said I was being nasty. I don't think I was being nasty. I think I was speaking the truth but he ain't ready to do anything and I don't know. He ain't ready to change his ways and my being critical of him, that is, accepting of the other boys' unwillingness to be bossed around by him, doesn't take him any place different from where he is."

—Transcribed Dictation, Diana Grossman Kahn, October 27, 1963

3. "It was his need to be close to his mother and to get something from females and that a child when he is young goes back and forth in his identifications and Steve's interest in big girls and women is a desire to get close and get something rather than to grow up and be that."

—Transcribed Dictation, Diana Grossman Kahn, Staff Meeting with Dr. Perkins, September 4, 1963

4. "He also wanted to know who determines whether Dr. B. continues here. Who would take over when Dr. B. left? Perkins replied that he thought that Dr. B. could stay here as head of the Orthogenic School as long as he liked. I don't know whether it was Steve that said that he guessed Dr. B. would work here until he died or whether it was Dr. Perkins who wondered if Steve was concerned with Dr. B.'s death because this is the middle of Dr. B.'s vacation absence."

—Transcribed Dictation, Diana Grossman Kahn, Staff Meeting with Dr. Perkins, September 4, 1963

5. "Incidentally, some time in the past two days, Steve has come up to me and put his arms around me, which he often does but has said, in a real low voice so I can hardly catch it. I think he said, 'My Diana.'"

—Transcribed Dictation, Diana Grossman Kahn, September 9, 1963

6. "I [Margaret] said, 'I think that if you want a visit, you should ask Dr. B.' Steve said, 'Well I do, but I am afraid. I am afraid Dr. B. would get angry at me.' I said, 'Why should he get angry if you know what you want and why you want it?' He told me that he was more afraid of Dr. B.'s words than of being hit. Because words go deeper and hurt more."

—Transcribed Dictation, Margaret Carey, August 8, 1966

7. Lecture Notes, "Understanding Human Behavior," Psychology 251, Bruno Bettelheim, University of Chicago, transcribed by Stephen Eliot, May 22, 1974.

8. "[Steve said that] Dr. B. is much better because he doesn't say things so flatfootedly. He says them with a twinkle in his eye."

—Transcribed Dictation, Margaret Carey, August 15, 1966

9. "Since I had told him that Ugo and I do not mate, he thinks that his rival must be elsewhere. So who else but the big boss, Dr. B.? This interpretation could make his fear a logical part of it because if he is scared that I am going to make him mate with me or if he has some fantasies that he is all too conscious of for his own comfort, and it is this particular fantasy which he thinks that Dr. B. would punish him so much for, then Dr. B. is the father and the rival—and he will not tolerate such fantasies."

—Transcribed Dictation, Diana Grossman Kahn, November 12, 1963

10. "The first thing he talked about was a 'bazooka' in his drawer. He explained that the bazooka was this scroll of Jewish writing inside of a little container that Jewish people put on their doors (mezuzah). I though it was interesting that he mispronounced it into something that shoots."

—Transcribed Dictation, Diana Grossman Kahn, October 24, 1964

11. "Steve spends about 45 minutes in the bathtub, comes out with his beach ball filled with water. He buries himself under his covers with it and comes out and tells me that he has been sticking his penis into it. Why does his penis get hard and stick out? he wonders. I don't think I answered that as he was going on. Supposing he started a baby in the ball, he continued, and in 9 months if it was a girl, would it have to go to the girls' floor or could he keep it with him? What would he do with it? I asked. He said, take care of it. I say that couldn't happen. How come? he asks. I say it never has, excepting I think that somewhere in this Steve has picked up the message of Christmas of the virgin birth and if Mary could do it, why can't Steve do it?

"He says, God is the father. I say well he would be the mother. He says that he would, except that he is a boy, so it would have to be a boy-mother. (I responded nonverbally, he just went on about this, but emotionally I guess I responded as if it was just the most natural thing in the world that God is his co-pilot and he is a boy-mother.)"

—Transcribed Dictation, Diana Grossman Kahn, January 2, 1964

6. *The Stage*

1. The essay appears in Bruno Bettelheim, *A Home for the Heart* (New York: Alfred A. Knopf, 1974), following p. 178, Plate 1.

7. *On Dr. B.*

1. Lecture Notes, Education 331, Bruno Bettelheim, University of Chicago, transcribed by Stephen Eliot, April 8, 1975.

2. Lecture Notes, Education 331, Bruno Bettelheim, University of Chicago, transcribed by Stephen Eliot, April 1, 1975.

3. Bruno Bettelheim, Monthly Parent Letter, February 22, 1965.

4. Lecture Notes, "Understanding Human Behavior," Psychology 251, Bruno Bettelheim, University of Chicago, transcribed by Stephen Eliot, April 1, 1974.

5. Lecture Notes, Education 331, Bruno Bettelheim, University of Chicago, transcribed by Stephen Eliot, May 27, 1975.

8. The Middle Period with Diana

1. "I took Steve to the lounge to tell him [he was going on a visit]. He was worried that it was a bad time for him to go on a visit and he really felt like he couldn't go because it was such a bad time. Why is it a bad time? I ask. He says, because you, Diana, have been yelling at me so much lately. In other words, it's true, as I've been dictating here, I have certainly been down on him because I have been swamped with his reaction to my vacation, which has lasted already two and half months, and his fears of rejection and all this and his rejecting me back and all this I haven't weathered very well. So what he's saying is how can I go home and you're throwing me to the lions if I don't have your full love and support and you send me home."

—Transcribed Dictation, Diana Grossman Kahn, November 19, 1966

2. "I began sessions with Steve. . . . It was difficult for me at first to take notes on Steve and it wasn't until some time that I realized there is so much and it is so facile and so clever that I think I almost felt overwhelmed."

—Transcribed Dictation, Margaret Carey, March 14, 1966

3. "He played almost constantly with the dollhouse. He had a very mean, utterly selfish, depriving woman, who he said was me, who simply herded the children, banged them around, everything for her own convenience. She even milked the cow and then threw the milk on the ground so that the boy wouldn't have any. The mother was not mean to the children, she was just somewhat indifferent. She fed them and she talked nicely to them, but the minute she could get away, she would dance and admire herself. There is a little baby doll dressed in baby clothes, which he makes into a fairy that has lived for two thousand years. The fairy is a kind of center of attention and preens and prides herself and shows herself off. There is no impression of good or bad, but she doesn't rescue any of the children on anybody's side."

—Transcribed Dictation, Margaret Carey, March 25, 1966

4. Lecture Notes, Education 331, Bruno Bettelheim, University of Chicago, transcribed by Stephen Eliot, May 5, 1975.

9. The New, Improved Mohawks

1. "I [Margaret] said, 'What do you want from sessions?' He was quiet for a time and then he said, 'That is a hard question. I don't know how to answer it. Do you ask everyone that? You have asked me before?' I said, 'Sometimes yes, sometimes no. But what about you?' He said to get better. I said what is better? Who is to say what is better? He said, like you say, warm inside. How do I do that? I said well what do you think gets in your way? He very quietly said it is my feelings. We got to what it is he wants for himself because I said I am only here to help you get it. He said it is hard to say what I want, a good life. I said, I guess all of us want a good life. But I think we all have different ideas of what a good life is. Like what is your idea? He was quiet and thoughtful and said to do like I want. But if you get married, you can't then because you have to think of another person. I said yes, that is true. We

talked and he was reluctant to go. We got to if the other person gives you something, then it might be worth considering the other person. Wouldn't it be a matter of choice as to where you got the most for yourself? He had complained you have to work it out. Then he told me that it frightened him in his stomach at the thought of making decisions alone yet. I said we will do that together until you feel comfortable of doing it by yourself."

—Transcribed Dictation, Margaret Carey, August 15, 1966

2. "Miracle of miracles happened this evening. Steve said, 'I've been very isolated lately,' and insisted that I play Flocks and Geese with him twice. I thought that this was marvelous. It never happened before that Steve should feel the need and carry it through to do something with somebody. Wow! Hurray! Goody!

"This continues for the next week or so that Steve spontaneously, without insistence, screams, tears, threats, requests, or begging from me, just goes and joins in the general hubbub and melee of the Mohawks that is the current imaginative play. The thing is, once he gets there, he doesn't do too well because he cannot help but be overbearing and run things his way. But what is so gorgeous to see is that there is a real desire in him to play. That is, he wants to. There is something in it for him, these stupendous Mohawk games of City, with blocks and cars going all around. One that he loved and got into a big hassle about was playing zoo with Sean's zoo set. Steve was so invested in taking care of the animals that he had his own very bizarre, very far out methods of zookeeping. That is, he had read about a zoo where certain animals were kept with certain other animals, which very much scared the other kids. They all objected to it. But he wanted things his way. So, once he gets there, it very difficult, and, furthermore, after all this time of Steve's overbearingness, nobody wants to play with him. They know how it is going to end up and they don't want to let him in. But he is trafficking with reality. He is getting in and he is trying. He is facing a little bit of what he does.

"A couple of days later, they were building a snow fort. Steve was in a nonsupervisory capacity. Somebody came along and asked if they could be the one to put up the next brick. Steve said, 'Don't ask me. I'm not in charge.'"

—Transcribed Dictation, Diana Grossman Kahn, January 5, 1968

3. Bruno Bettelheim, Monthly Parent Letter, February 4, 1964.

4. "Recently, he went to clinic and he had fantasies about his grandfather's stomach cancer and the fear that he would get cancer of the penis, which I told Dr. Wright, and he was very insulted that I exposed his crazy fantasies because intellectually he knew that he was being just anxiety ridden, although emotionally he really was scared of it, which was why I brought it out to Dr. Wright, but he was just furious at me for this.

"Also in clinic, he told Dr. Wright that he slept a great deal and he was afraid that he had a rare African sleeping sickness."

—Transcribed Dictation, Diana Grossman Kahn, May 27, 1968

10. *Back to Class*

1. "Allison was complaining in her miserable witchy voice how she didn't want to dance and she felt awful and blah, blah, blah, and just at that point Steve went over to Allison and asked her to dance, and Allison just adorably melted and just came off all of her complaints and her witchy voice and she was just absolutely adorable.

The two of them danced quite a while and they were very good together. It was really very nice to see them because underneath, and in spite, and in addition, and along with all the bickering, they really liked each other. And I was so pleased that tonight they were deserving each other in a positive way, and not just the other way, about deserving one another.

—Transcribed Dictation, Diana Grossman Kahn, October 31, 1966

2. Lecture Notes, Education 331, Bruno Bettelheim, University of Chicago, transcribed by Stephen Eliot, May 1, 1975.

12. *The First Leaving of Dr. B.*

1. Joyce McDougall and Serge Lebovici, *Dialogue avec Sammy* (Paris: Broché, 1984).
2. Genevieve Jurgensen, *La Folie des Autres* (Paris: Robert Laffont, 1973).
3. Lecture Notes, "Understanding Human Behavior," Psychology 251, Bruno Bettelheim, University of Chicago, transcribed by Stephen Eliot, April 15, 1974.

13. *Bert*

1. Lecture Notes, Education 331, Bruno Bettelheim, University of Chicago, transcribed by Stephen Eliot, April 17, 1975.
2. "In the midst of all this feeling, the suggestion was made that he go to school next year. I did not feel that there was any rush to send him to school, because his problem was not academic. I have struggled so long with his pushiness, achievement, [his feeling that] he could do anything, he needs guidance from nobody, well able to handle anything, and I thought that if you send him to school, he'll just start that all over again and we're getting his feelings and perhaps a chance to really work it out. Then when Mark, who was so willing to get into the basic problem, suddenly said he was, in essence, untreatable, that sent me into a fury, anyway I was very angry. Then I found that though we had agreed to talk about it again and I was genuinely willing to discuss it, though not on the basis that he was untreatable, I found that Mark had told Steve that he was probably going to go to school next year and Steve was in a panic, an absolute panic about it. His panic, as much as anything else, was that he felt that Mark had given up on him because Mark had told him he wouldn't get much through another year at the School.

   —Transcribed Dictation, Margaret Carey, May 4, 1972
3. "He said Steve's difficulty is his feeling about his mother's early depression and distance and then his rage and disappointment, and this needs to be interpreted to him. He did not get the satisfaction and sensitivity from his mother's body, so he turned to the man to find some part of his own body, his masculinity. . . . It was suggested that we explain to him that many facets of his personality are grown, but there's a part of him that is still very tiny and we need to get the two parts of him together."

   —Transcribed Dictation, Margaret Carey, May 4, 1972

14. Dr. B.'s Return and Life in the Adolescent Unit

1. "Since you last saw Steve, Mary left to go to another dormitory and Steve felt very badly. He had feelings that his anger at her had driven her away. He was very angry when she became involved with a boyfriend, another counselor, and he felt great disappointment at Mary, feeling betrayed that she had turned to another man. At the same time, he realized that John, his teacher, would be leaving and he was angry and depressed and expressed a sense of hopelessness and anger at having to be at the School. That he had me did not comfort him."

—Transcribed Dictation, prepared for consulting psychiatrist, Margaret Carey, October 15, 1973

As this note indicates, it was startling how much Margaret missed and how derivative this description is rather than showing any appreciation of the profound effects of what had been done to me. There was no questioning of the motives or if this was good for me or not. I was angry at Margaret, since she had not prevented this mess and indeed didn't help me realize that my feelings of hopelessness and despair were not just because of the past but because of the present, as mixed up as it was. No wonder I wanted out.

15. Dictation

1. Lecture Notes, "Understanding Human Behavior," Psychology 251, Bruno Bettelheim, University of Chicago, transcribed by Stephen Eliot, April 8, 1974.
2. Lecture Notes, Education 331, Bruno Bettelheim, University of Chicago, transcribed by Stephen Eliot, April 10, 1975.
3. E-mail, Diana Grossman Kahn, September 27, 2000.
4. "Steve talks a great deal in sessions, telling many important issues, insights about his early and primitive confusions. To interrupt in an effort to follow one thing does not work; he either says let me finish or he waits until I finish and then resumes his own train of thought. Recently I told him I felt as though I had been knocked down by a wave.

"I have always cared for him, he makes me feel his suffering and his need and I kind of ache to help him and sometimes he has succeeded in making me feel quire desperate as he makes it plain I don't help him, I don't ease his pain, in fact, I'm quite ineffectual and useless."

—Transcribed Dictation, prepared for consulting psychiatrist, Margaret Carey, May 5, 1974

16. Teddy

1. "He has been very involved with Teddy and he feels he was trying to be a good understanding kindly father to him. He had an understanding and he observed Teddy's baby needs, Teddy's way of seeing and thinking very closely. He was able to realize that he too had seen things in a similar fashion. He has always tended to be angry when his adult ways have been discouraged. To him adults have all the pleasures while children are given nothing and shut out."

—Transcribed Dictation, prepared for consulting psychiatrist, Margaret Carey, October 15, 1973

17. Ready for His Close-up

1. Lecture Notes, "Understanding Human Behavior," Psychology 251, Bruno Bettelheim, University of Chicago, transcribed by Stephen Eliot, May 22, 1974.
2. B. Bettelheim and D. Karlin, *Un Autre Regard sur Folie* (Paris: Stock, 1975).

18. Neither Fish nor Fowl

1. "I have been Steve's counselor for seven months. This time has been characterized by rather distinct phases when we have got on well, badly, or merely amiably.

"At first we spent many hours late into the night talking following arguments during the day as to whether he could go out for walks on his own and also as to how much time he could spend with Teddy in whom he has an enormous investment and interest. Since Christmas visits up till February there was a just a great deal of arguing as to what I would or would not allow him to do, which he would try and turn into issues of whether he was sane or not, challenging me to call him insane. Then, about a fortnight before his birthday, after he had a similar sort of row with Paulette, I started to talk to him and said that I felt that it was wrong for me to get angry at him as I didn't get either of us anywhere, although it seemed to me that he deliberately provoked many of the arguments. He agreed and said that it made him feel good to see us making fools of ourselves by shouting like that. There was a lapse of two weeks during which time we got on amiably but didn't say a great deal to each other. Then the day before his [nineteenth] birthday and for the few days following that he became remarkably open, soft, and presented his feelings of vulnerability to me with real feeling behind it. Just before his birthday, he had started reading *The Empty Fortress*, and he told me that he felt that he was getting more and more autistic and in contrast that he feels he is getting senile and that he is getting older and he feels that his problems will never be sorted out. He talked of how depressed and angry he felt and that really there was a hollow feeling inside him. He talked of his great anxieties to do even the most insignificant things and how he had great anxieties about his stomach although he was unable to elaborate on that."

—Transcribed Dictation, prepared for consulting psychiatrist, David Lerner, April 23, 1974

2. "Steve is now taking Dr. B.'s class in 'Understanding Human Behavior.' This has kept him in a state of anxiety, which leads to his openness. It raises the issues for him of whether he can cope with college in particular and the outside world in general. In addition, the course work turns up a variety of issues important to Steve."

—Transcribed Dictation, prepared for consulting psychiatrist, David Lerner, April 23, 1974

3. Lecture Notes, "Understanding Human Behavior," Psychology 251, Bruno Bettelheim, University of Chicago, transcribed by Stephen Eliot, April 10, 1974.
4. Ibid.

19. U-High

1. "In total picture, so invested as he is with his feelings, both introversive and externalizing, that he too often disregards the externals that lie before him. Thus

his reality testing suffers: in this he rates below the critical minimum of neurosis; but only in small degree. With regard to knowing the conventional he is in normal range. In his conscious thinking he is relatively intact, with only sporadic instances of confused or illogical thinking. Emotionally he, as of now, shows little understanding of the emotional needs of others; again because too introverted, too egocentric. Another character disadvantage is his low level of healthy self-assertiveness. . . .

"In sum, the absence now of the severe thought pathology that honeycombed his Rorschach pattern of February 23, 1963, and with impressive signs that he is mobilizing his ego and defenses—consciously struggling to extricate himself from the psychologic morass in which he had formerly floundered . . .

"So a transition stage with indication that with continued treatment of promise for an ultimate constructive integration."

—Samuel J. Beck, Ph.D., and Anne G. Beck, M.A., Test Results, July 5, 1974

2. "In his total intellectual functioning he is still taking losses, although without apparent thought pathology but emerging in erratic perceptions, due to his chronic troubled state. He is thus, in all, in a transition state: striving to climb out of his disorder, out of which he has progressed (from the first Rorschach) to what is now an ongoing neurosis."

—Samuel J. Beck, Ph.D., and Anne G. Beck, M.A., Test Results, July 5, 1974

3. Quoted from ibid.

4. "He talked about the fact that Dr. B. is going to be here next week, and he talked about his mixed feelings toward Dr. B. He said that he thinks of Dr. B. as very definite in his opinions, and that this is something which Steve both wants and needs and at the same time resents. He felt both secure in his relationship with Dr. B. and intimidated by Dr. B."

—Transcribed Dictation, Dr. Alfred Flarsheim, Consulting Psychiatrist, March 25, 1975

5. "On arrival, S was apologetic for having kept me waiting. Asked if there was some reason, he explained that he 'didn't want an I.Q. test': didn't think it could have 'any relevance'; that there was a 'hot' discussion with his counselor, following which he decided to come. I told him that while I appreciated his forthrightness, the fact that he had come was not sufficient reason to proceed—that unless he were willing to participate fully, there was no point in going on. I discussed some of dynamics involved, to which he responded; relaxed in his attitude, overcame in some measure his resistance. And it was clear very quickly that once we began, he wanted very much to succeed and he did his best. Here and there a superior smile, only once critical, concerning memory tests—he knows 'some stupid people who could look at a whole page and repeat it perfectly'! I explained that a photographic memory is a special talent that has nothing to do with intelligence—that what we were interested in here was the ability to concentrate. He grasped this and then went on to make a very strenuous effort. In the main S is confident; worked with almost no trial and error; but at one point, little insight into failure and see below. At the close S asked again some very relevant questions and commented that at first 'This wasn't what I thought—I didn't like to have someone pumping my brain in a way I have no control.' I further explained some of the specifics to which a psychometric evaluation could address itself. He listened with care; then asked some historical questions concerning our professional history; and he seemed genuinely pleased at what I told him. He then took his leave with a warm handclasp; apolo-

gized once again for having kept me waiting. In all, an intellectually gifted and very personable young man, struggling hard to maintain his integration; in some respects socially very adequate; sometimes symptomatic needs breaking through. His diction and language, very superior; ideas generally expressed with great clarity.

"As seen there is considerable spread in functioning levels. S is clearly a verbalist person and some subtest ratings in this area are well beyond his overall very superior rating. While significantly lower in the performance area, subtest scores are in the main steady within his own range. It is thus an uneven pattern, seen in individuals in whom intellectual controls are unsteady, due to emotional interference.

"On the verbal scale S rated above his own range in 4 subtests. His highest score is in *Information*, in which he discloses not only very wide interests but a very clear, precise grasp of his ideas. Very close is his *Arithmetic Reasoning*, succeeding in all except the last and most complex problem—i.e., a very high degree of concentration. In *Comprehension* (common sense) he was given the benefit of several doubts; some of his judgments disclose an egocentric twist with an underlay of social superiority; but with encouragement he improved his spontaneous, symptomatic responses. Thus, why better to give to charity than a beggar?—'I don't think it is!' (urged) 'If you give to a beggar he won't look for a job—a charity helps people,' i.e., a little more mature. Or, why should criminals be locked up?—'For punishment—society wants revenge' (urged) 'To keep from harming other others,' with its initial hostility.

"While his vocabulary is very wide, it is here that he could not recognize his own limitations. . . .

"While still maintaining his own superior range in *Similarities* (abstract reasoning) sporadic instances of only modest reasoning as in first and last?—'parts of a sequence—Jesus said the first shall be last and the last first'—a versatile but unique elaboration. Lowest score, at the bottom of his range, is in *Digit memory*: yet he tried hard and more important, he recognized his trend to confusion. In the verbal area then S is clearly gifted, and the inference is in order that he has even more potential than he now uses. While some immaturities appear, as well as some symptomatic needs, his clear verbal superiority is a major asset.

"In the *Performance* area, with one exception, all subtests are within his own range. This single exception, well above his average, is in the *Object Assembly*, in which he achieved the highest rating for all adults: disclosing a highly efficient as well as accurate grasp of the relationships between the whole and its parts. He also did well in the *Block Designs* (inductive reasoning) but he was a little slow, but accurate, as these designs became more complex. In *Digit Symbol* (new learning) again a little slow but accurate, suggesting some inflexibility. At the low end of his own average in 2 subtests: (a) *Picture Completion* (recognizing essential missing details) with loss of credit primarily due to slowness, and so some drag on his basic perceptual processes. And (b) in *Picture Arrangements* (sizing up a total human situation): now very uneven, especially as these became more difficult, with a final bizarre failure in the last of the series. Thus S is least effective in grasping or comprehending social situations. The inference is warranted that he will make some serious mistakes in his social judgments and in his personal relationships.

"Present findings classify S within the very superior group in intelligence. His gifted verbal abilities have been described. The difference between this and his ability to deal with concrete practical problems has been noted; as also the surfacing of symptomatic needs. But overall, even with the variations as above noted, his intellectual functioning is well intact. The losses that he takes are in the area of social and practical judgments. The expectation is that he can compete academically with the average of his age. Whether he can do so without the continuing support of a stress free environment is a question. In the light of the Rorschach test findings as of 7-5-74, he still needs continuing support to insure and further solidify the very real gains he has made in his struggle to extricate himself out of his deeply troubled psychological state. In view of his ability to overcome his initial resistance and that he functions as efficiently as he does, is evidence of ego reserves that can still be further liberated."

—Samuel J. Beck, Ph.D., and Anne G. Beck, M.A., Test Results, June 18, 1975

20. *Getting Ready for College*

1. Exactly one year and four months later, I showed up at the dean's office to say hello. He was the first person I went to see when I arrived in New Haven. In fact, he and Miss Bernardi were the only faculty I knew.

21. *Final Days*

1. Lecture Notes, Education 331, Bruno Bettelheim, University of Chicago, transcribed by Stephen Eliot, April 17, 1975.
2. Jacqueline Seevak Sanders, *Greenhouse for the Mind* (Chicago: University of Chicago Press, 1989).
3. Lecture Notes, Education 331, Bruno Bettelheim, University of Chicago, transcribed by Stephen Eliot, April 8, 1975.
4. David's dictated notes sum up where I was at the time, just prior to my leaving. Curiously, he described me and the other kids at Lab School as children, at a time when I was twenty-one and my classmates were eighteen. Thus, as kind and understanding as this description is, it also indicates all that had been wrong for me at the School for quite some time.

"Steve is leaving the School in three weeks' time, having spent just under thirteen years at the School. He is going on to school at the University of Chicago and hopes to transfer at the end of the year to Yale, where he was also accepted this year. He has chosen to stay in Chicago so he can continue to see Margaret in session, explicitly so that he can deal with his difficulties in relationships. He wants to go to Yale because he views it as a better school academically and because he sees it as a more undergraduate-oriented school and thus able to offer him more.

"Steve has done tremendously well at the School. When he came, he was diagnosed by the Becks as being psychopathic with a very poor prognosis for recovery. When I came to the School three years ago, he was very depressed, continuously struggling to get away from the School, from the dormitory, from me. At the point at which we told him he would be going to Lab School, he was terrified that he would not have the energy to do it and that indeed he wasn't capable of doing it. He now feels much more confident of himself and indeed has done excellently at his studies having had two years of straight A's. What has got more important to him is his having things to do with kids from outside the Orthogenic School and how he has handled those relationships.

"He has general difficulty that when he gets anxious he gets afraid of his own anxiety and thus loses sight of the initial difficulty. He tends to chase after people and impose himself on them when not wanted. This is troublesome to him, as he knows he does this and after an incident is capable of seeing the signs which could have indicated this to him but beforehand he is unable to recognize these signs. This has come out of his feeling very lonely and isolated, in comparison with the other children there, who have known each other for many years. He knows this but is afraid that no one would want to get involved with him very closely.

"The most painful thing he faces is his recognition of his own anxieties about closeness in a relationship."

—Transcribed Dictation, prepared for consulting psychiatrist, David Lerner, May 21, 1976